Attired in Deepest Mourning

Attired in Deepest Mourning

Eliza Joyce,
Mary Ann Milner and
Priscilla
Biggadike

Malcolm Moyes

Matador
Unit E2 Airfield Business Park,
Harrison Road, Market Harborough,
Leicestershire. LE16 7UL
Tel: 0116 2792299
Email: books@troubador.co.uk
Web: www.troubador.co.uk/matador
Twitter: @matadorbooks

ISBN 978 1803133 232

British Library Cataloguing in Publication Data.
A catalogue record for this book is available from the British Library.

Printed and bound by CPI Group (UK) Ltd, Croydon, CR0 4YY
Typeset in 12pt Minion Pro by Troubador Publishing Ltd, Leicester, UK

Matador is an imprint of Troubador Publishing Ltd

'*When we are born we cry that we are come to this great stage of fools*'

William Shakespeare, *King Lear*,
Act 4, scene 6, line 176

This book is dedicated to the memory of my mother,
Joan Moyes.

Contents

Acknowledgements

I would like to thank the British Library which, through its digital archives of C19th and C20th newspapers, enabled me to access with relative ease the news reports and articles relating to the trials of Eliza Joyce, Mary Ann Milner and Priscilla Biggadike, as well as their aftermath.

I would also like to thank the staff of various libraries for their unfailing support and courtesy in providing access to material in their local history collections, as well as obtaining scarce out of print books through the inter-library loan system: in particular, of Boston, Grantham, Sleaford and Lincoln.

I am also especially indebted to the Lincolnshire Archives and their excellent staff, who gave me access to various documents in their possession, and also permission to reproduce the three broadsides related to Eliza Joyce, Mary Ann Milner and Priscilla Biggadike.

For permission to use photographs of the Prisoners' Graveyard, I am grateful to Lincoln Castle and Lincolnshire County Council.

Finally, I would like to acknowledge the help of local historian, Martin Gosling, who kindly answered my various persistent questions about life in C19th Stickney.

Preface

History has the power to make spectres out of us all or to merely abandon us to an eternity of non-existence.

Even though dead and buried, the past, or parts of it, comes back to haunt the present, invoked by the invention of memory, the carefully curated lists of bureaucracy, the self-serving memoirs of the rich and powerful, the penetrating studies of academics, the mesmeric skills of performers, the fierce arguments of polemicists and the vacuous fictions of social media, to mention just a few of the malign necromancers and kindly mountebanks whose intention is to raise the spectre of those who once lived.

Brought back to the land of the living, such ghosts might be outraged, perplexed, amused, astonished, pleased, appalled, or totally indifferent to what they have become in their new existence beyond the grave: but they have lost all right of reply.

Because they have no right of reply, to argue the toss about what they have become, the historian must speak for them, as well as of them, and in so doing, perhaps invents new ghosts in the process to replace the old ones.

This book contains three new ghost stories which speak of, and for, the departed dead, whose elusive and slender spectral existences found in previous books, blogs and tour talks require a careful and respectful unmaking.

If the new spectres of Eliza Joyce, Mary Ann Milner and Priscilla Biggadike raised in this book turn out to be even more elusive and slender than those already in existence, then it has failed.

It may be, however, that the book will at least give all three women a more fitting epitaph than the initialled pieces of rough stone monuments located in Lincoln Castle, along with the decent burial which was denied them at the end of their short lives.

Chapter One

ELIZA JOYCE (1813-1844)

Eliza Joyce Timeline

March 17th, 1813: along with her twin brother, William, Eliza Chapman baptised in Irnham, daughter of John Chapman, farmer, and his wife Mary.

March 15th, 1841: Eliza Chapman married William Joyce, gardener, of Boston, a widower, at South Kyme.

11th October 1841: death of Emma Joyce, aged two years, daughter of William Joyce; attended by Dr Edward Ingram, Boston surgeon.

1st January, 1842: birth of Ann Joyce, daughter of Eliza and William Joyce.

22nd January, 1842: death of Ann Joyce, aged three weeks; attended by Dr Edward Ingram.

March, 1842: body of Emma Joyce exhumed and examined by Dr Edward Coupland on suspicion of arsenic poisoning: no evidence of arsenic found.

13th September, 1842: Dr Francis Snaith called to attend a very ill Edward William Joyce, son of William Joyce

16th September, 1842: arsenic purchased by Eliza Joyce from William Simonds, chemist, Boston.

17th September, 1842: Dr Snaith again called to attend Edward William Joyce, suffering from symptoms of arsenic poisoning.

22nd September, 1842; Eliza Joyce appears before Boston Magistrates on suspicion of attempted murder of Edward William Joyce. Released on bail, but committed to next session of Lincoln Assizes.

24th September, 1842: Eliza Joyce taken into the custody of her brother, Joseph Chapman, in Irnham, by Inspector Horatio Benjamin Cheney.

December, 1842: death of Edward Willam Joyce, aged fifteen years.

19th December, 1842: inquest on Edward William Joyce proves inconclusive.

8th March, 1843: trial of Eliza Joyce for attempted murder at Lincoln Assizes. Trial halted on a technicality. Eliza Joyce released on bail, with sureties from Joseph Chapman and Henry Briggs to appear at next Assize session in Lincoln.

18th July, 1843: trial of Eliza Joyce resumed in

Lincoln; acquitted of attempted murder by Grand Jury.

20th July, 1843: William Joyce issues a public disclaimer relating to any future debts of his wife.

21st July, 1843: Eliza Joyce admitted to the Boston Union Workhouse with her infant child, Betsy Joyce.

23rd August, 1843: Eliza Joyce leaves the Boston Union Workhouse with her child.

26th August, 1843: Eliza Joyce obtains a new order to be re-admitted to the Boston Union Workhouse with her child.

10th March, 1844: beginning of exchange of letters between Farndon Groom and the Board of Guardians, and ultimately with the Poor Law Commissioners, relating to William Joyce's refusal to pay for his wife and child whilst in the workhouse, as well as the behaviour of Eliza Joyce in the workhouse.

13th April, 1844: resolution of issue with William Joyce for repayment and non-payment of maintenance.

1st July, 1844: Eliza Joyce confesses to the murder of Emma and Ann Joyce in the workhouse, as well as the attempted murder of Edward William Joyce, to Dr Edward Coupland, Surgeon of the workhouse, and also to Thomas Wilson, Master of the workhouse.

8th and 17th July, 1844: Eliza Joyce interviewed by John Sturdy, magistrate and one of the Board

3

of Guardians, concerning her confession; warrant signed for commitment to Lincoln Assizes.

18th July, 1844: Eliza Joyce removed from workhouse and taken to Lincoln by steam packet.

22nd July, 1844: trial of Eliza Joyce in Lincoln, found guilty of murder and sentenced to death by Justice Thomas Coltman.

2nd August, 1844: Eliza Joyce hanged at Lincoln Castle by William Calcraft; buried in prisoners' graveyard, Lincoln Castle.

A full, true, and particular account of the Life, Trial, Confession, and Execution of

ELIZA JOYCE, Aged 31,

Who was Executed on the Drop at Lincoln, on Friday, August 2nd, 1844, for Poisoning Emma and Ann Joyce, her daughters.

At the Lincoln Assizes, on Monday 22 July 1844 Eliza Joyce, aged 31, a mild and not uninteresting-looking woman, the wife of a gardener, at Boston was arraigned upon, and pleaded guilty to, two indictments, charging her with the crime of wilful murder. The first indictment charged the murdering by poison (laudanum) in the month of October, 1841, of Emma Joyce, aged 18 months, the child of her husband by a former marriage. The second indictment charged the murdering by poison (laudanum) in the month of January, 1842, of Ann Joyce, aged six weeks, her own offspring by her marriage. The unhappy being was arraigned at the Spring Assizes last year upon the charge of administering to Edward William Joyce (a child of her husband's, of some years' growth) arsenic, whereby his death was caused, and to that indictment pleaded not guilty, and thereon, in consequence of proof to the name of William only, and not of Edward William, being offered, she was discharged, sureties being taken for her trial at the next ensuing Summer Assizes. She was again arraigned thereon at the Summer Assizes of last year, and acquitted As will be seen by her confession below, she now admitted the murder of the said Edward William Joyce, as well as the murders (all at different times) of Emma Joyce and Ann Joyce.

The shocking scene lasted but a very few minutes. The wretched creature only faintly uttered on each arraignment," I am guilty," and the Judge performed his sad duty in a few words and as short a time as decency and the observance of customary from would permit.

The following evidence was given before Mr. John Sturdy, Mayor of Boston, which embodies her confession on which she was committed.

Edward Coupland, of Boston, surgeon, was one of the medical officers of the Boston Poor Law Union. He had attended Mrs. Joyce, one of the inmates of the said Union, during her illness. On Monday the 1st of July, instant, he visited Eliza Joyce as usual, and in her conversation with him she alluded to the circumstances of the death of Mr. Joyce's son William, a boy about 14 years of age, and at the same time stated that she had admin-

istered arsenic to him. He then asked her how much ? She replied, "About a teaspoonful." He then went on conversing with her relative to the child three weeks old, and another little girl called Emma, observing that in the surgical examination of the body of the latter, which was exhumed for that purpose, he could not detect any arsenic. She then said, " Oh no, sir, I did not give her arsenic ; I gave her laudanum." He then asked if she had given anything to the other child, She replied, " Yes : I also gave it laudanum." Witness then said, " How much do you think you gave each ? She replied, " About a teaspoonful to the baby, and about two tea-spoonsful to the little girl Emma ;" but in a conversation he had with her on the following day, she stated that she gave two spoonfulls to the baby, and about four tea-spoonfuls to the girl Emma. Witness then asked her how much she had purchased. She replied "three-pennyworth" and that she obtained it at Mr. Smith's shop in Boston. Witness was the surgeon who examined the body of Emma Joyce, the daughter of William, after exhumation, owing to a suspicion that arsenic had been administered to it ; but on fully testing the contents of the stomach, and the parts immediately around it, he came to the conclusion that arsenic had not been administered. The child had been interred several months.

The woman having been sentenced to suffer death as above stated, tranquilly suffered herself to be removed from the bar.

Since her conviction the unfortunate woman has behaved in a manner befitting her in her dreadful situation. she has paid every attention to the spiritual instruction of the worthy chaplin.

On Thuresday afternoon the condemned sermon was preached by the Rev. Mr. Richter, chaplain to the castle, the discourse was impressive, and appeared to have considerable effect not only on the wretched woman but on the whole of prisoners present.

At the appointed hour, this day, the unfortunate culprit was conducted to the Drop, on the Castle walls, and underwent the sentence her crimes so justly merited, in the presence of an immense concourse of spectators.

A Copy of Verses.

Alas my heart was blinded thro,
By Satan's powerful sway :
That dreadful enemy of *men*
My reason took away.

I saw not then the dismal call,
The Judge of Judgment seat ;
The place where crime is doom'd to dwell
And there its deserts meet.

Hark I hear the prison door,
On its grating hinges turn,
A few sad mournful moments more,
And I'm for ever gone.

Hark the bell rolls, its sound
Calls her forth to die,
Beneath the fatal beam she stands
With tears in either eye.

Then on the platform she did stand
The convict then did cry ;
The drop it fell, and she was sent
To meet her God on high.

The halt's withdrawn—her spirits flown,
Its fatal doom to bear,
May God have mercy on her soul,
Through Christ our Saviour dear.

R. E. Leary, Printer, 19, Strait, Lincoln.

My Reason Took Away: The Life And Death Of Eliza Joyce

Introduction

Eliza Joyce, wife of William Joyce, of South End, Boston, was hanged in Lincoln Castle at midday, on the 2nd August, 1844, in front of a boisterous crowd, estimated to have been around five thousand people, many of them reported to have been women, all jostling for a grandstand view of the unfolding melancholic drama of judicial execution.

Compared to the convolutions and complications of many other C19th murder cases, the story of Mrs Joyce's misfortunes appears to have been a remarkably simple one. Contemporary and later accounts record a straightforward narrative of a woman accused of poisoning her teenage stepson, but acquitted by a Grand Jury; and then arraigned a second time, after confessing to having poisoned two infant daughters with laudanum, in addition to attempting to kill her stepson with arsenic. There was no incontrovertible evidence to convict Eliza Joyce other than her own words, freely uttered on her sick bed in the Boston Union Workhouse, to a reliable witness.

The lack of such staple sensational elements as sexual impropriety, unscrupulous avarice and shocking courtroom revelations, seems to support the comment made by Judith Flanders in her book, *The Invention of Murder*, that the trial and execution of Eliza Joyce aroused little interest, either locally or nationally. However, this overstates the case, in that the story was tracked assiduously between the 22nd September 1842 and the 9th August, 1844, by the *Stamford Mercury* and the *Lincolnshire Chronicle*, and was repeated or rehashed by various other British newspapers, as well as being mashed and mangled into shape by a souvenir broadside, printed in Lincoln, ready for peddling by the noisy patterers at the scene of the hanging. Perhaps even more telling, reports of the trial and sentencing of Eliza Joyce, and the background to the case, were circulating in London newspapers, including *The Times*, several days before they were reported by the Lincolnshire newspapers.

A close analysis of the case raises a number of awkward questions which indicate that the life and death of Eliza Joyce were not quite as straightforward as they were understood to be at the time.

Trial of Eliza Joyce for Attempted Murder, 8th March 1843

Mrs Joyce's first formal close encounter with the law was her appearance in front of a panel of Boston Magistrates on the 22nd September, 1842, which was reported by the *Lincolnshire Chronicle*. It was a very brief report, informing the reader that after a long investigation, Eliza Joyce had been brought before the panel consisting of Messrs W H Adams (Mayor), J Sturdy, J Elsom, J J Maclean and R W Stainbank, suspected of attempting to poison the eldest son of her husband, William Joyce, who was a market gardener in Boston. After the gathering together of depositions from several witnesses, including Mrs Joyce herself, she was committed for trial at the Lent Assizes in Lincoln, the following year.

The report in the *Lincolnshire Chronicle* on the anticipated opening of the Lent Session of the Lincoln Assizes on 6th March, 1843, made it clear that the judges, Sir John Gurney and Sir Edward Alderson, would have an unusually heavy workload in the week ahead. The forty-five offences for consideration included straw burning, sheep stealing, forgery, manslaughter, theft, breaking and entering, rape, poaching, assault, stabbing and an act contrary to the order of nature. Amongst this dismal litany of misdeeds, the report highlighted the case of Eliza Joyce, aged thirty years, currently out on bail, who was suspected of attempting to murder William Joyce of Boston.

The report in the *Stamford Mercury* was more exact in its detail, revealing that Mrs Joyce was accused of administering half an ounce of arsenic to William Joyce junior, with intent to murder, and was no doubt viewed by the newspaper as one of several crimes 'of a very heinous nature' found on the Lincoln Calendar.

The slightly different identities given to the alleged victim of arsenic poisoning in the two newspapers, on the surface, may seem superficial, but the confusion was to have serious consequences for the progress of the case against Eliza Joyce.

That one of the judges was an ailing Sir John Gurney, aged seventy-five years, and with a fearsome reputation for harsh sentencing and ignoring advice, would perhaps have filled some of the prisoners on the list with fear and trembling; and for a good number of them, such trepidation was to be in due course entirely justified.

The Crown Court session of the Assize, sitting on Monday, 6th March, 1843, did not begin, however, with the expected grave and sombre reflections appropriate to a court of law, but rather with low farce, which would not have been out of place in the satiric pages of *Punch*. The irascible elderly judge insisted that the Grand Jury must remove themselves from where they were sitting and relocate to the petit jury box 'on account of the indistinctiveness of his voice'.

It was not the most auspicious start to the smooth, fair and efficient administration of justice.

Once the Grand Jury had seated itself in the place nearer and more convenient to Sir John, they were treated to an address which praised the gentlemen of the jury for attending the session, attributing it to their desire to 'show their readiness to arrest the appalling progress of crime'. In his follow up remarks, the venerable judge did not mince his words nor did he spare local sensibilities as he drew attention to 'the number and enormity of the offences, <which> he did not expect in this county'.

The continuation of Sir John's address was not so much a judicial review of some of the cases to be presently considered by the Grand Jury, as a forthright lecture on human degeneracy and the responsibility of those placed in authority, such as Magistrates, Ministers and Parish Officers, to address such an intolerable state of affairs. In a particularly memorable phrase, an outraged Sir John called for the judicious exercise of 'restrictive influence' to curb vice, profaneness and immorality in the locality; in particular, such influence should be used to prevent drunkenness, which 'made a man a demon or a beast'.

Once the pulpit eloquence of the judge had subsided, he reviewed in more measured tones some of the more serious depositions which he had read, including those relating to the case of Eliza Joyce. Sir John instructed the Grand Jury, now in hearing range, that it must decide whether or not there was sufficient evidence to try the prisoner for attempted murder and therefore find a true bill.

The Grand Jury did think that there was a case to answer and consequently on Wednesday, 8th March, Eliza Joyce was tried for administering arsenic to William Joyce the younger, with intent to murder. She pleaded not guilty, but might well have had cause to feel uneasy about the outcome of her trial in that Sir John, when deciding the fate of several guilty felons the day before, had seemed determined to put the concept of 'restrictive influence' into robust practice.

Charles Goodhand, aged forty-four, a labourer of no fixed address, had been sentenced to fifteen years transportation for the crime of stealing a sheep from Francis Hewison of Candlesby, despite having pleaded guilty. Mr Goodhand's distressing story of sometimes having to sleep rough on frosty ground cut no ice with Sir John, who described the unfortunate man as 'an impudent thief.'

John Buttery, aged twenty, of Great Carlton, after having been found guilty of setting fire to a straw-stack, the property of Mr Robert Epton, had been sentenced to transportation for life. Sir John made no apology for the draconian sentence, explaining to the young arsonist that setting fire to a straw-stack was 'an atrocious crime' and that the Bench was determined to stop the practice by sentencing any perpetrator to a 'very severe punishment'.

Perhaps in an attempt to appeal to the more sentimental side of Sir John's nature, (should such an extraordinary thing have existed), Mrs Joyce appeared in court with an infant in her arms. It is an unremarkable detail, confirmed by several contemporary sources, but one which seems to have dropped out of modern accounts of the case: it is a detail which is significant in understanding some of the future difficulties of Mrs Joyce's life after the trial.

The accounts of the trial in the *Lincolnshire Chronicle* and *Stamford Mercury* vary very little in terms of the bare narrative essentials, although the latter newspaper was able to supply its readers with more detail, especially of Mrs Joyce's denial of guilt. It was established that arsenic had been bought by the accused from the Boston chemist and druggist, William Simonds. She had asked for white mercury to poison mice, but Simonds instead recommended an alternative compound for the destruction of vermin. Mrs Joyce, however, had refused the offer and instead purchased two ounces of arsenic.

The stepson of Mrs Joyce had been unwell since early September and had been left in her care by Mr Joyce, to ensure that he took his prescribed medicine. Unfortunately, the boy became very ill in the care of his stepmother, showing all the symptoms of arsenic poisoning. This was confirmed in the deposition of the Boston doctor, Francis Snaith, who had analysed the vomit of the boy and found the presence of arsenic. The boy had subsequently died in the December of

1842, it was true, but it was not from the effects of arsenic poisoning.

At the inquest into the boy's death, which had been held at the Ship Tavern, Skirbeck, before the Coroner, Charles Mastin, on the 19th December, 1842, two medical witnesses had examined the body of William Joyce junior. The post mortem revealed a large quantity of water in the chest, the pericardium in a highly diseased state, containing 'a large collection of matter', and that the liver was 'enormously large', weighing around four pounds. However, the two doctors were unable to say beyond doubt what had caused these unhealthy conditions, and a verdict to that effect was recorded by Mr Mastin. Neither of the newspaper reports of the Assize trial referred with any precision to the outcome of the inquest, beyond confirming that there was no clear evidence of death from arsenic poisoning.

Whilst the purchase of the arsenic by Eliza Joyce was not contested, the explanation of how the boy came to have the mineral in his stomach was disputed. According to Mrs Joyce, she had accidentally spilled a small quantity of the arsenic which she had purchased on the kitchen floor. To clean it up, she had used a spoon which she later also used to give her stepson his medicine.

According to the *Stamford Mercury*, the explanation from Eliza Joyce was seen as 'a subterfuge', simply because it was not possible for sufficient arsenic to stick to a dry spoon to account for the quantity discovered by Dr Snaith in the vomit of the boy. Further, but less convincingly, the purchased arsenic had been weighed and only one ounce and a half remained.

At this point in the proceedings the outlook for Eliza Joyce was looking bleak: arsenic had undeniably been bought by her, arsenic had been discovered in the body of the alleged intended victim left in her care and the explanation of innocence from the prisoner was barely credible. It would have come as no surprise if the Grand Jury, at this point, was leaning towards a verdict of guilty of attempted murder, and that Sir John was pondering another impressive demonstration of 'restrictive influence'.

However, to the surprise of the courtroom reporters, the judge suddenly stopped the trial in its tracks. Sir John realised, rather belatedly, that the integrity of the legal proceedings had been compromised, in that there was some confusion as to whom Eliza Joyce was actually accused of poisoning. On one hand, the intended victim was understood to be William Joyce, the name of her husband; on the other hand, the indictment had cited Edward William Joyce, the full name of her stepson, as the intended victim.

Consequently, Sir John directed the Grand Jury to acquit Mrs Joyce *pro forma*, whilst making it clear that the prisoner would not be escaping justice, as he would also be giving directions for a future re-trial.

Eliza Joyce was released on bail with the surety of her appearance at the next Assize session being guaranteed by Henry Briggs, proprietor of the Sun Inn, in Colsterworth, near Grantham, and Joseph Chapman, her brother, a farmer and maltster of Brickhill Lodge, Irnham, also near Grantham. Each of the men had agreed to stand the considerable bail money of £250 each.

It was the second time that Joseph Chapman had supported his sister in difficult circumstances in that after her appearance in front of the Boston Magistrates in September 1842, she was delivered into his custody in Irnham by Police Inspector Horatio Benjamin Cheney.

That Eliza Joyce does not appear to have returned to the marital home in Boston suggests that her relationship with her husband had unsurprisingly broken down, on account of his probable suspicions concerning his wife's guilt and the need to ensure adequate child protection for his son, should those suspicions be correct. The refusal by William Joyce to allow his wife to return to the marital home was a decisive one in the gradual downward spiral of her life, although perhaps not his first detrimental intervention. According to the account of the trial reported in the *Lincolnshire Chronicle,* Sir John Gurney remarked in his presentation of the Eliza Joyce case to the Grand Jury, that her husband had given evidence against her which had been admitted at the Coroner's inquest: Sir John was absolutely clear that this should not have happened and was legally improper.

Resumed Trial of Eliza Joyce for Attempted Murder, 18th July, 1843

The resumed trial of Mrs Joyce took place before Sir John Patteson at the Lincoln Summer Assizes, on Tuesday, 18th July, 1843, and was once again reported with great interest by both the *Lincolnshire Chronicle* and the *Stamford Mercury* newspapers. There were some inevitable differences between the two accounts, in terms of the emphases produced by the choice of reported details, as well as the mishearing or misspelling of names by the reporters. However, both newspapers published interesting new material dating back to the appearance of Eliza Joyce in front of the Boston Magistrates on the 22nd September, 1842, which had taken her to the Lincoln Assizes.

The number available for Grand Jury service on the day was unusually small, apparently, although the composition of the final selection was a reliable mixture of social standing and experience:

- Right Honourable Charles Tennyson D'Eynecourt (Foreman)
- Charles Allix
- Charles Henry Anderson
- Benjamin Bromhead
- Francis Browne
- Charles Chaplin
- Thomas Chaplin
- Robert Cracroft
- Richard Ellison
- Charles Fardell
- John Fardell
- John Goulden
- George Knollys Jarvis
- Theophilus Fairfax Johnson
- Charles John Munday
- Charles William Packe
- William Parker
- George Skipworth
- Richard Thorald
- Edward Wright

The 'slender attendance' of the Magistrature may have been a disappointment to the *Lincolnshire Chronicle*, but spirits were to be later buoyed by the attendance of Lord Brownlow, who seated himself to the right of Justice Patteson. In addition to his welcome presence, the noble Lord Lieutenant of the County was also observed to be 'in excellent health', as was the obsequiousness of the newspaper.

The address to the newly sworn Grand Jury by Lord Justice Patteson was in marked contrast to that by Sir John Gurney at the Lent Assizes. Whilst he acknowledged that there were cases of a serious nature to consider, his measured comments focused upon the practical issues of decision making, rather than upon the crimes as incontrovertible evidence of moral corruption at the heart of society. The most serious case and, in his estimation, the most difficult one for the Grand Jury to disentangle, was that of an alleged poisoning by a girl aged thirteen of her mother in Market Rasen, aided and abetted by a family servant aged eighteen, with the added complexity of the father of the girl being a probable accessory to the crime. Whilst the case was clearly a shocking and highly emotive one, the judge cautioned against finding a true bill which might result in premature acquittal through lack of definitive evidence against the accused. The jury might therefore consider the possibility of not finding a true bill until new and more compelling evidence emerged: the Grand Jury acted upon his advice.

The same pragmatic approach was also taken by Justice Patteson in relation to the resumed trial of Eliza Joyce: the main issue for the Grand Jury to note was that the accused had been acquitted at the previous Assize session on technical grounds relating to the inaccuracy of a name, but that outcome should have no bearing upon their deliberations; at the same time, however, it might become an issue for the court to consider in due course. What the judge meant by this remark is clarified in the report of the *Stamford Mercury*, in which he is quoted as referring specifically to the possibility that Mrs Joyce might make a double-jeopardy plea not to be tried a second time, a point of law which was not for the Grand Jury to consider.

The opening of the trial ensured that the mistake of an embarrassing administrative error was not repeated. The full name of the younger William Joyce being Edward William Joyce had been confirmed by the deposition of his grandmother, Rachel Tingle, (not Rachael Trayle as stated in the *Lincolnshire Chronicle*), and was later verified by the production in court by Inspector Cheney of a copy of the relevant entry in the *Boston Baptismal Register*, which read: 'Oct.4, 1827, Edward Willam, son of William Joyce and Elizabeth Joyce, gardener'.

In opening his case, the prosecuting solicitor, Mr Mellor, went through the sequence of events which led to the supposed attempt on the life of Edward William Joyce; but first, as an additional precaution, he pedantically reminded the jury that the alleged victim had been commonly known as William, but that he had the baptismal name of Edward William: clearly Mr Mellor was taking no chances.

Mr Mellor presented a strong case against Mrs Joyce, based upon the available evidence, some of which was already in the public domain from the abandoned first trial. On the 16th September, 1842, she had visited the shop of the Boston chemist, William Simonds, (not Simons, as reported by both newspapers), to purchase arsenic as a solution to a problem with mice. Mr Simonds had recommended Nux Vomica as an alternative, but Mrs Joyce persisted in her preference for arsenic. Despite his reluctance to sell such a dangerous substance to one person alone, the chemist sold Mrs Joyce two ounces of the poison, persuaded by her reassurances that she was well-known to Mr Simonds, and that her husband was aware of her intention to buy arsenic. The deposition of Mr Simonds was a nervous one in that he seemed to go out of his way to emphasise the sensible precautions he had taken in selling the arsenic: as well as warning Mrs Joyce about it being very dangerous, he had carefully wrapped it in two pieces of brown paper and had labelled it 'arsenic, poison'.

Cross-examined by Mr Miller, the defending solicitor, William Simonds was asked to explain the nature of Nux Vomica. The chemist said that it was used to poison rats and mice, but whilst being a deadly poison, it was not as deadly as arsenic – which perhaps seemed a somewhat sophistic fine distinction. The question from Mr Miller was probably intended to establish the idea of making a choice between two highly toxic substances to rid the house of vermin, as opposed to rejecting something less harmful to human beings in favour of something more deadly.

According to Mr Simonds, he told William Joyce about the purchase of arsenic the following day, who within fifteen minutes had returned with the poison, but wrapped in only one piece of paper, the outer one having been removed. The chemist then weighed the contents of the package and discovered that half an ounce of the arsenic was missing.

The deposition of the Boston doctor, Francis Snaith, (not Smith, as reported by the *Lincolnshire Chronicle*), explained that he had been called upon to attend Edward William Joyce on the 13th September, three days before the purchase of arsenic by Mrs Joyce. Under his care, the boy's health continued to improve over the next few days, until the 17th September, when he began to suffer from 'violent symptoms', consistent with having swallowed arsenic: the unpleasant symptoms were specified in the *Stamford Mercury* as 'violent pains in the stomach and bowels, as well as violent sickness, hiccups and purging.' According to the report in the *Lincolnshire Chronicle*, Dr Snaith testified that he had given the boy some medicine on the 16th September, but insisted that it did not contain any arsenic; and also, that on discovering how ill the boy was on the 17th September, he provided medicine as an antidote to the distressing effects of arsenic poisoning.

In order to confirm or deny his suspicions as to the cause of the painful symptoms experienced by Edward William Joyce, Dr Snaith had ordered that the boy's vomit should be preserved and sent to him for analysis. On the 20th September, he received a quart pitcher tied over and the contents were submitted to a series of chemical tests which Dr Snaith described in precise, scientific detail. The outcome of the tests confirmed the presence of arsenic in the stomach of the alleged victim.

In addition to his own tests, Dr Snaith had enlisted the support of Mr Henry Robert Gilson, (not Gillsen, as reported by the *Lincolnshire Chronicle* or Green as reported by the *Stamford Mercury*), to perform various experiments on the ejections from the stomach. Henry Robert Gilson of Skirbeck, noted in the report as an expert in Chemistry, appears also to have been an expert in Botany, whose help was acknowledged by Pishey Thompson in his *History and Antiquities of Boston* (1856). The ingenious methodology of Mr Gilson was documented in impressive detail: he too discovered traces of arsenic and so corroborated Dr Snaith's findings.

The timeline and events of Dr Snaith's treatment of the sick boy were confirmed by the testimony of Rachel Tingle, the boy's grandmother, for whom William Joyce had sent on the 17th September. On arrival at the house, she had found him very ill and had been directed by Dr Snaith to preserve the boy's vomit, which she dutifully did, delivering it to his surgery. Mrs Tingle was scrupulously precise in the expansion of her evidence: Phoebe Wilkins, the servant of Dr Snaith, had received the pitcher containing vomit, which she placed in his surgery; a certain Mr Henry Tomlinson had then removed the pitcher to the back surgery, where it remained untouched until the return of Dr Snaith.

The testimony of Rachel Tingle was reported only by the *Lincolnshire Chronicle*.

Inspector Cheney confirmed that he had taken Eliza Joyce into custody at her brother's home in Irnham, on the 24th September, and that she had told the inspector that if she had given her stepson poison it had been a complete accident caused by the spillage of arsenic on the kitchen floor and her clearing it up with the spoon used to administer his medicine.

William Henry Adams, the mayor of Boston, proved the deposition of Edward William Joyce made in front of the Boston Magistrates before his untimely death. The examination of the alleged victim had provided a detailed account to Adams of the events which took place in the very early hours of the 17th September, 1842. Both the *Lincolnshire Echo* and the *Stamford Mercury* published a version of the deposition from Edward William Joyce, but the latter provided significant additional information about the boy's medical history prior to the 17th September, which the other newspaper chose to omit.

According to the version of the deposition published by the *Lincolnshire Chronicle*, on the night of the 16th September, 1842, the boy's father had retired to bed, leaving him in the care of his stepmother. At around midnight, she had given him his medicine in a wine glass, which had made him violently sick and his heart beat abnormally fast. He told his father in the morning about the uncomfortable experiences he had endured and that he was so ill he refused any more of the medicine. The symptoms of nausea and thirst had continued for two or three days.

The version of the deposition reported in the *Stamford Mercury* concurs almost word for word with that found in the Lincoln newspaper, but prefaces it with the Edward William Joyce's description of his illness prior to the alleged poisoning. He had become unwell about a month earlier with a swelling of the eyes and then of both legs. This was followed in subsequent days by a further swelling of the whole body, although he did not feel any pain. Some days after this, he became very sick and vomited violently, accompanied by some purging. On becoming worse, Dr Snaith was called, but the patient continued to be ill and remained very ill, up to and including the night when his father went to bed between 10 and 11 o'clock, leaving him in the care of his stepmother.

The final sentence of the deposition, also omitted by the *Lincolnshire Chronicle*, was that he had been 'on middling terms' with his stepmother.

The Mayor also proved the deposition of Eliza Joyce, made under voluntary examination, which had told the story of the spilling of arsenic in the kitchen and trying to gather it up with a spoon subsequently used to administer medicine to the alleged victim. The only additional material to the narrative heard at the first trial was that she had swept what arsenic she could not gather under the fender.

The most interesting information from Mr Adams was that Eliza Joyce had refused to sign the deposition. It was a curious detail, mentioned only by the *Lincolnshire Chronicle*, which seemed to have been passed over without further comment.

Unfortunately, neither newspaper provided any report of the summing up of the case by Justice Patteson. However, both ended their reports with the address on behalf of Eliza Joyce made by Mr Miller, which went some way towards the ultimate Not Guilty verdict. According to the *Lincolnshire Chronicle*, which is the most detailed summary of the case for the defence, Mr Miller gave 'a long and powerful address on behalf of the prisoner'. His argument focused upon a lack of motive, especially when there was no ill-feeling between Mrs Joyce and her stepson; the presence of arsenic in only the very small quantity of a fraction of a grain; and that if poison had been taken by the boy, it was the result of an unfortunate accident.

If the summary of Mr Miller's speech is accurate the case for the defence was built upon the medical and scientific evidence, the deposition of the alleged victim and the explanation of Mrs Joyce herself.

Unless it was omitted from the newspaper reports, it is surprising that Mr Miller did not pick up on a strange inconsistency between the deposition of Dr Snaith and that of Edward William Joyce, which amounted to a complete contradiction.

Dr Snaith had asserted that he attended the boy on the 13th September, although he did not go into detail about the nature of the boy's illness. What he did say was that his health continued to improve over the following few days and that he administered medicine on the 16th September. Unfortunately, the improvement was reversed in the early hours of 17th September, when Edward William Joyce became very ill, showing symptoms of arsenic poisoning. The account of his illness by the boy told a quite different story: he had been unwell for some time before the doctor was summoned to treat him on the 13th September on account of the increasing severity of his symptoms. What had started as an odd, but painless swelling of the body, had turned into violent vomiting accompanied by purging, which worsened after his stepmother gave him the medicine presumably prescribed by Dr Snaith on the 16th September. The unhappy coincidence of the symptoms of violent vomiting accompanied by purging before the 17th September, recorded in the deposition of Edward William Joyce, being the same symptoms identified as supposed arsenic poisoning on the 17th September, might have been probed by Mr Miller. Similarly, the lack of precision from Dr Snaith concerning the prescribed medicine, as well as his overstated optimism about the improving health of the boy in the days prior to the alleged poisoning, might have given rise to questions about the doctor's judgement, as much as his memory.

Whilst it is hardly definitive evidence for questioning the doctor's competence, the notice of his death on the 3rd April, 1844, not only highlighting his local eminence as an apothecary, but also his 'advanced age', might have produced some unease.

The acquittal of Eliza Joyce on Tuesday 18th July, 1843, by a Grand Jury which included such highly influential and respected figures as the MP Charles Tennyson D'Eynecourt of Bayons Manor, Richard Ellison of Boultham Park, Charles Chaplin of

Blankney Hall, Charles Allix of West Willougby Hall
and George Knollys Jarvis of Doddington Hall, might
have given her hope for a better future.

William Joyce: The Facts and the Fictions

Such hope, however, was dashed by a legal notice
which appeared in the *Stamford Mercury*, on Saturday,
21st July, just days after her acquittal:

> '*Notice is hereby given, that I will not be answerable
> for the payment of any Debt or Debts, which my
> Wife, Eliza Joyce, may contract from the date hereof.
> Dated this 20th day of July, 1843*'.

It was signed, William Joyce, South End, Boston.

The husband of Eliza Joyce was clearly trying
to sever all ties with her: as a moral liability, he had
probably refused to let her back into the marital
home after she appeared in front of the Boston
Magistrates on the 22nd September, 1841; now, as a
financial liability, William Joyce was trying to evade
any pecuniary responsibility for her plight.

In the newspaper reports on the case, William
Joyce had rarely been mentioned, beyond his
occupation as a market gardener, once running a
beer house and living at South End in Boston. He had
gone to bed and left his stepson with Eliza Joyce on

the night of 16th September, 1842; on the morning of 17th September, he was told by his son, showing symptoms of arsenic poison, that he felt very ill after taking his medicine from his stepmother; later on, in conversation with the chemist, William Simonds, he discovered that his wife had purchased arsenic on the previous day. After the unexplained death of his son in early December, 1841, he provided incriminating statements about his wife to the inquest, held on 19th December, which were ruled as inadmissible in court.

Based upon such fragments, the image of William Joyce is one of an upright man with a steady job, seriously concerned about the welfare of his son and disturbed by the behaviours of his wife to such an extent that he refused to have her back in the house. It is an image which sits comfortably with the description of him in the report of Eliza Joyce's execution, as 'a remarkably inoffensive man', who despite his misgivings about the conduct of his wife, had been willing to support her when she was compelled to enter the Boston Union Workhouse.

The evidence from official records of the time, however, suggests that the image of the straightforward, upright sobriety of William Joyce, created by the media, is as open to question as the reliability of courtroom journalism.

The 1841 Census records that the Joyce household consisted of nine people, not the four implied by the newspapers. Of the nine people living at South Street, two were unrelated to William Joyce: John Vickers, a fifteen year old gardener and servant, and Ann Bradshaw, of the same age and also a domestic servant. In addition to Eliza Joyce, there were two of the three children who were to became part of the poisoning story: Edward William Joyce, aged thirteen, born in 1828 and Emma Joyce, aged one, born in 1840: Ann Joyce, the third child allegedly poisoned, had not yet been born. In addition, and never mentioned in any newspaper report, were three other children: James Joyce, aged nine, born 1832; Henry Joyce, age seven, born 1834; and Harriet Joyce, aged three, born 1838.

As with Census records in general, the accuracy of the entry for the Joyce family is open to scrutiny: official records of births, deaths and marriages indicate several alternative, perhaps more reliable facts. Mrs Joyce was baptised in Irnham, along with her twin brother William Chapman, on 17th November, 1813, the daughter of John Chapman, farmer, and his wife Mary: on 6th June, 1841, and so on Census day, she would have been twenty-seven, not twenty-five years old. Further, Emma Joyce (recorded as Ama Joyce in the Census), was born in the final quarter of 1839, probably October, not 1840; Emma was buried on the 14th October, 1841, and was recorded as having died aged two years which, whilst not contradicting the age of one year in the Census return, does modify the age of eighteen months for her death published in the newspapers. Similarly, the *Boston Baptismal Register* exhibited in court by Inspector Cheney showed that Edward William Joyce was born on 4th October, 1827, not 1828, although he would still have been thirteen years old on Census day.

The newspapers reported that Eliza Joyce was the second wife of William Joyce and that Edward William and Emma were the children of his relationship with his deceased first wife. No details about the first Mrs Joyce ever emerged in the newspaper reports, other than her mother, Rachel Tingle, having provided corroborating evidence concerning the illness of her grandson and one of her granddaughters. However, Elizabeth Joyce (née Tingle) is recorded as having died in 1839, aged thirty-four, and was buried on the 10th November in Boston, which meant that she left William Joyce with four, possibly five young children, including one who was only a few weeks old at the time of her mother's death. William Joyce remained a widower, until he married Eliza Chapman, eldest daughter of the late John Chapman, formerly a farmer at Irnham, and later an innkeeper in Colsterworth, at South Kyme on 15th March, 1841: the marriage details were conspicuously celebrated by an announcement in a column of the *Stamford Mercury*.

The same kind of complication and uncertainty concerning the children of the Joyce family emerges in an examination of the 1851 Census. Seven years after the execution of his wife, William Joyce had evidently prospered as a market gardener and seedsman, now employing two men in his business. He had remarried, again to a much younger woman, Amelia, who bore him a son, also named William, in 1850. James Joyce, unmarried, still lived at home, and was employed as an architect's clerk, as did thirteen years old Harriet, still a scholar. The most interesting addition to the Joyce household is Betsy Joyce, aged eight, who was born in Boston, in 1843, and is almost certainly the infant whom Eliza Joyce held in her arms in court and whom she took with her into the Boston Union Workhouse, after her acquittal in July, 1843. Betsy died on the 16th October, 1853, aged ten, another addition to the sad catalogue of premature deaths in the Joyce household.

Curiously, records of births, deaths and burials in Boston note the death of a Bets<e>y Joyce, daughter of William and Elizabeth Joyce, on the 14th February, 1840. Bets<e>y Joyce was born on the 22nd April, 1832 and so died before her tenth birthday: she may well have been the twin sister of James Joyce, also born in 1832.

The unfortunate William Joyce seemed to lose a lot of children prematurely.

That William Joyce took in his infant daughter at some point before or shortly after the execution of his wife is to his credit. However, it is difficult to know whether this was an act of natural parental kindness, social pressure or a legal compulsion to do his duty, after having abandoned the infant Betsy to a grim life in the Boston Workhouse with her mother.

Newspaper reports mention in passing that William Joyce had supported his wife financially whilst she was in the workhouse, an assertion which is at odds with his public disavowal of responsibility for her debts, as she was on the point of entering the Boston Union Workhouse. Moreover, it is a total contradiction of a more uncomfortable reality, revealed in a series of letters published on the 26th April, 1844, by the *Stamford Mercury*.

Described as 'a singular case', the newspaper reproduced an exchange of letters between Mr Farndon Groom, a recently appointed member of the Boston Board of Guardians, the Clerk to the Board of Governors and the Poor Law Commission, at Somerset House, written between the 10th March and 13th April, 1844. The correspondence, as well as modifying the image of William Joyce as being 'inoffensive', provides a valuable insight into the life of Eliza Joyce in the workhouse, before her confession of guilt.

The initial letter of the exchange, written by Mr Groom, is clear and precise, providing useful official facts and figures relating to Mrs Joyce, which otherwise would have been lost. The tone is one of respectful enquiry into the rules of the workhouse and their implementation, especially in relation to the non-payment of maintenance; it also touches upon the brutalities which inmates of the workhouse might have to endure.

According to Mr Groom, Eliza Joyce entered the Boston Union Workhouse on 21st July, 1843, having obtained an order for admission to the workhouse from the Relieving Officer, on behalf of herself and her infant. Mr Groom pointed out that William Joyce had refused to have his wife in the house and was also 'in good circumstances' – a euphemism for being able to meet his financial obligations. On the following day, the Board of Guardians had met to discuss the Admissions book, including the case of Mrs Joyce and her child; more specifically, the refusal of her husband to pay for their maintenance in the workhouse.

On the 23rd August, 1843, Mrs Joyce and her infant left the workhouse, but returned three days later, having obtained a fresh order from the Relieving Officer; at the time of writing, Mrs Joyce was currently still resident in the workhouse. On her return to the workhouse, her case had been reviewed by the Board and it was moved that the Clerk to the Board should write to the Overseers to summon William Joyce before the magistrates to explain why he was not paying any maintenance for his wife and child. The meeting, consisting of only six of the Guardians, did not second the proposition. The case was discussed further in the afternoon sitting of the Board, at which it was resolved that Eliza Joyce should not have any visitors whilst she remained in the workhouse.

A concerned Mr Groom followed his narrative with three urgent questions:

- Can the Board of Guardians, under the circumstances, legally allow Eliza Joyce and her infant to remain in the workhouse, and charge her husband maintenance?
- Can the Board of Guardians, under such circumstances, deny Mrs Joyce the privilege of being visited by her friends and relatives?
- Can the Board of Guardians punish Mrs Joyce if she refuses to work, or does not comply with the rules of the workhouse?

Mr Groom signs his letter off by regretting not having raised the case at an earlier date, but he had hoped for some resolution to have been reached by way of an arrangement between husband and wife, but he accepted that this was now unlikely.

The second letter, dated 16th March, 1844, was written by the Boston solicitor, J G Calthrop, Clerk to the Boston Union, acknowledging receipt of a letter from the Poor Law Commissioners, concerning the issues raised by Mr Groom, which was read before the Board of Guardians on that day. Details of the letter are not quoted, but it seems clear that the Commissioners had requested confirmation that the concerns raised by Mr Groom were true and possibly invited the Board of Guardians to respond to those concerns. Calthrop's letter said that he has been instructed by the Board to confirm that the contents of Groom's letter were true, but the Board had no observations to make on the case. It was a masterpiece of prevarication and evasion, ending predictably with a request for further instructions.

The third letter, dated 4th April, 1844, responded to Calthrop with clear and unambiguous directions concerning the financial issues raised by Mr Groom. It started with a mild rap on the knuckles, advising the Board of Guardians that their course of action was not the one which should have been pursued. William Joyce, because he was 'in good circumstances' was liable for Mrs Joyce's costs and there was 'not sufficient reason for allowing her to become chargeable to the parish'. Just in case the Board of Guardians did not grasp the point, the Poor Law Commissioners tartly pointed out that the workhouse 'was intended as an asylum for the destitute, not as a residence for persons in a position of Mrs Joyce, possessing means of subsistence independently of parochial support'.

Perhaps as a gesture of support for the Boston Board of Guardians, the letter acknowledged that William Joyce's refusal to allow his wife back into the marital home was beyond their control. However, his refusal to support his wife, exposed him to the penalties of the Vagrant Act. In short, by law, William Joyce remained responsible for his wife whilst they were still married and he had the means to support her.

The final paragraph of the letter advised the Board not to relieve Eliza Joyce, 'either in or out the workhouse', unless she became destitute as a result of William Joyce continuing to refuse any maintenance: in which case 'the compulsory provisions of the law should be put in force against him'.

The resolution to isolate Mrs Joyce and the possibility of punishing her for refusing to work or comply with workhouse rules were passed over in silence.

The final letter, penned by Calthrop, dated 13th April, 1844, in response to the advice from the Poor Law Commissioners, informs them that it had been considered by a large meeting of the Board of Guardians, which by a majority of thirteen votes to four resolved that as long as the husband continued to repay the full expense of the maintenance of his wife and child in the workhouse, no proceedings would be taken against him under the Vagrant Act. In addition, he noted that expenses had now been paid up to 23rd March and that

William Joyce had expressed his willingness to continue maintenance of his wife and child.

The speedy resolution of the issue before any further unwelcome intrusions by the Poor Law Commission would have been advantageous to the Board, but more so to William Joyce. The Boston Union Workhouse in the past had contracted William Joyce to supply potatoes and being prosecuted under the Vagrants Act would not have been good for either his business relations or his social pretensions to respectability in the town.

Breaking the law would also have been something of an embarrassment in that William Joyce seemed to be a man who firmly believed in the strict rule of law, and who made good use of it to protect his own interests. Understandably, he had not been happy that his fruit gardens were the regular target of local ne'er-do-wells, for example, whom he took to court on several occasions to receive their just desserts. Three youths, James Clarke, Robert Burnett and Charles Fisher, all of Boston, received two months hard labour for stealing a quantity of cherries; a boy named William Warrener was given seven days hard labour for stealing an unspecified fruit; and Charles Hotchkin, a man with the unenviable curriculum vitae of being 'a prowling marauder', as well as 'a drunken vagabond', was handed down a sobering sentence of three months hard labour for stealing some apples. It is perhaps indicative of William Joyce's priorities at the time that his prosecution of William Warrener, the child robber, took place three days before the execution of his wife.

Some years after Mrs Joyce had been hanged, William Joyce became embroiled in a legal case involving the Great Northern Railway Company in 1848, relating to a compulsory purchase order on some of his land and gardens, in order to accommodate its Bawtry to Peterborough line. William Joyce appears to have been a man whose life was defined by profit and loss columns, as well as by a no-nonsense strict observance of the law, as he saw it. That a complex dispute concerning the compulsory purchase of his land, involving the interpretation of the Section 15 of the Railway Class Act and a serious difference of opinion concerning the value of his land, should have gone to the Court of Chancery, with all its attendant legal fees, is indicative of William Joyce's singlemindedness, as well as his financial security.

William Joyce died on the 11th December, 1888, a comfortably well-off man, with a personal estate worth in excess of £1400.

Trial of Eliza Joyce for
Wilful Murder, 22nd July 1844

Once William Joyce had been compelled to pay workhouse maintenance for his wife and infant child, Eliza Joyce was no longer a burden to the parish, but it seems she became, more and more, a burden to herself.

On the 1st July, 1844, lying on her sickbed, Mrs Joyce reportedly confessed to Dr Edward Coupland, the workhouse Surgeon attending her, that she had poisoned her two infant daughters, Emma Joyce and Ann Joyce, as well as her teenage stepson, Edward William Joyce. On the 8th July and the 17th July, she was interviewed by John Sturdy, the mayor, who was also one of the Board of Guardians, concerning her confession to murder, who consequently signed a warrant for her arrest. Mrs Joyce was taken by steam packet from Boston to Lincoln the next day, to be tried for murder .

The wheels of legal bureaucracy had turned remarkably quickly.

Thomas, Lord Denman and Justice Thomas Coltman, arrived to open the commission in the city and county courts at 11 o'clock on Saturday, 20th July, 1844. They were met by the High Sheriff, the Honourable Charles Thomas T Clifford and his civic retinue at the Great Bar Gates, no doubt reinforcing to the most casual onlooker the power of traditional ceremonial and the hierarchical grandeur of the law. Their Lordships were greeted grandly and in the evening they were entertained splendidly by John Kaye, the Bishop of Lincoln, at the episcopal palace at Riseholme, two miles from the city. The day after, both men piously attended the divine service at the Cathedral, where the sermon was preached by the Precentor. On the following Wednesday evening, two days after the sentence of death had been served upon Eliza Joyce, the Judges and the High Sheriff dined comfortably with the Reverend Humphrey Waldo Sibthorp at Washingborough, perhaps discussing, amongst other things, the recent remodelling of Hagnaby Priory, the family seat of Thomas Coltman.

After the formality of swearing in the Grand Jury, Justice Coltman began his address: whilst the cases for consideration were not distinguished by their number, the list did contain 'crimes of great enormity'. The main focus of his attention was not the case of Eliza Joyce however, but of Elizabeth Johnson, also accused of child poisoning, at Benington. It may be that the reasons for the Eliza Joyce case being only mentioned in passing was that she had pleaded guilty, and therefore was a formality, and also because the case of Elizabeth Johnson was complex and problematic, involving what Coltman termed 'some nice points of law'.

The earliest report of the trial was in *The Times*, published on 24th July, 1844, two days before the accounts in the *Lincolnshire Chronicle* and the *Stamford Mercury*. Whilst there are verbal reminiscences and inevitable duplications suggesting a possible familiarity with the report in *The Times*, it is not always clear whether the Lincolnshire newspapers were consciously making use of it or whether they were drawing upon an intermediate source, which itself was relying upon the account of the trial in *The Times*.

The report on Eliza Joyce's trial appeared in the newspaper's Crown Court section, with the strapline *A Series of Murders*. The report was used in various forms, attributed and unattributed, on the same day, by other London newspapers, such as the *St James's Chronicle*, *Pictorial Times* and *Morning Post*. It was also used a few days later in London, by *The Weekly Dispatch*, *The Shipping and Mercantile Gazette* and *London Evening Standard*, amongst others, moving out into the provinces, where it appeared partially or almost verbatim. In addition, large chunks of the report were later used in the broadside published in Lincoln, as part of the commercial exploitation of the execution of Mrs Joyce.

The opening of the report in *The Times* created the impression, or perhaps the illusion, that the reporter had been present in the Lincoln courtroom, describing Mrs Joyce as 'a mild and not uninteresting looking woman'.

The minimal business of the court was economically summarised and the demeanour of the condemned woman described sympathetically. The clichéd epithets of 'wretched' and 'miserable' were used, but without any sense of triumphalism or melodrama. Observing that those present were unlikely to leave without having had their hearts touched and their spirits left incapable of enjoyment for some time, came close to hyperbole and sentimentality, it is true; but what followed created a sense of the dignity of Eliza Joyce in her darkest moment in court. If accurate, her response to being condemned to death was one of 'patient calmness and contrite sincerity'; her resolution was evident, but appropriately subdued, indicative of 'an awfully acute mental agony that we never yet have seen so strikingly evinced by any male criminal so sentenced for an offence of any kind'.

It was an overtly sympathetic description of Mrs Joyce, perhaps too sympathetic to be of interest to the *Lincolnshire Chronicle*, and especially the *Stamford Mercury*, who both had their own less charitable versions of the accused. In addition, there may have been some reluctance to make use of what followed in *The Times* report, as some of it was contentious and, in several respects, demonstrably inaccurate.

The bare-bone account of the background to the trial, describing the two indictments against Eliza Joyce of poisoning her children, as well as her acquittal on the charge of poisoning Edward William Joyce, wrongly stated that Ann Joyce died at the age of six months. A sense of the reporter's uncertainty about some of the finer details of the case was also indicated by his vague assertion that Edward William Joyce was 'of some years growth' when he died.

The court proceeding against Eliza Joyce consisted of very little more than a reading of the indictment, the receiving of the plea with the usual formalities and then the passing of the death sentence. The information related to witness depositions which the newspaper had subjoined for the benefit of the reader had not been made public in court.

The Times therefore provided a useful account of the witness depositions, which was recycled more or less intact by many other newspapers, excepting the *Lincolnshire Chronicle* and *Stamford Mercury*.

The list of depositions started with both of Mrs Joyce's confessions to John Sturdy, on the 8th and the 17th July, the second interview adding more detail relating to the poisoning of Ann Joyce.

The initial deposition from Eliza Joyce focused upon the poisoning of her stepson, Edward William Joyce. Mrs Joyce now confessed to having given the boy two teaspoonfuls of the arsenic purchased in Boston. According to the report of the examination by John Sturdy, Eliza Joyce admitted that she had not told the truth in an earlier deposition denying any administration of arsenic to her stepson.

This was followed by an admission that about eight months after her marriage to William Joyce, she administered laudanum to Emma Joyce, the child of her husband's first wife: the substance was purchased from another Boston druggist, Mr Smith. She estimated that she had given Emma about two teaspoonfuls at about 6 o'clock in the evening, and she had died almost immediately after a fit. Dr Ingram had been sent for, but he arrived too late to save the child; she had not told the doctor about the laudanum.

When Emma Joyce had died in October, 1841, Eliza Joyce was pregnant with Ann Joyce, who was born in the following January. She was given two teaspoonfuls of the laudanum from Mr Smith, which sent the infant into convulsions. Once again, Dr Ingram was called out and his solution to the problem was to put the baby in a warm bath, but she died the following night.

Mrs Joyce was unable to explain why she had poisoned three children: she and Mr Joyce 'had words' during her period of rest after the birth of Ann, but in general they were on 'middling terms'. She had been induced to make her confession because her mind was 'so burdened that she could not live, and she hoped, as she had now confessed, she should be better'.

According to the report, she had made a similar confession to Susanna Francis, the workhouse Nurse, Mr Wilson, the Master of the workhouse, and also to Dr Coupland, the workhouse Surgeon.

The second statement made to John Sturdy, on the 17th July, was less extensive, and to some extent, went over old ground in its recollection of dates and events; however, it provided some interesting domestic details about the poisoning of three weeks old Ann.

A day or two before Ann died, Eliza Joyce had the child upstairs in bed with her, who was apparently in good health . She took a bottle out of a box, which contained laudanum, and gave the infant two teaspoonfuls of it. Some laudanum remained in the bottle which she placed back in the box by her bedside. She thought that she remembered putting the bottle in the cupboard the next day.

Soon after having given Ann Joyce the laudanum, the child went into fits, at which point her husband sent for Dr Ingram. The nurse came upstairs and removed the child from the bed, although Mrs Joyce said nothing about the laudanum.

Ann Joyce continued having fits almost all of the following day, and died the following night.

The statement finished with a repetition of her comment about her relationship with her husband in general being on middling terms.

The confessional statements by Eliza Joyce were followed by the deposition of Ann Howard, the Boston nurse, who had attended her confinement. The fifty-four year old widow provided a good deal of precise information, some of it possibly prejudicial to Mrs Joyce.

The account provided by Mrs Howard in her deposition was impressive in its precision after over eighteen months. Around 8.30 on the evening of Thursday, 20th January, 1842, she remembered undressing Ann Joyce who was, she recalled, quite a healthy child. After undressing the child, she had placed it in bed with her mother, left the bed chamber, and went downstairs for about an hour. Mrs Howard was quite insistent that as far as she was aware nobody else was in the bedroom during that time. At 9.30, she returned to the room reportedly to feed the baby. On removing the child from the bed, she noticed that its hand was doubled up near its chest and that the mouth was so rigid that she was unable to feed it. Mrs Howard, in some alarm at not being able to get the child's mouth open, alerted Mrs Joyce to the difficulties by asking her what was happening. The alleged reply was an astonishing one in view of the gravity of the situation: 'Oh dear, I don't know; for it's been restless ever since it's been in bed'.

At this point, the nurse placed the baby back into bed with her mother and also climbed into the bed herself to monitor the child. About half an hour later, she noticed that Ann Joyce had gone into convulsions and commented to Mrs Joyce that she thought the child was dying. If Mrs Joyce's initial response to her child's problems was oddly unconcerned, her reaction to the convulsing baby next to her in the bed, bordered on the incredible. She told the nurse to inform her husband about what was happening so that he could send for Dr Ingram, but her reported initial response to Mrs Howard's fearful declaration was casual to the point of complete indifference: 'Oh dear, do you think so?'

The apparent lethargy of Mrs Joyce in dealing with a life-threatening emergency was emphasised by the reported reactions of both William Joyce and Dr Ingram: the former 'immediately' went for medical assistance, whilst on arrival, the doctor 'immediately' ordered the child to be placed in a warm bath.

According to Mrs Howard, Ann Joyce's convulsions continued throughout the night, but by around 9 o'clock, she was much better, the convulsions having almost ceased. Mrs Howard left the house an hour later and did not return until about 8 o'clock that evening, when she found the baby once again convulsing. At about 1 o'clock in the early hours of the morning, the baby died.

The report in *The Times* of Mrs Howard's deposition also included material, which was not mentioned in any later reports, relating to the ill-health of Ann Joyce. The child's mouth was not only mishapen, but was also black above the top lip, which disappeared after she died. In addition, Mrs Howard presented further information which possibly reinforced a sense of Mrs Joyce being partially insensible to the death of her child: 'Mrs Joyce did not fret, but appeared to mourn.' The deposition also drew attention to the fact that there was a cupboard in the chamber where Mrs Joyce slept, containing a number of bottles, but Mrs Howard was unsure as to whether they contained medicine 'or other matter'.

The reference to a collection of bottles in the cupboard next to the bed would seem almost trite in its unexceptional nature and may account for it not having been included in some later versions of Mrs Howard's deposition. In any case, the fact of the bottles being in close proximity to Mrs Joyce's bed was mentioned in her second deposition to John Sturdy, so it was hardly a shocking revelation of a secret stash of poison.

However, the reported depositions in *The Times* also included one from a woman who was never mentioned again, except by those newspapers which were quoting from *The Times* verbatim.

Mildred Morley, the wife of James Morley, a shipwright of Boston, had been in the service of William Joyce for a short time. During that time, when Edward William Joyce was ill in the front bedroom, she found three or four small bottles in a cupboard. One of the bottles was about half full of laudanum. Even more sinister, perhaps, was the fact that the label had been torn off, although luckily, the eagle-eyed Mrs Morley was still able to read the contents from the remaining pieces of the label stuck on the bottle. There had been labels on the other bottles and they too had been removed. If it was true, it was hardly compelling; if it was untrue, Mrs Morley's story fittingly found the oblivion which it probably deserved.

The deposition of Ann Howard looked back over eighteen months; that of Rachel Tingle, aged sixty-seven, also a widow, and the mother of William Joyce's first wife, looked back even further, to the death of her granddaughter Emma in October 1841. Mrs Tingle remembered having been at the house of William Joyce on the Sunday before Emma had died: however, she could not remember the precise day of the month. She recalled that whilst her granddaughter was unwell she was still able to play, which she did for most of the day. Mrs Tingle went home between 8 and 9 o'clock at night, returning at 10 o'clock the following morning. She discovered Emma playing under the stairs, as on the previous day. Mrs Tingle asked Mrs Joyce if she wanted her to stay and look after Emma, but her offer was declined with the words 'You need not stay', which Mrs Tingle interpreted as a rather curt response. Mrs Tingle left the house and did not return until the following evening, having heard that Emma had died.

Beyond the implication that Mrs Joyce had been discourteous to Mrs Tingle, with the additional more sinister suggestion that she did not want her in the house, the deposition seemed to add very little to an understanding of the case. Except that, according to the report, Mrs Tingle also insisted that on finding little Emma dead, Mrs Joyce 'said very little about the death of the child'.

Any reluctance by newspaper editors to use the version of the Eliza Joyce case published in *The Times* without a degree of scepticism, was perhaps confirmed by the account of the deposition of Dr Edward Ingram.

The deposition of Dr Ingram reflected his involvement with the Joyce family and the death of their two infants. He had been called out to attend Emma Joyce, but he had arrived to find her dead; he had also been called out to attend the infant Ann, whom he found to be having convulsions. He treated her with the necessary medicines both on that day and following day, when she appeared to be no better. Despite the professional treatment of Dr Ingram, the infant died.

In relation to Emma Joyce, he could not remember whether she had been eighteen months or two years of age at the time. He thought that he first attended her in late September, but definitely on the 11th October, when he found the child dead. He could not recall what had been wrong with Emma Joyce nor could he remember whether or not he had examined the child after she had died.

The doctor's memory was slightly more clear concerning his attendance of Ann Joyce, although far from exact about details. He remembered attending the infant about 1 o'clock in the morning of 21st January and finding her in convulsions. She was provided with a quantity of medicines, but he was called again the following day, and finding her no better, he provided additional treatment. Unfortunately, the child died during the course of the night.

The narrative of the events in relation to Ann Joyce is not entirely clear, however, producing a divergent account from that of both Mrs Joyce and Mrs Howard. Most puzzling was his failure to mention the initial treatment of a warm bath when attending Ann Joyce.

In the final analysis, the inability of the doctor to recall basic medical procedures and his vagueness concerning what medicines he had dispensed, would not have inspired confidence in the accuracy and usefulness of his deposition.

The report of the depositions of Edward Coupland and James Wilson appeared to be more helpful, although not entirely free from uncertainties, especially in relation to the quantities of laudanum allegedly used by Eliza Joyce.

Dr Edward Coupland had been the first person to hear Eliza Joyce's confession, on Monday, 1st July,

1844. According to the doctor's deposition, he had been attending Mrs Joyce for a prolonged period and stated that she had been in the workhouse for some time. During a daily visit, she confessed that she had administered arsenic to Edward William Joyce. The doctor asked her how much arsenic she had used, to which Mrs Joyce answered a tea-spoonful, adding that she had only done it once.

The conversation then turned to the death of both Emma and Ann, the doctor having been involved in the exhumation of the body of the former on suspicion of foul play, but without having found any traces of arsenic. Eliza Joyce confessed to Dr Coupland that she had used laudanum to kill the two girls, not arsenic. Once again, the doctor wanted to establish the quantity of poison used. A spoonful for the baby and two for the older girl, was Mrs Joyce's response, although these quantities were to change in a later conversation to two spoonsful for Ann and four for Emma. The laudanum, she confirmed, had been bought from the shop of Mr Smith in Boston.

Dr Coupland had been of the opinion that there would be little point in exhuming the body of the infant Ann, due to her having been interred so long ago.

The final deposition published was that of James Wilson, the Master of the Boston workhouse, to whom Mrs Joyce made her confession on the 1st and

2nd July, 1844. Mrs Joyce confessed to administering two teaspoons of arsenic to her stepson and the same quantity of laudanum to Emma, the daughter of her husband by his former wife, and Ann, her own child. Not surprisingly, Mr Wilson asked why she had done such things, to which he received a melancholic response which said a good deal, yet said so little: 'I don't know except I thought it was such a thing to bring a family of children into this troublesome world'.

The report of the trial in the *Lincolnshire Chronicle* was relatively short: the lack of any courtroom drama meant that the focus was upon the background to the trial, didactic sermonising and the occasional dramatic invention to enliven a foregone conclusion.

The newspaper had a firm grasp on such basics as names and dates, but the overuse of the formulaic utterance of 'it is said' and its variants, suggest an insecure reliance on anecdote and hearsay, which in turn produced errors and fanciful speculations passed off as truth. The reporter was aware that William Joyce had refused to have his wife back into his home, but mistakenly said that the refusal was based on his prescient suspicion that she had murdered the two infants, as well as his son. In addition, William Joyce had also generously given his wife an allowance to support herself, but after a short time 'she began to waste away' and entered the workhouse.

In the absence of any legal drama, the reporter indulged himself and his readers in human drama. The reason for Mrs Joyce's admission to murder in the workhouse, allegedly in her own words, was that 'her existence was complete hell on earth', whose only relief was a full confession, despite knowing that she would be hanged. The appearance of Eliza Joyce at the bar was an opportunity to create a scene of utter human wreckage. The prisoner was 'bent double with sickness and misery' and seemed 'the very impersonation of wretchedness'. The purple prose ended with a variant of a phrase used several times by Dickens in his work, describing a very weak Eliza Joyce who had to be assisted up the steps of the dock and into a chair, as being 'attired in deep mourning'.

The report of Lord Justice Coltman's summing up of the case, with its dry formalities relating to painful duty, passing the awful sentence of the law and the condemned prisoner seeking forgiveness from God, was perhaps something of an anti-climax after the powerful evocation of human dejection in the dock. However, the report did at least end with an intriguing and perhaps puzzling explanation – admittedly hearsay – for Eliza Joyce having poisoned her own children: she had been afraid of having a large family.

The *Stamford Mercury*, published on the same day as the *Lincolnshire Chronicle*, produced two separate accounts: a short one in the section of the newspaper appropriately titled 'Friday's Express', and a second, much longer one found on the previous page, which provided the reader with material previously unreported about the case.

The first report rapidly established that 'the unhappy woman' had been condemned to death, after admitting to the murder of her children. She had since entertained the hope of a royal pardon to avoid her ignominious fate, but clearly this would be in vain. Whilst her health was said to have recently improved, she had the appearance of someone 'weighed down by a consciousness of deep guilt as well as bodily suffering.' At this point, the reader might well have had some sympathy for the felon; however, any such delicate feelings were luckily averted by the reporter's cautionary note. An understanding of the woeful story of Eliza Joyce was essential for the vicious, the cruel and the reckless in society, if they were to avoid 'the extremity of horror' to which 'the unrestrained passions of mankind' might lead them. The report insisted that Eliza Joyce did not have the slightest chance of avoiding being hanged, but that would not be the end of her difficulties. The short notice of Eliza Joyce's impending fate ended with a chilling melodramatic flourish, reminding the reader of her imminent appointment with the Almighty: first execution 'and after that, the Judgement'.

It may be that the report, in its tasty concoction of casual triumphalism and self-righteous moralising was intended to tempt the reader into looking back at the details of the case available in the expanded version of the story, found on the previous page in the Crown Court section of the newspaper.

The extended report of the trial focused upon the details of the circumstances surrounding the confession of Eliza Joyce in the workhouse and some of its key players. Some of the comments, made in passing, suggest strongly that the newspaper had useful sources of good information, probably from inside the Boston Union Workhouse, which it used to supplement its account of the trial: it was, of course, the *Stamford Mercury* which had published the revelations about the refusal of William Joyce to pay for his wife's residence at the workhouse.

After a brief overview of the charges against Eliza Joyce of poisoning two infant children with laudanum, the report began its construction of the criminal identity of the woman by reminding the reader that she had been acquitted in July, 1843, of the poisoning of her stepson. During the course of that trial, Mrs Joyce 'appeared a fine healthy woman' and 'seemed quite unconcerned at the grave charge.' It was not an observation made in the newspaper's report at the time, but in the context of having later confessed to murder, it created a retrospective image of Eliza Joyce as being either supremely arrogant or naively unaware.

It was noted by the newspaper that William Joyce 'from a grave sense of her guilt', refused to have his wife back in the marital home, and she was sent to the Boston Union Workhouse with the infant which she had held during the course of the trial. Whilst there is some question about the accuracy of the chronology of her rejection by William Joyce, the newspaper asserted quite rightly that Mrs Joyce struggled to make her husband maintain her once she was in the workhouse. The most interesting assertion, however, was that 'all her friends forsook her'. Unfortunately, there is no elaboration of this claim, and it certainly does not appear in any other account; in addition, the truth of it does not sit easily with the exchange of official letters published by the newspaper itself in March 1844, in which it was revealed that the Board of Guardians had agreed to deny Eliza Joyce any visiting rights.

Inevitably, the explanation for Mrs Joyce's confession was overwhelming remorse for what she had done; almost equally inevitably, the confident image of her at the first trial was overtly contrasted with that of her at the second, in which she was described as 'thin and pale, and seemed utterly woe-begone'. In a variant of the version published in the *Lincolnshire Chronicle*, the torment in Eliza Joyce's mind was characterised by the infernal image of living 'in hell-flames.' The truth and accuracy of both versions is perhaps questionable in that the *Lincolnshire Chronicle* version prefaced its description with, 'She is said to have declared', whilst the *Stamford Mercury* modified its claim to absolute truthfulness with, 'It is understood that.' Whatever the truth of the matter, both reports created a rhetorical journalistic appropriateness by linking Eliza Joyce with the pangs of a guilty conscience and the horrific, but just, punishment of sinners in the afterlife.

Of Eliza Joyce's guilt there could be no doubt, according to the report: after having been removed from the workhouse she had repeated her confession to the Chaplain of the Lincoln County gaol on the morning of the trial; in court, she had pleaded guilty to the charges of murder, 'in a tremulous voice'. On putting on the black cap, it was observed that Lord Justice Coltman 'appeared greatly affected.' The nature of his Lordship's discomfort, however, was not so much to do with sadness at the execution of a young woman, but more to do with outrage at the brutality of the crime. It was not his Lordship's first experience of capital crime, having sentenced James and William Lightfoot to be hanged at Bodmin gaol in 1840 for the merciless beating to death of Nevill Norway, However, he declared to Eliza Joyce that the destruction of her innocent children was the most shocking case he had ever had to pass sentence upon. There was no possibility of any reprieve and the only advice he could offer to her was 'to seek mercy through the redeeming merits of our Saviour.' At which point, his Lordship passed the sentence of death.

Charting the different versions of the trial and sentencing of Eliza Joyce in contemporary newspapers often creates a sense that an accurate representation of people and events was secondary to a well-packaged product, constructed from whatever materials were to hand at the time. The silent reinvention of the story, adding bits here and bits there from versions published in other places hardly mattered it seems, as most consumers would have been content to read an engaging human-interest story in their local newspaper and then just move on to the next column. Mrs Joyce, like many others on trial for their lives in the C19th, became a flexible concept rather than a human being, as fragments of her story were recycled, arranged and rearranged, over time and place.

Whilst the selection of materials and the way in which they were manipulated provide an interesting insight into a newspaper's values, its decisions concerning what information not to use as it ran the risk of producing an inconvenient narrative disruption, are often equally instructive.

This is especially evident in the absence from many newspapers of the most compelling part of report of the trial in *The Times*, which was an astonishing extended analysis, amounting to a strident manifesto, which followed the sympathetic description of Eliza Joyce in court. It was surprising, both in tone and content, on several fronts: first, it strongly called for an enquiry into 'the whole conduct, over the long space of time in question, of the husband of this unhappy convict'; secondly, that before sentencing Eliza Joyce to public execution, due diligence demanded a more robust understanding of all the circumstances and impulses which had resulted in a woman killing her own children, including her state of mind at the time.

The plight of Eliza Joyce, and by extension, others like her, was compared to the recent case of the Frenchman, Augustus Dalmas, who had brutally cut the throat of his lover, Sarah MacFarlane, on Battersea Bridge, in April, 1844. Dalmas was sentenced to death, but on the evidence of his prior erratic and violent behaviour, the result of a head injury sustained after falling from a ladder, he was judged to be insane. He was incarcerated in Bethlem Royal Hospital as a lunatic, but was transported for life the following year to New South Wales.

As the concepts of 'partial insanity' and 'a diseased perception of the great principles of right and wrong' had saved Dalmas from the full penalty of the law, the same should have been applied in the case of Eliza Joyce. 'Women do not, in cold blood, destroy their own innocent offspring', asserted the report, in its final paragraph.

Such radically sympathetic journalism in a case of infanticide in a society which idealised motherhood would not have been easy reading for many.

It is no surprise that few newspapers made use of the highly combustible thundering from *The Times*, even if they drew upon the account of the witness depositions. Where newspapers did make use of the forthright opinions of *The Times*, they usually did so with a more conservative edited version, as in the *Devizes and Wiltshire Gazette*, Thursday, 25th July, which circumspectly omitted material bluntly critical of the legislative status quo.

As well as being a plea for a more enlightened understanding of the relationship between the irrational and the criminal, especially in the case of women, it was also a barely disguised attack on public execution. The horrified description of 'a woman, upon the scaffold, before the brutal gaze of a huge mass of heartless, if untempted, ruffians', left no doubt where the writer stood on the issue.

Incarceration and Execution of Eliza Joyce at Lincoln Castle

The reports of the execution of Eliza Joyce, 2nd August, 1844, in the *Stamford Mercury* and the

Lincolnshire Chronicle, were extensive, reminding the reader of the background to the case, as well as feeding the unsavoury popular taste for melodrama and retribution. Both created a convenient image of Eliza Joyce, not especially sympathetic to her beyond the usual tired epithets of 'the unfortunate woman', 'the unhappy culprit' and 'the wretched woman'.

It is clear that the account in the *Stamford Mercury* was the earlier of the two, in that the version in the *Lincolnshire Chronicle* explicitly corrects a supposed error relating to the construction of the gallows, found in the Stamford newspaper. Inevitably, the reports overlapped in many respects, although the *Stamford Mercury*, published some extraordinary claims concerning the private life of Eliza Joyce which damned her even more than she had damned herself.

As a preface to the culmination of 'the fateful history', the *Lincolnshire Chronicle* focused upon creating an image of William Joyce as an industrious citizen caught up in very unpleasant circumstances. He had lived 'a tolerably happy life' with his wife, this in part being due to his disposition which was 'remarkably inoffensive'. Even after the notoriety of her 'two escapes from the halter', William Joyce paid for her support in the Boston Union Workhouse: the report failed to mention that he had come very close to being arrested under the Vagrant Act for refusing to support his wife and infant child when he had the means to do so.

That Mrs Joyce was hanged on the strength of her own confession provided the newspaper with an opportunity to create a lurid narrative of a monstrous sinner, beyond redemption, consoled only by the kindness of a prison Chaplain and Governor.

Before confessing, Eliza Joyce had been sustained by 'a callous indifference' to what she had done; believing herself to be on the point of death in the workhouse, however, she was overcome by 'the horrors of a guilty conscience'. Compared to the frightful secrets which she had kept hidden for so long, the 'grim destroyer had no terrors for her.' In her distressed confession, Mrs Joyce, was crying out as did Cain, the archetypal killer, whom God refused to grant the release of death, 'my punishment is greater than I can bear'.

The power of confession was once again emphasised by the repetition of the story that Mrs Joyce again admitted her 'destruction of two female children' in gaol, to the prison Chaplain, the Reverend Henry Richter. Her act of contrition apparently lifted her spirits 'as if an incubus had been lifted from her mind', even to the extent of her thinking that she might be given royal clemency. Unfortunately, such hope was confounded by Richter's spiritual direction: the circuit judges had left the city, so she should now prepare herself to meet 'the Judge whose laws she had awfully outraged'. This perhaps blunt spiritual advice was tempered, it seems, by the Reverend Richter's sermon in the prison chapel on the day before her execution. The sermon was heard respectfully and with great attention by all the prisoners, especially by Eliza Joyce, who 'listened with almost breathless eagerness to the words of grace and hope which fell from the lips of the reverend gentleman'.

The praise for the professionalism of the cleric was also extended to the prison Governor, John Nicholson, who visited Mrs Joyce after chapel and who had been 'unremitting in the performance of every attention to the unfortunate woman consistent with his painful duties'. As well as visiting Mrs Joyce in her cell, Captain Nicholson was thoughtful enough to delay the construction of the gallows until the early morning of the execution, rather than on the day before, so that Mrs Joyce was spared having to look upon the place of her impending death for too long. It was cold comfort, but suggests a modicum of humanity towards her.

The description of the final hours of Eliza Joyce evoked an image of resolution and self-possession, even as she gazed at the gallows from her cell. In addition, the newspaper created a sense that she responded graciously to the spiritual consolation she had been offered and that during her final hour in the chapel, she had joined in the service 'with a sincerity which must have been gratifying to the Rev. Chaplain'.

Reading accounts of the lives of prisoners in the last days before their execution as reported in C19th newspapers often creates a sense of a glossy well-tempered fiction when it involved religion and its representatives in their worthy attempts to save the souls of the wretched. It is difficult, of course, to contradict such accounts in the absence of any modifying or contrary alternative narratives, which might rub the shine off such highly polished surfaces.

It is fortunate, therefore, that a detailed account of the Reverend Richter's prison ministry has survived. Whilst most of the entries are just brief records of whom he visited and when, some of them depart from such dull routine, with remarks about the prisoner, and they occasionally preserve snippets of conversation. Whilst the general tenor of his comments on Eliza Joyce do not create a dramatically different narrative, they do produce a more complex one than that implied by an incubus having been 'lifted from her mind' by confessing her crimes to the Chaplain and her listening to an uplifting sermon 'with breathless eagerness', just hours before being hanged in public.

The Reverend Richter ministered to Mrs Joyce from Saturday, 20th July to the morning of her execution on Friday, 2nd August, 1844. On his first encounter with her, she 'persisted in her innocence', which was surprising in that she had already confessed her guilt. The following day, Mrs Joyce was 'much depressed and very unwell', but appeared to be 'very penitent'. On Monday, 22nd, July, Richter visited all the prisoners who were to be put on trial that day and not surprisingly found them all to 'very much distressed'. The fate of Mrs Joyce was recorded briefly, as a curt fact: 'Eliza Joyce condemned'.

From Thursday, 25th July onward, Richter visited Eliza Joyce privately, rather than as part of a group of prisoners. On the following day, he found her 'more composed', but expressed the hope that she would now be penitent. The sense that the reverend gentleman now saw it as his task to probe the guilt of Mrs Joyce, to get beneath the surface of things, is evident from his visit of Saturday, 27th July, which ruefully noted: 'Can get no motive for the crime she committed'.

On Sunday, 28th July, the Reverend Richter visited Mrs Joyce to prepare her for receiving the sacrament, something to which she presumably assented and which the Chaplain viewed as some kind of spiritual progress. The following day, such optimism appeared to have been justified by Mrs Joyce requesting that he gave 'credulity to her declaration of penitence...acknowledging the greatness of her crime, the justice of her punishment, but her hope of forgiveness'. However, what may well have been seen as a triumphant sign of God's grace at work by the

Chaplain, such a plea was probably more to do with feelings of guilt for the distress she had caused her family, rather than any hope of personal salvation. The reason she gave for her contrite declaration was she hoped that 'the feelings of her husband and relations and friends may be soothed with the hope that she leaves the world penitent'.

Henry Richter's sense of Mrs Joyce being on a spiritual journey seemed further justified by her still seeming 'very penitent' on Wednesday 31st July and receiving the sacrament. On the following day, she heard the condemned sermon in the chapel, but the Chaplain does not record any sense of its impact on her: the absence in his account of any reference to 'breathless eagerness' perhaps tells its own story.

The final entry concerning the Chaplain's ministrations to Mrs Joyce in Lincoln prison was written after her execution and in many ways is the most interesting. It is a compound of well-worn facts about her crimes, her demeanour on the morning of the execution along with interesting information which might otherwise have been lost.

His potted history of Mrs Joyce's crimes listed her victims, although Richter wrongly identified Emma Joyce as her own child, her acquittal in Lincoln and her later conviction after a voluntary confession of guilt. The emphasis of the Chaplain was upon the remorse of Mrs Joyce, quoting her words of the 29th July spoken 'with the hope of forgiveness', and her receiving the comfort of the sacrament a short time before being hanged. In one final flourish, Richter recorded that the resolve shown in her sorrowful feelings was 'wonderful and never forsook her to the last.' To support his commentary, the Chaplain recalled a conversation which he had with Eliza Joyce on the night before her trial, asking her if she 'intended to persist in her confession'. She had replied that this would be the case 'for I wish the law to take its course'. It was an attitude of virtuous resolve which she also showed on the morning of her execution, according to the Chaplain.

The narrative up to this point was a somewhat cardboard one, an assurance, at least to himself and his superiors, of a professional job of work well done. What followed provided an almost accidental alternative narrative to that of popular journalism and, ironically, of the Reverend Richter himself.

According to the prison Chaplain, on leaving the chapel 'for the drop', Mrs Joyce begged him to try and reconcile her husband with her infant child whom she was leaving behind; at the same time, she 'expressed a wish that her brother and relatives might be informed of her deep sorrow and penitence. That so they might not have hard feelings against her'. As in her declaration of sorrow on the 29th July, there is more than a hint that her penitential tears were for the pain which she had caused her family, rather than any concern for her soul, as well as being a mother's anxiety for the future of her infant child.

In a moment of common humanity and decency, Richter promised to write to or see her husband: whether he did is not recorded in his journal, but the child, Betsy, was eventually brought up in the Joyce household.

His kind gesture was rapidly followed by a vexed declaration that 'from first to last I could derive from her no motive'. Accessing the deepest secrets of the woman condemned to death was clearly the driver of his professional pride and it was therefore a source of great frustration that he had failed to make any progress in solving the riddle of Eliza Joyce. It is not clear whether the conversation which he transcribed took place on the morning of the execution or before, but the words of Eliza Joyce had a familiarity to them in their dreamy elusiveness, reminiscent of her conversations with Mrs Howard, as Ann Joyce lay dying. Richter asked Mrs Joyce directly if she was motivated by the wish to rid herself of children not her own. Mrs Joyce's response was as unhelpful to the Chaplain as it was enigmatic: 'I suppose it must have been so'. Perhaps sensing that he was getting somewhere in resolving the issue of motivation, he followed up with the obvious question as to why she had destroyed a child of her own, if that was the case. Eliza Joyce replied with a not very obvious answer: 'Oh I cannot tell'.

At this point in the journal, in a desperate and not very convincing attempt to square the circle, Richter penned his own explanation. 'It strikes me', he wrote, 'that she might have destroyed her own with the others to make their deaths less suspicious.'

The explanation failed to take account of its illogical chronology: the Chaplain clearly did not have a vocation for criminal investigation.

The extended entry returned to safer and more familiar territory when it recorded that up to the time of the murder, Eliza Joyce had had little to do with religion and at the Assize trial of 1843 was described as a Dissenter. He seemed, in the end, to take comfort from her profession of the Christian faith and implied reconciliation with the Anglican communion through her penitential utterances and her taking of the sacrament.

At least the execution had followed procedure correctly 'with dignity and order' and all who attended the execution treated Mrs Joyce with respect and decorum, for which 'she expressed her thankfulness'.

The final mention of the troubles of Eliza Joyce was written by the Reverend Richter the next day, recording the unexpected spiritual bonus that 'Joyce's past seems to have made a fearful impression on all of them. The woman Jessup seems much affected'.

That Elizabeth Jessup should have been 'much affected' is hardly surprising: she had been tried and acquitted of murdering her four month old daughter, on the grounds of insanity. In response to being asked why she had cut her own child's throat, she replied using words which might have been spoken by Mrs Joyce herself: 'she talked about her desolate children'.

The *Lincolnshire Chronicle* claimed that the time and date of the execution of Mrs Joyce had not been generally known and so was surprised at the number of men, women and children gathered in the Castle yard and at other vantage points, who had travelled from local villages and further to see the spectacle.

The description of the final five minutes of the life of Eliza Joyce, restrained, detached and slowed down by a plethora of detail, emphasised the austere ritual of public execution in Lincoln. The bleak cortege began its sombre journey at 11.55, departing from the door of the gaol, led by two bailiffs holding symbolic rods and followed by the Chaplain, the Under-Sheriff, the Surgeon, the executioner, two gaolers and Mrs Joyce attired in black.

And the bell tolled.

The sanitised dignity of such a dreadful procession, across the green to the flight of steps by the side of the gate, along the constructed platform and on to the roof of Cobb Hall, created the illusion of civilised decorum, which the *Lincolnshire Chronicle* was at pains to maintain in its report. Inevitably, the human realities which occasionally disturbed the smooth surface of ceremony also had to be accommodated by the newspaper. Mrs Joyce carried a prayer book in her hand, but appeared to be 'too overcome' to read any comfort it might offer; she walked towards her death 'with a tolerable firmness', but occasionally had to be supported; on the recently constructed platform, she stopped and turned 'as if to take a lingering farewell', but at the same time, 'her face and features wore an aspect of ghastly agony'.

The pace of the narrative increased as the executioner performed his routine of pinioning the arms of the condemned prisoner and then pulling down the white cap over the face, before the final ascent to the noose.

According to the report, as the clock struck midday, the rope was adjusted, the burial service was read and the huge crowd fell silent.

The report ended with the reassurance that Eliza Joyce died without a struggle and that the correct protocols were followed: her body was cut down after an hour and buried in the ground at the back of gaol.

The report in the *Stamford Mercury*, in its lack of contextual information, assumed a familiarity with the background of the case of Eliza Joyce. After it highlighted size of the crowd, estimated to be between five and six thousand, it focused instead on her workhouse confession. Her mind had been filled with 'the horrors of remorse' and the weight of her conscience had reduced her to 'the lowest state of physical disability.' Despite knowing that confessing her crimes would result in her execution, followed by facing the 'Tribunal of her Maker', Mrs Joyce had felt compelled to unburden herself.

What followed was a series of snapshots of Eliza Joyce's final days in Lincoln Castle gaol. She was constantly attended by the Chaplain and seemed to have become truly penitent. The condemned sermon was preached on Thursday, 1st August, taking as its text Psalm 51, verse 14: 'Deliver me from blood guiltiness, oh God, thou God of my salvation, and my tongue shall sing aloud of thy righteousness'.

On the day of her execution, despite an awareness of the preparations on the roof of Cobb Hall, Mrs Joyce remained unaffected and even held on to the hope of a royal reprieve. However, the report revealed that the prisoner really wished to die in order to relieve herself of a guilty conscience.

In contrast to the *Lincolnshire Chronicle*, the description of the walk from the gaol to the place of execution was minimal and impressionistic, noting that she walked more firmly than she did at her trial, although at one point, she appeared to be close to fainting, but adding the surprising detail that just before mounting the platform, she stopped and spent a short time in devotion.

Even more surprising perhaps, once on the platform, Mrs Joyce asked for something to cover her face. Calcraft, the hangman, either in obedient response or as part of the ritual of execution, put the cap on her, which she reportedly pulled down over her chin: a feat which may have been quite difficult with her arms pinioned.

Having reported that Eliza Joyce died with scarcely a struggle, the routine report suddenly came to life.

The reactions of the large crowd did not involve awed and respectful silence, as reported in the *Lincolnshire Chronicle*, but rather its opposite. Some indulged in 'profane and brutal observations, betokening rather a fiendish pleasure at the sight than the sad and painful reflection it was designed to produce'.

It was a concern which Sir John Gurney would have heartily applauded.

The *Stamford Mercury* was moving towards its final word on the theme of dreadful warnings to the living from the dead. The report insisted that drunkenness, murder, a hell of mind and the scaffold were surely compelling reasons to learn a moral lesson from the life and death of Eliza Joyce. She had committed murder, but could not explain the reason for it, merely stating that it was a hard thing to bring up children in such a troublesome world. However, the explanation for the murder of her own children was clear enough to the *Stamford*

Mercury: she was 'addicted to intemperate habits, and becoming listless and lazy, she did not like the trouble of a family'.

Having asserted that Eliza Joyce was an alcoholic, the report reminded the reader that she had been in the prime of life and respectably connected; her relationship with her husband, once again described as 'a remarkably inoffensive man', had been a reasonably happy one. It hardly needed to be made explicit to the reader that alcohol was responsible for the loss of respectability and the disintegration of family life, as well as the death of her children.

The report ended, as did that in the *Lincolnshire Chronicle*, by reminding the reader that Eliza Joyce was the grim successor to Elizabeth Warriner, the previous woman to be hanged in Lincolnshire, who had also poisoned the son of her husband's first wife with arsenic.

The report of the execution of Eliza Joyce appeared in a large number of newspapers beyond Lincolnshire. On the whole, they were short space fillers, probably because the big story of the week was the execution in Nottingham of William Saville, who had cut the throat of his wife and three children with a razor. The punishment of an impenitent brutal murderer was sensational in itself, but it was given added value by the number of fatalities and injuries caused by a crowd surge crush.

It is no surprise that these short reports contributed nothing different to the story of Eliza Joyce. The only exception to this was that which appeared in the *North Star and Leeds General Advertiser*, on the 10th August, 1844. It reported that a large crowd had gathered to watch the execution, which included people who had travelled fifty to sixty miles; a large number had also travelled from the southern parts of the country (*sic)* where Mrs Joyce was known personally.

If such a precise knowledge of the composition of the crowd was dubious, the additional information about the personal life of Mrs Joyce was ludicrous. Admittedly based on common rumour and without a secure foundation, she was also guilty of two other murders: her young lover, killed many years previous in a fit of jealousy, and also, her own father.

Having taken its lead from the *Stamford Mercury*'s perhaps flexible approach to the truth, nothing had been added to the story of Eliza Joyce's troubled life, other than crass piffle of the most lurid kind.

The two reported explanations given by Mrs Joyce for her crimes were rather enigmatic, but both involved the difficulty, as she perceived it, of being responsible for children. In her workhouse confession to James Wilson, responding to his question concerning her motivation for killing her own children, she stated that 'it was such a thing to bring a family of children into this troublesome world' – an explanation scoffed at by the *Stamford Mercury*, which preferred its own version of neglect rooted in alcohol. The *Lincolnshire Chronicle*, using an unattributed source, more cautiously and less scathingly, reported that Eliza Joyce had been afraid of having a large family.

That Mrs Joyce should have allegedly expressed a fearfulness about having a large family has some credibility. On marrying William Joyce in March 1841, she had taken on the responsibility of four children; by January 1842, she had an additional child and most likely become pregnant again soon after, still only aged twenty-eight. Rather than an abdication of personal responsibility, as suggested by the *Stamford Mercury*, it may be that Eliza Joyce was simply overwhelmed by present difficulties and future expectations.

The diatribe in *The Times* concerning the injustice of Mrs Joyce's state of mind not being considered before sentencing her to death, encapsulated a deep sense of unease about judicial due process and its lack of understanding about emotional disturbance as a possible explanation for a criminal act.

Patrick Wilson in *Murderess, A Study of the Women Executed in Britain since 1843*, suggested somewhat vaguely that the root of Eliza Joyce's crimes was melancholia. He also speculated that when she attempted to poison her stepson she 'may have been insane', her mind having been deranged by the sudden natural deaths of Emma and Ann Joyce.

Katherine Watson, in her book, *Poisoned Lives: English Poisoners and their Victims*, is more circumspect in her analysis, suggesting that Eliza Joyce was suffering with mental health problems, 'perhaps depression exacerbated by alcoholism'. The explanation of the poisoning of the three children in terms of mental illness is a credible one, although its exacerbation by the consumption of alcohol is debatable. She also indirectly raises the more specific possibility that Mrs Joyce was suffering from puerperal insanity, a condition which was becoming better understood by the middle of the C19th and developing its own taxonomies, although this was clearly not the case in Boston and Lincoln.

Recent research on puerperal insanity and the impact of its symptoms upon the lives of nineteenth-century women and their families is certainly helpful in an understanding of the case. The behaviour and words of Eliza Joyce, if correctly reported, share many of the destructive symptoms of the condition. Her seeming emotional detachment from the death of the two infants referred to by Mrs Tingle and Mrs Howard in their depositions, for example, might be seen as symptomatic of puerperal insanity, rather than construed as evidence of an appalling lack of any maternal feelings. The very act of child killing itself might similarly be understood as an extreme of such mental derangement, rather than of brutal wickedness.

Whilst she did not experience the grinding poverty often associated with cases of puerperal insanity, from the outset of her married life she was living under the pressure of close circumstances with a large number of children, and soon to increase. Her killing of Emma took place in October 1841, when she was around six months pregnant; her killing of Ann took place in January 1842, just three weeks after giving birth; and the attempted murder of Edward William took place in September of the same year, by which time, she was almost certainly pregnant with Betsy.

Women suffering from puerperal insanity in the nineteenth-century and beyond sometimes ended their own lives. In one of the few reported cases in Lincolnshire close in time to the Joyce case, for example, Sarah Kempstead, aged forty-three, the wife of the toll-bar keeper, near Crowland, hanged herself, on account of being 'afflicted with a deep despondency of spirits, brought on by puerperal fever, which she could not get the better of'. Clearly Eliza Joyce did not commit suicide in the literal sense, but her confession to infanticide with the inevitable death penalty, was certainly a suicidal act which would bring an end to her physical and mental torment.

That Mrs Joyce endured distressing mental health problems might be seen as speculative in the absence of definitive evidence. However, the daily journal of

Ralph Howett, the Lincoln prison Surgeon, provides some substance to such speculation.

Howett attended Eliza Joyce between Friday, 19th July and Friday, 2nd August, the day of her execution: he sometimes saw her twice a day, depending upon her state of well-being on the morning of his visit. His remarks on Mrs Joyce create a picture of uneven physical and mental health, which is occasionally at odds with the more upbeat account of the Chaplain, Henry Richter.

His initial examination pronounced her to be 'in a delicate state of health', recording after a later visit during the day that Mrs Joyce was 'weak and delicate and complains of having no appetite'. In addition, she was badly constipated, and required 'opening medicine'. On Saturday, 20th July, she showed improvement, but on the following day, she had become 'feverish and restless'. The pattern of day-to-day volatility continued on Monday, 22nd July, the date of her trial before Justice Coltman. On the day, she appeared to be rather better, but on the following day Mrs Joyce was 'very low and nervous and poorly, and very distressed at her sentence.'

Perhaps now realising that there was probably little hope, she deteriorated over the following few days. From the 24th to the 26th July, her mental equilibrium was clearly disturbed, causing her loss of both sleep and appetite. The report of the doctor for Thursday, 25th and Saturday, 27th July make for very difficult reading: on the Thursday, after a bad night, she 'continued in a state of depression'; on the Saturday, Mrs Joyce was 'in great distress and agitation, having just seen her brother.' Surprisingly, in his *Journal* for that day, the Chaplain makes no reference to her having been visited by her brother or its impact on her – being rather more concerned, it seems, with her possible repentance.

In the evening of her brother's visit, Mrs Joyce became less agitated and also ate a small amount of food. She remained in this state for the next few days, described by Howett as either 'composed' or 'tolerably composed'; less convincingly, perhaps, Mrs Joyce was also described as 'rather less depressed' or 'more composed than could be expected.'

The *Journal* entry for Thursday, 1st August, the day before her execution, has the feel of a summative assessment of the prisoner probably intended to reassure Lord Brownlow, who would be signing the document off at the 3rd October Gaol Session, that all was well in Lincoln Castle. Mrs Joyce was now 'in a decidedly improved state of health since she came into prison and her mind is in a surprisingly calm and resigned state.' Unfortunately, the optimism of Howett had to be modified that evening, as Eliza Joyce reverted to being 'a good deal agitated, the Chaplain having just left her'. The connection between the agitation of Mrs Joyce and Henry Richter having left the prison cell is not explained; nor is the Chaplain's *Journal* entry for that evening of any help, as he merely records visiting Eliza Joyce, and two other female prisoners.

Perhaps the imagined terrors of what was to come the next day is explanation enough.

Howett's final visit to Mrs Joyce, on the morning of her execution, described her as being 'surprisingly calm and composed and apparently resigned', a rather more understated description than that of Henry Richter, convinced of the efficacy of his spiritual guidance in raising the spirits of a young woman about to die. The prison doctor's final mention of Eliza Joyce, writing at 1.30 in the afternoon, maintained a sombre professional distancing, merely noting that she had been executed and 'is now put into her coffin and screwed down.'

Should an understanding of the crimes of Eliza Joyce have been informed by contemporary medical thinking about the maternal illnesses, puerperal in particular, rather than welcomed as exemplary material for the instruction of the vicious, the cruel and the reckless, the final outcome of her life might have been different.

If Mrs Joyce was suffering from mental health problems of any kind, her subsequent misfortunes of being disowned by her husband, coping with financial uncertainty and enduring being isolated inside the brutal regime of the workhouse, where she had all visiting rights removed, would only have intensified those problems. In less than two years, her life had slid slowly out of control from comfortable respectability into the depths of a squalid sink of workhouse misery, alongside the other assorted casualties of an unequal and unjust society.

There is a sense that Mrs Joyce might well have been a strong and difficult woman for men in authority to manage: she refused to take no for an answer from the chemist when initially being denied arsenic; she had reportedly refused to sign her deposition for the Boston Magistrates; and she had truculently refused to do such tedious work as unpicking oakum in the Boston Union Workhouse. However, by 1st July, 1844, that strength seems to have reached its limit when she confessed her crimes to Dr Edward Coupland, after having endured several weeks of physical and mental debilitation.

During her final grim days of confinement in the condemned cell at Lincoln Castle, feeling the moments tick away, it was reported by both Lincolnshire newspapers that Mrs Joyce was hoping Queen Victoria would intercede and save her from the rough, bungling hands of William Calcraft, the hangman. If true, it was a strange and forlorn hope, as unreal as it was pathetic, an apparent sad grab at an illusory straw by a woman at the end of her tether and soon to be at the end of a rope.

Even if Her Majesty had been informed about the desperate plight of one of her subjects, soon to die ignominiously in a county which she had once briefly visited, it is unlikely that she could have been of much help to Eliza Joyce. At the time, the Queen was facing her own difficult, but very different confinement, in Windsor Castle, but with a much happier outcome, having given birth to a son, Prince Alfred Ernest Albert, second in line to the British throne, on the 6th August.

As a guest of the Second Marquess of Exeter, the Queen did eventually come to Lincolnshire that year, revisiting the splendid comforts of Burghley House at Stamford, on the 12th November, by which time, of course, Eliza Joyce had become the very uncomfortable judicial statistic of being the most recent reluctant guest of the Lucy Tower graveyard.

The temporary stay of the Queen at Burghley House was marked by a very fine oil painting by the portrait and landscape artist Henry Brian Ziegler; the permanent stay of Eliza Joyce, now in the shadow of two yew trees, was indicated by a rough stone engraved with her initials, now partially effaced, marking the spot.

APPENDIX

Key Players In The Story Of Eliza Joyce

ADAMS, William Henry. Mayor of Boston, editor of *Boston Herald* newspaper and magistrate, interviewed Eliza Joyce, 22nd September, 1842, concerning death of alleged poisoning of her stepson. Elected to Boston Board of Guardians, March 1844.

ALDERSON, Sir Edward Hall. Present at suspended trial of Eliza Joyce at Lincoln Assizes for suspected poisoning of her stepson. Resident of Great Yarmouth, Norfolk.

ALLIX, Charles. Member of Grand Jury at resumed trial of Eliza Joyce at Lincoln Assizes. Resident of

West Willoughby Hall, Ancaster.

ANDERSON, Charles Henry John. Member of Grand Jury at resumed trial of Eliza Joyce at Lincoln Assizes. Resident of Lea Hall, Gainsborough.

BRADSHAW, Ann. Age 15, servant, living with family of William Joyce at South St, Boston, in June, 1841.

BRIGGS, Henry. Landlord of Sun Inn in Colsterworth. March, 1843, put up £250 surety as part of the bail terms for Eliza Joyce, after court proceedings against her were stopped on a technicality.

BROMHEAD, Benjamin. Member of Grand Jury at resumed trial of Eliza Joyce at Lincoln Assizes at Lincoln Assizes. Resident of Grecian Place, 13 Minster Yard, Lincoln.

BROWNE, Francis. Member of Grand Jury at resumed trial of Eliza Joyce at Lincoln Assizes. Resident of Welbourne.

CALCRAFT, William. Public executioner, summoned from Newgate to hang Eliza Joyce. Paid £11/3/0 for his services.

CALTHROP, J G. Solicitor and Clerk to the Boston Union Workhouse.

CHAPLIN, Charles. Member of Grand Jury at resumed trial of Eliza Joyce at Lincoln Assizes. Resident of Blankney Hall, Lincolnshire.

CHAPLIN, Thomas. Member of Grand Jury at resumed trial of Eliza Joyce at Lincoln Assizes.

CHAPMAN, Joseph. Brother of Eliza Joyce, farmer and maltster, resident at Irnham, Lincolnshire. 10th March, 1843, put up £250 surety as part of the bail terms for his sister, after court proceedings against her were stopped on a technicality.

CHENEY, Police Inspector Horatio Benjamin. Delivered Eliza Joyce into the custody of her brother, Joseph Chapman, after her appearance in front of the Boston Magistrates' Bench. Produced copy of baptismal record of Edward William Joyce at resumed trial of Eliza Joyce.

COLTMAN, Justice Thomas: sentenced Eliza Joyce to death for child murder at Lincoln Assizes, Resident of Hagnaby Priory, near Spilsby and 8 Hyde Park Gardens, London.

COUPLAND, Edward. Medical Officer of Boston Union Workhouse and Registrar. Conducted autopsy on Ann Joyce in March, 1842, after exhumation of body on suspicion of arsenic poisoning. Heard the confession of Eliza Joyce on 1st July, 1844, in the workhouse, concerning the poisoning of three of her children. Resident of Strait Bargate, Boston.

CRACROFT, Robert. Member of Grand Jury at resumed trial of Eliza Joyce at Lincoln Assizes. Resident of Hackthorn Hall.

D'EYNECOURT, Rt Honourable Charles Tennyson, MP. Foreman of the Grand Jury at the resumed trial at Lincoln Assizes,. Resident of Bayons Manor, Tealby.

ELLISON, Richard. Banker. Member of Grand Jury at resumed trial of Eliza Joyce at Lincoln Assizes. Resident of Boultham Park, Lincoln.

ELSOM, J. Magistrate, interviewed Eliza Joyce, 22nd September, 1842, concerning alleged poisoning of her stepson.

FARDELL, Charles. Member of Grand Jury at resumed trial of Eliza Joyce at Lincoln Assizes. Resident of Holbeck Lodge, Ashby Puerorum.

FARDELL, John. Member of Grand Jury at resumed trial of Eliza Joyce at Lincoln Assizes. Resident of Eastgate, Lincoln.

GILSON, Henry Robert. Analysed the content of Edward William Joyce's stomach for traces of arsenic, at the request of Dr Edward Snaith. Resident of Skirbeck, Boston.

GOULDING, John. Member of Grand Jury at resumed trial of Eliza Joyce at Lincoln Assizes.

GROOM, Farndom. Miller, elected to Boston Board of Guardians, March, 1844, raised the issue of William Joyce's refusal to pay for Eliza Joyce's stay in the workhouse.

GURNEY, Sir John. Sentencing judge at suspended trial of Eliza Joyce at Lincoln Assizes , 6th March, 1843, for suspected poisoning of her stepson. Resident of London.

HOWARD, Ann. Nurse, attended Ann Joyce. Gave evidence at the trial of Eliza Joyce for murder, at the Lincoln Assizes. Resident of Boston.

HOWETT, Ralph: Surgeon of Lincoln Castle prison: attended Eliza Joyce. Resident of Low Hill, St Mary le Wigford, Lincoln.

INGRAM, Dr Edward. Surgeon, attended Emma and Ann Joyce. Elected to Boston Board of Guardians, March 1844. Resident of 40 Market Place, Boston.

JARVIS, George Knollys. Member of Grand Jury at resumed trial of Eliza Joyce at Lincoln Assizes. Resident of Doddington Hall.

JOHNSON, Theophilus Fairfax. Member of Grand Jury at resumed trial of Eliza Joyce at Lincoln Assizes. Resident of Holland House, High Street, Spalding.

JOYCE, Ann. Born 1st January, 1842, daughter of William Joyce and Eliza Joyce, died 22nd January, 1842.

JOYCE, Betsy. Daughter of William and Eliza Joyce, born 1843, died 16th October, 1853.

JOYCE, Bets<e>y. Daughter of William and Elizabeth Joyce, born 22nd April, 1832, died 14th February, 1840.

JOYCE, Edward William. Son of William and Elizabeth Joyce (nee Tingle), born 4th October 1828, died December 1842.

JOYCE, Eliza (nee Chapman). Baptised 17th

November, 1813, married William Joyce on the 15th March, 1841, at South Kyme, Lincolnshire. Hanged at Lincoln Castle, 2nd August, 1844, for infanticide.

JOYCE, Elizabeth (nee Tingle). Born 1805, married William Joyce on the 22nd June, 1826, buried St Botolph's, Boston, 10th November, 1839, age 34.

JOYCE, Emma. Born October 1839, daughter of William and Eliza Joyce, buried 14th October 1841, aged two years.

JOYCE, Harriet. Born 1838, daughter of William and Elizabeth Joyce.

JOYCE, Henry. Born 1834, son of William and Elizabeth Joyce.

JOYCE, James. Born 1832, son of William and Elizabeth Joyce.

JOYCE, William. Market Gardener. Resident of South-End, Boston.

JOYCE, William. Father of William Joyce, resident of South Kyme in June, 1841.

MACLEAN, J J. Magistrate, interviewed Eliza Joyce, 22nd September, 1842, concerning death of alleged poisoning of her stepson.

MASTIN, Charles. Boston Coroner, carried out post-mortem examination on body of Edward William Joyce.

MELLOR, J W. Counsel for Prosecution in resumed trial of Eliza Joice at the Lincoln Assizes on the charge of attempted murder of Edward William Joyce.

MILLER_____ . Counsel for the Defence in resumed trial of Eliza Joice at the Lincoln Assizes on charge of attempted murder of Edward William Joyce. Probably the Sergeant Miller who later presided over many cases on the Midland Circuit with great distinction.

MORLEY, Mildred. Worked in service for William and Eliza Joyce. Gave evidence at the trial of Eliza Joyce, at the Lincoln Assizes. Resident of Boston.

MUNDAY, Charles John H. Member of Grand Jury at resumed trial of Eliza Joyce at the Lincoln Assizes. Resident of Ormsby Hall.

PACKE, Charles William. Member of Grand Jury at resumed trial of Eliza Joyce at the Lincoln Assizes. MP for South Leicestershire. Resident of Prestwich Hall, Leicestershire and 7 Richmond Terrace, London.

PARKER, William. Member of Grand Jury at resumed trial of Eliza Joyce at the Lincoln Assizes. Resident of Hanthorpe House, Hanthorpe.

PATTESON, Lord Justice Sir John. Presided over the resumed trial of Eliza Joyce, at the Lincoln Assizes, on the charge of administering poison to her stepson, Edward William Joyce. Resident of Feniton Court, Honiton, Devon.

RICHTER, Reverend Henry William. Chaplain of

Lincoln Castle prison and Rector of St Paul in the Bail, Lincoln. Resident of 23 Minster Yard, Lincoln.

SIMONDS, William. Chemist and druggist, Market Place, Boston. Sold arsenic to Eliza Joyce on 16th September, 1842. Gave evidence at the re-trial of Eliza Joyce for attempted murder.

SKIPWORTH, George. Member of Grand Jury at resumed trial of Eliza Joyce at the Lincoln Assizes. Resident of Moorton House, South Kelsey.

SMITH, Thomas. Chemist and druggist of Post Office Lane, Boston, sold laudanum to Eliza Joyce.

SNAITH, Dr Francis: attended Edward William Joyce; carried out an examination of his vomit to determine the extent of arsenic in his stomach. Gave evidence at re-trial of Eliza Joyce for attempted murder and at the trial of Eliza Joyce for murder, at the Lincoln Assizes. Resident of Pump Square, Boston.

STAINBANK, R W. Magistrate, interviewed Eliza Joyce, 22nd September, 1842, concerning death of alleged poisoning of her stepson.

STURDY, John. Magistrate, interviewed Eliza Joyce, 22nd September, 1842, concerning death of alleged poisoning of her stepson; Guardian of Boston Union Workhouse, interviewed Eliza Joyce after her confession to murder.

THORALD, Richard. Member of Grand Jury at

resumed trial of Eliza Joyce at the Lincoln Assizes. Resident of Weelsby House, Clee.

TINGLE, Rachel. Housekeeper to Rachel Hopkins, infant school mistress, resident 49 Field St, Boston. Mother of William Joyce's first wife, verified details of the baptismal name of Edward Willam Joyce at the second trial of Eliza Joyce on 18th July, 1843. Gave evidence at re-trial of Eliza Joyce for attempted murder and at the trial of Eliza Joyce for murder, at the Lincoln Assizes

VICKERS, John. Gardener and servant, age 15, living with the Joyce family at South St, Boston, in June, 1841.

WILKINS, Phoebe. Servant of Dr Francis Snaith.

WILSON, James. Master of Boston Union Workhouse. Interviewed Eliza Joyce twice after her confession of murder. Gave evidence at trial of Eliza Joyce for murder at the Lincoln Assizes.

Chapter Two

MARY ANN MILNER (1818-1847)

Mary Ann Milner Timeline

3rd March, 1840: marriage of John Milner, aged twenty-two, to Mary Ann Jekyl, aged twenty, at Barnetby le Wold.

April 1847: Mary Ann Milner buys arsenic from local grocer, William Percival.

2nd June, 1847: Mr William Milner and Mrs Mary Milner, father and mother-in-law of Mary Ann Milner, taken ill.

5th June, 1847: death of Mrs Mary Milner.

15th June, 1847: death of Ellen Jickels, aged four months, niece of Mary Ann Milner.

26th June, 1847: death of Hannah Jickels, sister-in-law of Mary Ann Milner from arsenic poisoning.

28th June, 1847: inquest at Barnetby le Wold before Caistor solicitor and coroner, George Marris, on the body of Hannah Jickels, wife of Thomas Jickels, agricultural labourer. Inquest adjourned.

6th July, 1847: resumed inquest after exhumation of bodies of Ellen Jickells and Mary Milner, concluding that both had died from arsenic poisoning.

Mary Ann Milner, committed to Lincoln Castle on charge of murder.

17th July, 1847: arrival in Lincoln of the Rt Honourable Thomas Lord Denman and Sir Robert Monsey Rolfe to open the Lincoln Assize session.

19th July, 1847: confession of guilt by Mary Ann Milner to the Reverend Henry Richter, Prison Chaplain.

20th July, 1847: trial of Mary Ann Milner in front of Sir Robert Monsey Rolfe and the Grand Jury; Messrs Wildman and Dennison for the Prosecution; Mr Miller for the Defence.

On the first charge, Mary Ann Milner found not guilty of poisoning Mary Milner; on the second charge of poisoning Hannah Jickels, found guilty, and condemned to death by hanging.

29th July 1847: Mary Ann Milner seen in her cell by Reverend Henry Richter allegedly around 8.00; Mary Ann Milner last seen alive by the Matron, Mrs

Emily Johnson, allegedly around 9.15. Suicide of Mary Ann Milner in condemned cell, sometime after 9.15, possibly in the early hours of 30th July.

30th July, 1847: discovery of dead body of Mary Ann Milner by Mrs Emily Johnson; Mr William Melson, Chief Turnkey, summoned to cut the body down; Governor, Mr John Nicholson and the Surgeon, Dr Ralph Howett, summoned. Rev Henry Richter hears about the death of Mary Ann Milner, allegedly sometime after 9.00.

Scaffolding on Cobb Hall dismantled; crowd dispersed.

31st July, 1847: inquest into death of Mary Ann Milner at Lincoln Castle before Coroner, James Hitchens: verdict of suicide.

Mary Ann Milner buried in prisoners' graveyard, Lincoln Castle.

1703

An Account of the Trial, conviction and Condemnation of M. Ann Milner, at Lincoln Assizes July

20th, 1847 for the Murder of Hannah Jickells at Barnetby le-Wold.

Mary Ann Milner, aged 27, was charged with having wilfully murdered Mary Milner at Barnetby-de-Wold in the parts of Lindsey, by administering a quantity of arsenic.

After a very long trial of six hours, his Lordship summed up, when the jury consulted for a few minutes and returned a verdict of not guilty.

The prisoner was then arraigned under a second indictment charged with the murder of Hannah Jickels, on the 24th of June, by administering poison.

Mary the wife of William Winter said she lived under the same roof as the deceased although in a separate house. She saw the deceased on the 24th of June who was in good health at that time; in the evening deceased went to Kettleby, and the prisoner who was her sister-in-law went into her house to her husband, she remarked it because it was a strange occurrence—next morning she saw the deceased who was in good health; at about half-past 8, and saw her again at 10. She afterwards went into her house and found her down upon her knees vomiting violently; and declaring she was poisoned by eating pancakes at the prisoner's. Witness held her head, afterwards she assisted her up stairs where she continued very sick—she was so weak as scarcely to be able to speak, but complained of her throat and mouth, which she said were very hot; she was thirsty and appeared in great agony, as she frequently threw herself up and down the bed—she asked for her husband and he came home at about 1 o'clock—as the prisoner at about half-past two o'clock said was "Hannah Jickels has been eating pancakes along with you and has been poisoned with them?" Prisoner turned white but made no answer. She then told her that deceased said so, Eliz. Thompson was by at the time this was said. Witness then went to deceased's bed-room followed the prisoner deceased was throwing up very violently, prisoner said to her "do you think I would put anything into the cakes and poison you?" deceased made no answer—she asked deceased if she had taken anything herself, deceased replied she never had any poison in her house. She several times declared she should die as she had been poisoned by eating the pancakes—deceased died at 6 o'clock that evening. She (the witness) ordered her daughter to throw away that which the deceased had thrown up into a wash tub, her daughter and so the deceased also threw up in some other vessels, and she declared that to be saved for the surgeon to analyze, and particularly told the prisoner not to throw it away, it was however thrown away and upon asking the prisoner why it was thrown away, she replied it was offensive to the room; the vessels were well cleaned out. Prisoner was in the room when the deceased died, and remarked that she died like her poor mother Milner and deceased's child which had died on the 13th of June. On the day deceased died the prisoner came to her house and said that as the deceased had no fire would she have some pancakes with her at her house for breakfast, she (the prisoner) had had some, and could easily fry another for deceased, deceased said she was very fond of them, she had been thinking of frying herself one but had no eggs, and would therefore go to prisoner's house.—The prisoner at the same time said, "Hannah does not blame me in the least for putting anything into the cakes."

Elizabeth Winter the daughter of Mary Winter, remembered the day of deceased's death; saw her in the morning of that day in the garden, she was in good health and spirits at that time it was 9 o'clock; saw the wash-tub and emptied it, there was something like bread or pancake in it with phlegm, she threw it on the ash hill, and afterwards pointed out what she had thrown there, to some men who took it up.

William Booth, a shoemaker in company with G. Watson, searched a dunghill and was shewn by Elizabeth Winter, a quantity of matter, which he delivered to the constable Mackerill.

Constable Mackerill received the matter and gave it to the coroner, and afterwards to Messrs. Patteson and Moxon.

Wm. Percival a shopkeeper at Barnetby-de-Wold knew the prisoner; sold her 9 oz. of arsenic when she applied for it, he said it was an awkward sort of thing to sell, but as she was not a person likely to kill herself he did not object. She said she wanted it to kill mice, and that the dog got thin which she before had, and he died in the most excruciating agony. He recommended the antimonial wine for the deceased.

Mr. James Burdett Moxon, a surgeon residing at Glandford Brigg, attended the deceased and found her vomiting and purging, she was so weak she seldom spoke, but complained of pain in her stomach. He was suspicious of poison at first seeing her. Prisoner and her mother Sarah Jickels were in the room. He asked the prisoner a question relative to the cause of the deceased's illness, the prisoner said she had had some pancakes with her, he examined the matter which the deceased vomited and it looked like partly digested food. He applied several tests all with similar results, which quite satisfied him that arsenic was in the stomach to the amount of 30 grains; 10 or 12 grains was quite sufficient to kill any person, 4 grains had been known to kill a person.

Mr. Milner made a very eloquent appeal on behalf of the prisoner, and the Judge summoned up, dividing the evidence into sections. The Jury must be convinced that the deceased died from the effects of poison, and his lordship then read over, and commented upon, the evidence of the surgeons. The next question was how was it administered and recapitulated the evidence relative to the cake, and then, if the poison was administered in the cake, was it done by the prisoner, she intending to murder the deceased—upon all these points the jury must satisfy themselves and return the verdict according to the evidence.

The jury consulted for some minutes and then returned a verdict of Guilty.

During the whole trial the prisoner remained firm and collected, nor did her demeanour alter when the jury returned their verdict, or when his lordship passed sentence.

In passing sentence his lordship alluded to the dreadful crime of murder, and said he confessed he almost felt in trouble for the security of our lives, and of the consumers of trial by jury, if the gentleman had come to any other conclusion, than the one they had just expressed, after the careful and minute sitting of the evidence; for how many other murders she might have committed it was not for them to determine, for her crimes she would have to seek intercession for mercy with her Maker. She seduced her unfortunate victim under her roof to partake of her hospitality, and in the face of one of her children administered to her poison and sent her to her long account. It was hardly necessary in this case to say that on this side the grave she need not hope for mercy, and advised her to employ the time she had to live, in seeking instruction which would assist in reconciling her with that God whose laws she had so outrageously violated. His lordship then in a very solemn tone of voice sentenced the prisoner to Death.

R. E. Leary, Printer, 13 Strait, Lincoln.

Hidden in Fearful Mystery: The Life and Death of Mary Ann Milner

Introduction

The death of thirty-eight year old Hannah Jickels after eating an arsenic-laced pancake prepared by her sister-in-law, Mary Ann Milner, on Saturday, 26th June, 1847, no doubt made a telling contribution to the media-manufactured mythology that North Lincolnshire was fast developing an unenviable reputation for such appalling crimes.

The arrest and trial of Mrs Milner was reported by the press with its usual toxic mix of fact, fiction and outrage, and the execution of the young woman would no doubt have received similar coverage, had it taken place. However, in its stead, she provided an alternative tasty narrative for newspapers to consume by committing suicide in the condemned cell, probably less than twelve hours before her execution was due to take place at noon, Friday, 30th July, 1847.

Deprived of its usual opportunities for mealy-mouthed sensationalism, the press now found itself reporting not only a shocking subversion of well-established judicial procedures and public entertainment, but also an unedifying aftermath of recrimination, evasion and denial, as the city respectables and the morally upright smartly ducked for cover.

Nothing was ever straightforward with Mary Ann Milner, it seems: even her maiden name, recorded as Jekyl on her marriage certificate, is an unusual variant amongst the many versions of Jickels/Jickells/ Jeckill/Jeckills found in contemporary press reports and official documents.

Based upon what is known about Mary Ann Milner before her arraignment for murder, there is little indication that her life would involve anything other than an unexceptional existence in an unexceptional North Lincolnshire village, four miles from the unexceptional market town of Brigg.

Her marriage to John Milner, originally from nearby Somerby by Bigby, on 3rd March, 1840, at the parish church of Barnetby le Wold, seemed predictable in terms of a prescribed, but assured future, in a well-established Lincolnshire agricultural community. Both of their respective fathers were labourers, as was John Milner himself; Mary Ann is recorded as the ubiquitous domestic servant at the time of her marriage; and the opportunities for both husband and wife to significantly change the direction of their lives were limited by a lack of that most basic functional literacy of being able to write their name.

Described in White's 1842 *Directory* as 'a pleasant village on a lofty acclivity', with a modest population of seven hundred and five occupying around two and a half thousand acres of land, Barnetby le Wold, on the surface, seemed to offer few surprises which might disturb White's topographical restraint. Even though the village was in a state of demographic and economic transition in the 1840s, with the development of the local railway network and the influx of men to build and service that development, it continued to maintain a relatively undisturbed low profile. Few of its inhabitants appeared in front of a magistrate, an unfortunate exception being seventeen– year old Thomas Maunders, sentenced at the Lindsey Sessions to seven years transportation for stealing a quantity of wheat and beans. Lord of the Manor, William Abrahams, ensconced in what White termed his 'neat mansion', seemed content to just get on with the efficient management of his farm estate of nine hundred acres and win prizes year on year for his English Leicester sheep at the North Lincolnshire Agricultural Show, presided over by the Earl of Yarborough. He also dutifully attended the AGM of the Caistor Association for the Prosecution of Felons and, following the compelling logic of enlightened self-interest, actively supported the founding of an Association for the Protection of Property against Incendiarism, proposed in 1845, also presided over by the Earl of Yarborough.

Meanwhile, the Wesleyans, Primitive Methodists and Independents, made quiet progress in establishing a benign presence in the village, as the numbers attending the decaying parish church of St Mary's slowly declined.

Virtually the only hint of any scandalous departure from the comfortable normalities of life in Barnetby le Wold, at the time, was the premature death of Elizabeth Kitchen, wife of William Kitchen, who was an opium addict and who died in late May, 1847, allegedly from an overdose.

The alarmed article in the *Stamford Mercury* 25th October, 1850, reporting an outbreak of theft and senseless damage to property, as well as the harassment of local worshippers as they left chapel, captured a sense of unease in the village, now allegedly 'infested with a band of lawless vagabonds, thieves and window smashers'. That the article described this shocking threat to property and public safety in contrasting terms to 'a once quiet village', underlined the apparent conservative equanimity of Barnetby le Wold life in the 1840s.

Perhaps more representative of the village's steady state character, was the life of the much-respected Methodist tailor, William Abey, who died on the 15th October,1847, aged 88, and who had famously lived in Barnetby le Wold for sixty-four years.

The grim act of suicide, by the less than much-respected Mary Ann Milner, alone in the bleak semi-darkness of a prison cell, using her own red handkerchief, a nail fixed on a cupboard door and probably a chair, was explained by one commentator as an attempt to prevent the people of Barnetby le Wold, many of whom had made a special journey to Lincoln, from enjoying the public spectacle of her death. The plan clearly worked and the authorities had the tricky task of dispersing a large and hostile crowd which had gathered in the area around Cobb Hall, expecting some free lunchtime entertainment.

What Mary Ann Milner could neither have planned nor have predicted was that her act of self-destruction would incongruously find its way a few days later into an electioneering speech by Sir Charles Anderson, one of the most powerful men in the county, alongside his severe lambasting of Sir Robert Peel's political chicanery over the Corn Laws and a robust defence of sturdy English Protestantism, currently under siege from pernicious Popish plots.

Nor could Mrs Milner have anticipated that her suicide would, in due course, lead to a more humane duty of care for condemned prisoners in their miserable final hours of life.

The world beyond Barnetby le Wold was first alerted to the troubles of Mary Ann Milner by both the *Lincolnshire Chronicle* and the *Stamford Mercury* on Friday, 9th July, 1847, which published very similar reports relating to the inquest on the body of Hannah Jickels, wife of Thomas Jickels, labourer, which had taken place on Monday, 28th June. The opening paragraph of the brief report expressed concern that a growing trend of 'the horrible and dastardly crime of poisoning' in the area was becoming as alarming as that observed in Norfolk. It was a sensational claim, but given some substance by the decision of George Marris, the Coroner, to adjourn the inquest in order to allow the exhumation of the body of Ellen Jickels, the infant daughter of the deceased Hannah Jickels, recorded in the parish Burial Register as having been interred on the 18th June. In the light of further evidence heard at the inquest, Mr Marris also required the exhumation of Mary Milner, the mother-in-law of Mary Ann Milner, who had been buried on the 7th June.

The inquest resumed on Friday, 6th July, concluding with the report from the surgeons, James Burdett Moxon and Robert Henry Paterson, both of Brigg, on the exhumated bodies, that both showed signs of a fatal ingestion of arsenic.

Mary Ann Milner was committed to Lincoln Castle for trial and the scene was set for a lurid narrative of serial poisoning in a small Lincolnshire community.

Trial of Mary Ann Milner for the Wilful Murder of Mary Milner (First Indictment), 20th July 1847

The report of the trial from both newspapers was published Friday, 23rd July, but was preceded by a short interim notice, published Friday, 16thJuly in the *Stamford Mercury,* whose headline 'The Murder by Poison at Barnetby le Wold' suggested that the case against Mary Ann Milner was already clear cut. It was very much a taster for the ensuing report of the trial, noting that it was likely that Mrs Milner would be indicted on three distinct charges of murder. In addition, it had been discovered that the father-in-law of the accused had only just escaped death after eating the same food which had poisoned his wife, and that he had been very ill since the death of his wife.

The prospect of a media circus generated by a story of multiple poisonings was greatly enhanced by the news that around twenty witnesses had been bound over to attend the Assizes on Tuesday, 20th July to present their evidence.

The weight of witness numbers descending on the courtroom, as well as the pre-trial perceptions of the popular press, did not bode well for Mary Ann Milner.

The pomp and ceremony which preceded the opening of the Lincoln Summer Assizes on Saturday,

17th July, was reported by the *Lincolnshire Chronicle*. The showpiece formalities, described in unusually modest terms by the newspaper, still managed to capture the moment of civic and judicial grandeur. The Right Honourable Thomas Lord Denman and the Honourable Robert Monsey Rolfe, arrived on the Lincoln and Nottingham Railway train at 3 o'clock precisely, and were welcomed by the dignitaries of the city. The report seemed especially impressed by the magnificence of the Sheriff's carriage, which was 'of a beautiful description', and which was drawn through Lincoln by 'four splendid horses'.

Lord Denman, the incumbent Lord Chief Justice of England, was neither overawed nor distracted by the excitement of the occasion, getting straight down to practical business immediately after reaching Lincoln Castle.

First, the Grand Jury was appointed, consisting of a substantial number of successful Lincoln shopkeepers and manufacturers, located on Lincoln High Street:

- T Newton (Foreman)
- T Bainbridge
- S Bayles
- S Blow
- C H Bodens
- S Bonsor

- J Dymoke
- J Flint
- T Garton
- W H Hyde
- F Johnson
- W H Jones
- C Pennell
- J Plumtree
- J W Reeve
- R Seely
- A Shuttleworth
- J Slack
- G Spenser
- W Singleton
- J S Wilkinson

Then, Lord Denman moved briskly on to share his reflections upon the Lincoln Calendar. He observed that the list of prisoners presented to him was a long one, but his disappointment was not simply with the city, but with the country as a whole, throughout which there had been no recent discernible decrease in criminality. The reason for this, Lord Denman opined, was plain and obvious: the administration of justice had become lax and this had inevitably created a mindset in the populace that crime 'was not so serious'. More specifically, that the pernicious doctrine of extreme mercy rather than justice now pervaded the

courts to such an extent that the administration of the
law had degenerated into 'a disposition to trifle with
crime'. The experienced judge was clearly in a state of
some distress as he pointed his lordly finger at the main
culprits: prosecutors were guilty of either delaying
or abandoning prosecutions; juries were culpable of
favouring prisoners through misguided 'false notions
of mercy or compassion'. The result of such dereliction
was catastrophic, according to the learned Lord, as it
encouraged the vicious to commit crime with impunity
and placed society in great jeopardy; furthermore,
such 'tampering with justice' could only lead to 'the
indulgence of passion and a disregard of duty'.

Perhaps in a late attempt to redress the balance, Lord
Denman offered some much needed encouragement
to his listeners. Progress had been made relating to
the education and moral improvement of prisoners
whilst serving their sentence, thus guaranteeing a
more effective integration of the convict into society
on his or her release. However, just in case the
Grand Jury might become too complacent, having
enjoyed this cautious note of optimism, his Lordship
strongly warned them against being led astray in
their deliberations by 'charitable considerations': in
the final analysis, courts existed 'in order to punish
criminals for the prevention of crime'.

During the course of his optimistic discourse
about prisoner rehabilitation, Lord Denman did

allow himself one more unguarded moment of unqualified congratulation to the prison system: the treatment of prisoners in gaol was now 'honourable to the humanity of the country'.

It was a terrible irony to which no reference was ever made during the inquest into the suicide of Mary Ann Milner in gaol.

At 9 o'clock, Tuesday, 20th July, the trial of Mrs Milner commenced under the watchful eye of Lord Justice Rolfe. The case for the Prosecution was presented by Mr Wildman and Mr Dennison, whilst the case for the Defence was undertaken by Mr Miller, who had successfully defended Eliza Joyce at her resumed trial for attempting to poison her stepson four years earlier.

Mary Ann Milner was facing three indictments for poisoning and potentially three difficult trials during the course of the same day. The *Lincolnshire Chronicle*'s account of the first trial, indicting the prisoner on suspicion of having murdered her mother-in-law with arsenic and having attempted to murder her father-in-law, also by poison, was detailed, but created the impression of being more in a hurry to get to the second indictment than to report accurately on the first.

Rather than describing the unfolding courtroom drama, witness by witness, the newspaper chose to summarise the background information of the case, supplemented by evidence, occasionally vaguely attributed, which had emerged during the proceedings: the same slightly disjointed impressionistic approach was used, but with a little more clarity, by the *Stamford Mercury*. It may be that both newspapers, knowing the outcome of the first and second indictment, decided that the latter, involving the drama of a death sentence, would be more interesting to its readers.

However, it is clear from reading a report of the first indictment in the *Evening Mail*, a London newspaper published on the same day as the two Lincolnshire newspapers, that such a rapid summary of proceedings produced a misleading account of the trial and the case. By focusing in forensic detail on the many witness depositions, the version in the London newspaper created a significant representation of the social context of the alleged crimes and the life of Mary Ann Milner in Barnetby le Wold.

The report of the trial in the *Evening Mail* was a very long one, large parts of which appeared in other London newspapers, such as the *Evening Chronicle* and the *London Evening Standard*, with the odd snippet of additional information, some of it real, some of it thinly disguised dramatic invention.

Large parts of it were also later pilfered by the broadside, published in Lincoln by R E Leary, which gave an account of the trial and condemnation of

Mary Ann Milner. The account was presumably an enterprising last-minute production to replace a scrapped memento of Mrs Milner's execution. The occasional structural awkwardness of the narrative and the unfortunate misnaming of Mr Miller, the Defence lawyer, as Mr Milner, perhaps indicate the time pressure under which it was hastily produced.

The opening of the report, as with many other C19th newspaper accounts of murder trials, tried to create a sense of immediacy by describing a densely packed courtroom anticipating the drama to come. Similarly, it described the prisoner in the dock as 'a good looking and rather lady-like young woman' who pleaded not guilty to the charge 'in a firm and audible voice'. The humanising of Mary Ann Milner may have been true, partially true or mere journalistic embellishment, of course: neither of the Lincolnshire newspapers included such material.

The report in the *Evening Mail*, like the two Lincolnshire newspapers, focused upon the key judicial point of a possible motive for the crime, outlined by Mr Wildman in his opening address. Both the mother and father-in-law of Mary Ann Milner had been in a burial club and she had benefited from the subsequent pay out. According to the *Lincolnshire Chronicle*, Mrs Milner had received £5 from the burial club which she had spent on mourning clothes for herself and the deceased's family. It was a well-worn motive for murder, identified in many criminal investigations of the period, and a familiar motif in the narrative of what Judith Flanders has called 'the burial club bogey'.

The first witness to take the stand was seventeen-year old Elizabeth Milner, the daughter of the deceased, who along with her twelve year old sister, Hannah, had still been living with her parents. Elizabeth Milner was not mentioned by name in either of the two Lincolnshire newspapers, and only in passing by the *Stamford Mercury* as a daughter who appeared to play only a minor part in the unfolding tragedy. The precise details of what Elizabeth Milner said in court were left unsaid or were obscured by the general comment used by both newspapers which noted the extremely long and minute evidence lasting over two hours: a convenient formula which enabled both reports to skirt quickly over many mundane details which were arguably essential to the reader's better understanding of the events in Barnetby le Wold.

Elizabeth Milner recalled both her mother and father being ill on the morning of Wednesday, 2nd June and being concerned enough to go to Brigg 'to fetch Mr Moxon', the doctor. She returned home between 2 and 3 o'clock, to find her mother complaining of 'a sick headache', although she did manage to come downstairs to eat some tea, before returning to bed.

The next day she was better, although remained in bed complaining of being thirsty. On Friday, she remained in the same condition, but by the Saturday Elizabeth Milner was alarmed by what she called her mother's 'dangerous state'.

In response to her mother's condition, Elizabeth Milner gave her raspberry vinegar and water to drink, as well as brandy and water. She also made her some gruel of which she ate a small quantity and her father ate the rest. In the afternoon, she left the house for about half-an-hour to clean the local chapel, leaving Hannah in the house with her parents.

Mary Ann Milner had been in and out of the house in the course of Thursday, Friday and Saturday and was apparently aware that Elizabeth Milner cleaned the chapel every Saturday afternoon. After returning home and finding her mother a great deal worse, she went to fetch Mary Ann Milner to the house, who went upstairs to check on the health of her mother-in-law. After walking Mary Ann Milner back to her house, Elizabeth Milner returned home at around 10.30 pm to find her mother dead.

Elizabeth Milner then referred back to the day of her mother's exhumation. Mary Ann Milner had expressed surprise at what was happening and said that the only thing that she had brought into the house was a rice pudding, which both her father-in-law and young Hannah Milner had eaten. She also confirmed that Mary Ann Milner had received £5 from her mother's burial club fund which in part was spent on clothes for mourning; she also mentioned that Mary Ann Milner had 'managed the funeral', probably meaning all other associated expenses. Elizabeth Milner mentioned, in passing, that since her mother's death, her father now belonged to a burial club, a detail, which contradicted the report in the *Stamford Mercury* that both parents belonged to it, as well as Elizabeth Milner's reported earlier words.

The cross-examination of Elizabeth Milner by Mr Miller probed her account in order to obtain clarity concerning when Mary Ann Milner was actually at the house and therefore had an opportunity to harm her mother-in-law. It was established that she had not been in the house whilst Elizabeth was in Brigg on the Wednesday, but that she had gone to fetch the prisoner at about 10.00 pm on the Saturday evening, just half an hour before her mother died. It was also established beyond doubt that Mary Ann Milner had 'purchased mourning and paid for everything'. Mr Miller also probed the professional services of Dr James Moxon: he had turned up at the house, but it was whilst Elizabeth Milner was out cleaning the chapel, and by the time she had returned, he had been and gone.

What medical care Moxon actually provided for Mary Milner on his visit remains unknown.

Elizabeth Milner was re-examined by Mr Dennison, which seemed to establish very little other than that she had fetched Mary Ann Milner to the house at 6 o'clock on the Saturday evening, who had later left to summon another woman. Several neighbours were with her mother that evening, from 7 o'clock onwards, she said, until 10 o'clock, just before her mother had died.

The second witness was Hannah Milner, the younger sister mentioned several times in the testimony of Elizabeth Milner. Her existence was never mentioned by either of the Lincolnshire newspapers, despite her being a key witness to the events of Saturday 5th June.

Under questioning from Mr Dennison, twelve-year old Hannah recalled being at the house of Mary Ann Milner on the day of her mother's death. Just after dinner she had been asked by Mrs Milner to go to Mr Scott's shop to buy half a pound of sago, allegedly on the recommendation of medical advice. On her return from the shop, Hannah handed over the parcel of sago: Mary Ann Milner then removed some of the sago and gave Hannah the rest to take home for her mother.

Hannah recalled Elizabeth going to clean the chapel in the afternoon and also recalled, in contradiction to her sister, that Mary Ann Milner had come round to the house, bringing with her a boy, younger than herself. Whilst at the house, Mrs Milner had gone upstairs to see her mother-in-law and had left the young boy in Hannah's care. Hannah could not remember whether or not Mary Ann Milner left the house before Elizabeth returned from cleaning the chapel. What she did recall, and once again contradicting the account of her elder sister, was that Mary Ann Milner visited the house whilst Elizabeth Milner was in Brigg on the Wednesday to summon the doctor. Further, she had brought a rice pudding, some of which both she and her father ate. After her mother's death she recollected seeing sago in a cup in the cupboard.

The cross-examination by Mr Miller appeared to be a brief one in which he highlighted Mary Ann Milner having bought mourning clothes for the family: luckily for Mr Miller, Hannah was wearing the mourning dress purchased for her by Mary Ann Milner for all to see. She also told the court that she had ten other brothers besides John Milner, the husband of Mary Ann Milner. It seemed a disconnected and random piece of information which Mr Miller had elicited.

The next witness to give her testimony was Jemima, the wife of the village butcher, James Sharp. She remembered the deceased and her husband having been taken ill, both complaining of 'heat of the throat'. Mrs Sharp was at the house on the Thursday, where she encountered Mary Milner, the sister-in-law of the deceased. Jemima Sharp recalled returning to her house with Elizabeth Milner, where she handed over some raspberry vinegar, which was later administered to the deceased. On Friday, Mary Milner was no better than she had been on the Thursday, which agreed with the testimony of Elizabeth Milner. However, what followed from Jemima Sharp seemed to contradict Elizabeth Milner on at least one important point. Mrs Sharp had visited the deceased at 7 o'clock on the Saturday evening and had found Mary Milner in great distress 'tearing at her throat'; she died between 10 and 11 o'clock that night, in the presence of her son, John Milner, a woman by the name of Hannah Metcalfe and Mrs Sharp herself. At some point later, although it was not made clear when, she had a conversation with Mary Ann Milner in the home of the deceased concerning the gruel prepared for the deceased. According to Jemima Sharp, Mary Ann Milner had told her that she was the one who had cooked the gruel and that her appreciative mother-in-law had asked for more. According to Elizabeth Milner, it was she who had cooked her mother some gruel: whether it was the same gruel remained ambiguous.

Mr Miller did not cross-examine this witness, it seems.

The next witness was Mary Milner, the sister-in-law of the deceased referred to in the account of

Jemima Sharp. Mary Milner told the court that both her brother and his wife were ill on the Wednesday morning, although her brother had been ill a few days before that. Both were suffering badly from purging and sickness and she remained at the house until the Friday. She left that night because Mary Ann Milner who 'had been backward and forward that day', had said that she would help Elizabeth Milner to take care of the elderly couple. On returning to the house at 7 o'clock on Saturday evening, she found that Mary Ann Milner was still there; other neighbours also visited the house that night. She recalled seeing a saucepan on the hob, which appeared to have sago in it. It was removed from the hob after the death of her sister-in-law.

Martha Milner, another daughter of the deceased, had visited her mother's house between 12 and 1 o'clock, on the day after she died. She testified seeing Mary Ann Milner in the house, who told her that she had given her mother some sago at about 6 o'clock on the day of her death, who had said that it was good and asked for more. Martha Milner had seen a saucepan in the house on the Sunday morning containing clean water; there was also a basin containing sago. She claimed to have visited Mary Ann Milner later and had the same discussion about the sago, as before, adding that Mary Ann mentioned that she did not make any more sago for her mother-in-law as she was called upstairs to deal with the deceased who was having a fit.

If the testimony of Martha Milner amounted to very little more than a repetitious confirmation that Mary Ann Milner had made some sago for her mother-in-law, the appearance of the Barnetby le Wold grocer, William Pilkington, in contrast, presented important circumstantial evidence of which the Prosecution might make good use. Its importance was clearly recognised by the *Stamford Mercury* which published more or less the same version of Pilkington's deposition found in the *Evening Mail*. The evidence of the shopkeeper was precise and unambiguous: Mary Ann Milner had purchased two ounces of arsenic from him about eight to ten weeks before the death of her mother-in-law, having obtained it to deal with an infestation of mice. Pilkington had been reluctant to sell such a dangerous substance, but as he had known her for some years and, perhaps flippantly, thought her of sound enough mind not to poison herself with it, he did so. He also recalled that Mary Ann Milner had assured him that she had bought arsenic before to kill vermin and was aware of the destructive power of the substance, having observed its distressing effects upon a dog which had accidentally eaten it.

Pilkington also remembered speaking to Mrs Milner just after the death of her mother-in-law. She had told Mr Pilkington about the untimely death, but said that she thought there would be no need for an investigation by the Coroner. The shopkeeper had enquired if the cause of death was cholera, to which Mary Ann Milner allegedly replied, 'Nothing of the sort'.

Mr Pilkington was quite insistent that he had never sold arsenic to either Mary Milner or her husband, William, although this was not reported in the *Stamford Mercury*.

In a sense, the recollections of William Pilkington were familiar territory to Mr Miller. When defending Eliza Joyce, he had heard similar evidence of arsenic being reluctantly sold to a local woman who wanted it for killing mice. His cross-examination, however, was more interested in Mrs Milner's remark about the Coroner. Pilkington was asked if it was he who had raised the issue of a Coroner's intervention, to which he replied in the negative – probably much to Mr Miller's disappointment.

The evidence of Thomas Havercroft, a local carpenter, probably seemed the most superfluous of the morning, merely confirming the formalities of him having made Mary Milner's coffin, nailed it down, opened it up on the 2nd July for the exhumation and being present when the examination of the body took place. Unsurprisingly, Thomas Havercroft was not mentioned in either of the two Lincolnshire papers.

The final depositions were from the medical practitioners who had been involved in the case.

Dr James Moxon had attended William Milner on the 1st June, as he was purging and vomiting, which he suspected to be symptoms of English cholera.

He had examined the body of Mary Milner after exhumation, along with his colleague, Dr Paterson, concluding that the deceased's stomach contained a large quantity of arsenic; further, that the inflammation of both the stomach and intestine confirmed arsenic to have been ingested. The quantity of poison found in the body of the deceased was sufficient to cause death.

Moxon then shifted his testimony from the scientific to the anecdotal, recounting a discussion he had with Mary Ann Milner in the street, on the day of Mary Milner's death. She had enquired about her health and he had told her that she was rather better, but still rather ill. Mrs Milner had then asked him if he had observed any symptoms of poison? The doctor had been surprised by the question and asked why she had made such an enquiry? Mrs Milner replied that she had been told by someone that the doctor had mentioned the subject in the house. According to Moxon, he made no reply, but did concede that he had mentioned poison during the course of the day, claiming that he had suspected poisoning from his observation of the deceased's symptoms and her having become ill so soon after her husband.

In his cross-examination, Mr Miller was clearly asking the doctor about the possibility of an 'arsenous substance' existing naturally in the human body in some minute form. Moxon said that he had read about the idea, but did not believe it. His scepticism was supported by the intervention of Justice Rolfe who informed the court that the theory had been propounded in the past ten or twelve years, but had been discredited.

The case for the Prosecution ended with the evidence of Dr Paterson who also attended William Milner, his last consultation having been on the 6th July when he found him in a 'very reduced state': his arms and feet were paralysed. He had originally been summoned by John Milner, the husband of Mary Ann, and he appeared to be suffering from English cholera. Paterson had later changed his diagnosis as the symptoms developed, deciding that William Milner was suffering from arsenic poisoning. He concurred with his colleague's analysis of the amount of arsenic in Mary Milner's exhumed body being sufficient to cause death.

The indictment for murder concluded with Mr Miller delivering 'a powerful speech' for the Defence which focussed upon a lack of motive and the inconclusiveness of the evidence connecting Mary Ann Milner with the administration of poison. The *Stamford Mercury* was more helpful than the *Evening Mail* in its more expansive report on Miller's concluding speech, in particular, his dismissal of the flimsy and incoherent circumstantial evidence presented by the Prosecution. At best, the evidence merely pointed a finger of suspicion at Mary Ann Milner and it was quite possible that arsenic may have been accidentally introduced into the food consumed by William and Mary Milner. Given the numerous nationwide press reports of such accidental contamination before the regulation of the sale of arsenic in 1851, and even beyond, it was a credible defence. In addition, the attempt by the Prosecution to construct a motive of financial gain from a burial club pay out had 'signally failed', as she had used the money to buy mourning clothes for the family and pay all the funeral expenses. In a moment of theatrical outrage, Mr Miller strongly suggested that it was 'monstrous' to construe her kindness towards the deceased during her illness as acts leading to a suspicion that Mary Ann Milner was a murderer.

Rolfe summed up the case in detail and the jury did not take much time to return a verdict of Not Guilty.

Trial of Mary Ann Milner for the Wilful Murder of Sarah Jickels, (Second Indictment), 20th July 1847

The more meticulous, stage by stage presentation of the business of the court by the *Evening Mail*, did not necessarily guarantee greater accuracy, but in comparison with the two Lincolnshire newspapers, it did ensure greater clarity. A comparison between the three accounts not only highlights different ways of reporting a trial, but also indicates how those differences might account for divergent versions of the truth. Sometimes the divergence is only a minor one, a question of nuanced emphasis or unimportant fact; but occasionally, the outcome is more significant. In the *Stamford Mercury*, for example, it was confidently reported that Mary Ann Milner was in her mother-in-law's house both whilst Elizabeth Milner was at Brigg seeking medical help and whilst she was cleaning the chapel: on the latter occasion, she had taken the opportunity to boil some gruel for Mary Milner, whose condition then deteriorated, leading a few hours later to her death. It made for a rapidly expounded sensational narrative, but when placed side by side against the slowly unfolding narrative found in the *Evening Mail*, it is obvious that the *Stamford Mercury* had fabricated a highly selective version of events. The piling up of circumstances detrimental to Mrs Milner, presented as fact, was an unacknowledged pastiche of the deposition by twelve year old Hannah Milner, which completely contradicted the version of events heard in court from Elizabeth Milner: Mary Ann Milner was not at the house on either of the occasions in question, as far as Elizabeth Milner knew.

The stolid exposition of the trial by the *Evening Mail*, communicating little sense of drama and tension, was nevertheless the ideal vehicle for capturing the sense of a claustrophobically tight-knit village community, living in each other's pockets on Gravel Pit Lane, and their response to the unexpected and inexplicable. Memories of what happened were sometimes muddled, personal animosities seemed to bubble beneath the surface and witnesses, who did not seem to be of any great help in defining what really happened, were summoned to tell their stories.

More importantly, for a retrospective understanding of the case, it helped to clarify what Mary Ann Milner was later to say in gaol after she had been condemned to death.

The inconsistencies and vagaries of some witness statements, creating a sometimes cluttered narrative of domestic trivia, no doubt helped Mr Miller to dismantle the case against his client with some ease. The second indictment against Mary Ann Milner, of wilfully murdering Hannah Jickels, her sister-in-law, which followed straight on from the first indictment, however, presented a different set of challenges.

The first difficulty was recognised by Lord Rolfe when he acknowledged that the impartiality of the Grand Jury might have been compromised by having heard the first indictment. He therefore offered the Defence the opportunity to have a different jury, an option which Mr Miller was happy to take. Unfortunately, the offer from Lord Rolfe had to be quickly withdrawn as the Deputy Clerk of the Arraigns, Mr Collison, pointed out that most, if not all of the Grand Jurymen who had not been called to service for the first indictment, had actually been in court to hear it. Either magnanimously or pragmatically, Miller agreed to have the same jury; in response, Justice Rolfe, somewhat optimistically, instructed the gentlemen of the jury to dismiss all knowledge of Mary Ann Milner from the first indictment 'as if they had heard nothing to her disadvantage'.

Surprisingly, neither of the Lincolnshire newspapers recorded this potential difficulty for the Defence. Less surprising was that it should have been allowed to happen at all, perhaps suggesting the assumption of a foregone conclusion, as much as an embarrassing administrative bungling.

The report of the second indictment in the *Evening Mail* used the same structure as for the first.

The first witness to be heard was a Mrs Mary Winter, the wife of Walter Winter, a railway policeman. In terms of proximity to the alleged victim of the crime, Mrs Winter could not have been better placed, living next door to the house in which Hannah Jickels died on the 26th June.

She recalled standing near her front door on the evening of the 25th June after Hannah Jickels had taken

Mrs Winter's daughter, Elizabeth, to Kettleby, a small village just a mile or so up the road from Barnetby le Wold. She observed Mrs Milner go into the house of Mrs Jickels, along with her husband; Mr Jickels was in the house at the time. This piece of domestic trivia seemed quite remarkable to Mrs Winter at the time, as neither Mary Ann nor her husband usually visited the house. Mary Winter helpfully finished this section of her testimony by informing the court that Mary Ann Milner's maiden name was Jickels, perhaps to confirm the perceived oddness of her not visiting her brother and sister-in-law with any regularity.

The next morning, at around 8.30, Mrs Winter saw Hannah Jickels, opposite her front door, and she appeared to be in good health. At 10 o'clock, she entered the house of Mrs Winter, staying for a short time, before returning home, as she was feeling unwell. Mary Winter followed her into her house where she discovered Mrs Jickels on her knees, vomiting, but managed to get her up the stairs into bed, where she continued to be very ill, saying very little. She complained of pains in her throat and mouth, and of being very thirsty. Hannah Jickels was in such distress that 'she threw herself about on the bed as if in great pain'.

Other people were alleged to have been present in the house at the time.

Mrs Winter commented that she left to fetch Mrs Milner, but had met her on the way. The ensuing conversation related to Hannah Jickels having told her that she had eaten pancakes with Mrs Milner that morning, and that she was poisoned. According to Mrs Winter, Mary Ann Milner looked pale and made no response. The conversation was witnessed by Elizabeth Thompson who was nearby at the time.

Once in the house, Mrs Winter went upstairs into the bedroom of Hannah Jickels, and was followed by Mary Ann Milner. The latter asked her sister-in-law if she thought that she had put something in her pancake that morning: according to Mrs Winter, Hannah Jickels said nothing in response.

What followed from Mrs Winter was not so much useful material for the jury to consider, as evidence that the garrulous witness had difficulties in presenting a coherent narrative. She reverted to the encounter in her own kitchen with a rendition of the story which was more dramatic than the earlier one presented to the court. Whilst in the kitchen with Mary Winter, Mrs Jickels declared that she thought she was going to die, having told her the story of the pancakes. Once in her own kitchen, the deceased repeated her story about having eaten pancakes with Mary Ann Milner and once again declared that she was going to die; not surprisingly, Hannah Jickels expressed a need to see her husband, who returned home at 1 o'clock.

At this point, and perhaps in hindsight rather surprisingly, Mrs Winter instructed her daughter to throw away the contents of a wash bucket into which Hannah Jickels had vomited: the dutiful daughter deposited the contents on the ash heap and returned the wash bucket to the house. Perhaps realising her error, Mrs Winter then told her daughter and the deceased not to throw anything more away, until the doctor had examined it.

Meanwhile, Mrs Jickels continued to 'vomit violently and was much purged'.

After Hannah Jickels had died, Mrs Winter asked Mary Ann Milner what she had done with 'the stuff', to which she replied that she had thrown it away 'as it was offensive to the room'. Without any awareness of inconsistency, it seems, Mrs Winter told Mary Ann Milner that she should not have done so.

Mrs Milner, she said, was close by when her sister-in-law had died and she casually commented that she had died in much the same manner as her mother-in-law and her niece, Ellen Jickels.

During the course of the day, Mary Ann Milner had recounted the story of inviting Hannah Jickels to breakfast for pancakes after having spoken to her through the window of her house, to ask if she had had breakfast.

In a final flourish to her sometimes disjointed story, Mrs Winter revealed that Mary Ann Milner had claimed that 'Hannah does not blame me for putting anything in the pancakes'.

Cross-examined by Mr Miller, it was confirmed that Mrs Milner's claim was voiced before Hannah Jickels died: it had taken place downstairs whilst the deceased was upstairs.

The version of Mrs Winter's testimony recorded in the *Lincolnshire Chronicle* was virtually the same as in the *Evening Mail*: it added the odd insignificant detail, but helpfully included the time of death as being 6 o'clock in the evening. The *Stamford Mercury* covered the same ground, albeit maintaining the same breakneck speed reporting style of the first indictment.

Elizabeth Thompson, who lived only a few doors away from Mrs Jickels, provided a brief statement which confirmed the claim that Mary Ann Milner had turned pale when confronted by the thinly veiled accusation that she had poisoned the pancakes which she had cooked for her sister-in-law.

Elizabeth Winter, the daughter of Mary Winter, supported the narrative of her mother 'in almost every particular'. In addition, she claimed to have heard Mary Ann Milner say to her son on the morning of the death of Hannah Jickels: 'Come John, come along, Bella (meaning the deceased's daughter) is to have some pancakes with us'. The remainder of her evidence referred to her throwing the vomit from a vessel on to the ash hill, adding that it appeared to contain phlegm and pancake. She stated that she later showed three men where she had thrown Mrs Jickels' vomit.

If Mary Winter, by virtue of living next door to Hannah Jickels, could lay claim to having presented a reliable testimony, the next witness might have made a similar claim, having lodged along with her husband in the house of Mary Ann Milner from the 21st to the 26th June. Unfortunately, neither the *Evening Mail* nor the *Lincolnshire Chronicle* or the *Stamford Mercury* could agree upon the woman's identity. In the *Evening Mail*, she was Mary Watson; in the *Lincolnshire Chronicle*, she was Mary Dixon; and in the *Stamford Mercury*, she was Elizabeth Dixon. Whatever name she went by, the witness was in the right place, at the right time, to report to the court on the crucial events of the morning of Saturday, 26th June.

According to this particular witness, Mary Ann Milner had made herself some pancakes for breakfast before she went out, returning a few minutes later and then frying another pancake. Hannah Jickels came round to the house with her daughter and sat down to eat the freshly made pancake. She also saw the child eat pancake, but would or could not say if it was the same one as her mother was eating.

All three newspapers agreed upon the details of the statement made by the witness and the *Stamford Mercury* was bold enough to give the husband of the witness an occupation of railway timekeeper, whilst the *Lincolnshire Chronicle* went one better and also provided him with the name of Robert Dixon.

Mrs Jemima Sharp had appeared at the first indictment, presenting important evidence relating to Mary Ann Milner having cooked gruel for her deceased mother-in-law. She had also supplied raspberry vinegar to Elizabeth Milner to give to her mother in her time of illness. In her latest visit to the witness stand, Mrs Sharp revealed that she had visited Hannah Jickels and had given her some antimonial wine recommended by the grocer, Mr Percival. She also said that she had spoken to Mary Ann Milner that evening who had recounted having breakfast pancakes with her sister-in-law. In addition, Jemima Sharp remembered what Mrs Milner had allegedly said about the similarities between the death of her mother-in-law and her sister-in-law mentioned to Mary Winter, using virtually the same words.

The report in the *Stamford Mercury* attributed to Mrs Sharp the claim that she had warned Mary Ann Milner to keep 'what was cast up' to enable the doctor to identify any substance which she had taken. If true, Mrs Sharp once again was speaking with a voice remarkably similar to that of Mary Winter earlier on in the trial.

It was no surprise that Mr Miller homed in on the dubious health benefits of antimonial wine. Under cross-examination, Mrs Sharp passed the buck to her supplier, Mr Percival, and quite remarkably, she claimed to be unaware that the mineral concoction could produce violent vomiting.

There followed a rapid succession of various witnesses who played a marginal part in the drama. William Booth, one of the many shoemakers in Barnetby le Wold, along with George Watson, testified that they had retrieved 'a quantity of matter' from the ash heap, which they thought consisted chiefly of wheaten flour. This had been passed on to Mr Mackerill, the Constable, who confirmed that he had delivered the parcel into the safe keeping of the surgeons, Mr Moxon and Mr Paterson, for analysis.

William Percival made a second, but undistinguished appearance, repeating that he had sold arsenic to Mrs Milner a few weeks ago. He discreetly failed to mention selling antimonial wine to Jemima Sharp.

Before any medical opinion was presented, the court was told of a voluntary statement made by Mary Ann Milner at the Coroner's inquest. The contrasting ways in which the statement was reported is quite extraordinary: the *Lincolnshire Chronicle* was quite perfunctory, dismissing Mrs Milner's statement as involving a 'a contradiction or two, but of no great importance'; slightly more expansive, but hardly more sympathetic, the *Stamford Mercury* described the statement as being 'at some variance with the facts proved', and that she had protested her innocence. The version of the statement, published in the *Evening Mail*, was more specific, and whilst being at odds with the statements of the witnesses, it was hardly 'of no great importance'. Mrs Milner denied that Mary Winter had spoken with her about the making of a pancake; more crucially, she declared that the deceased, herself and the two children had all eaten the same pancake.

The evidence from the two medical experts reported by the *Evening Mail* was brief and to the point. Moxon and Paterson had examined the vomit retrieved from the ash heap and the contents of the stomach of the deceased. Having submitted both to 'the strictest chemical tests' they both concluded that the cause of death was metallic poison.

In contrast, the two Lincolnshire newspapers gave extensive details of the scientific evidence submitted to the court, in terms of process and outcome. They also provided more anecdotal material which related to exchanges between Mary Ann Milner and James Moxon in particular, concerning the production and consumption of the pancakes.

In the *Lincolnshire Chronicle*, Moxon told the court of his visit to see Mrs Jickels, finding her vomiting and purging; she was so weak that she seldom spoke, other than to complain of pains in her stomach. The doctor said that he had immediately suspected poisoning.

In response to a question from James Moxon, Mrs Milner confirmed that she had eaten pancakes with the deceased that morning. He examined matter which the deceased had vomited and it appeared to be partly digested food; whilst he was in the room, she vomited, and his observations on the fresh vomit led him to conclude that her illness was not caused by the administration of poison. His conclusion was perhaps supported by Mary Ann Milner mentioning that her sister-in-law was feeling unwell before eating the pancake. Before he left the house between 2 and 3 o'clock that afternoon, he asked Mrs Milner if the deceased had taken anything, to which she replied in the negative. This may or may not have been true at the time, given that Mrs Jickels had certainly, at some point, consumed raspberry vinegar with water, as well as brandy and water; it is also possible that she had been given antimonial wine.

Moxon stated that when he left the house he still had suspicions that Hannah Jickels had been poisoned, and therefore returned the following day, only to find her dead.

After an exposition of the various scientific tests carried out on the stomach and intestines of the deceased, Moxon returned to his various conversations with Mrs Milner. He had asked Mary Ann Milner if her sister-in-law had eaten the same pancake as herself, to which she replied that it was made of the same butter (*sic*) as her cakes were. The day after the death of Hannah Jickels, Mrs Milner had also expressed the hope that the doctors had not found anything and 'that she would be clear'.

The doctor told the court that if poison had been administered then antimony 'would not be a bad treatment': in the context of tracking the events of Saturday, 26th June, it would have been a natural medical observation to make; as a detached sentence at the end of his deposition, as reported by the newspaper, it created a sense of special pleading.

The account in the *Stamford Mercury* also published the scientific information from the autopsy, although not as extensively as the *Lincolnshire Chronicle*. It also reported the conversations between Moxon and Mrs Milner, albeit in slightly different words. In addition, the newspaper also provided an expanded contextualised version of the comment made by the doctor on the administration of antimonial wine. Moxon had been aware that antimony had been administered to the deceased, but two ounces of wine would contain only half an ounce of antimony, and that would not be enough to kill someone, he explained to the court, and 'would not yield arsenic results'.

Only the *Lincolnshire Chronicle* reported the cross examination of the witness by Mr Miller, who had pressed Moxon on the wisdom of administering antimony to a patient who was clearly very ill indeed. Moxon endorsed the status of antimony as a recognised medical treatment, as well as defending the conclusions he had reached after his examination of the remains of Hannah Jickels.

With absolute confidence, he asserted that antimony was not an irritant poison. However, he then appeared to modify his position: he had read Alfred Swaine Taylor's *Medical Jurisprudence*, 'a work of note amongst medical gentlemen', and on reflection, he remembered that tartar emetic or antimony in large quantities was considered an irritant poison. Mr Miller seems to have asked the logical question in the light of Moxon's statement: if the same tests had been applied to the stomach of the deceased should antimony have been ingested, as opposed to arsenic, would it have produced the same outcomes? Moxon replied in the negative.

The concluding speech by Mr Miller in defence of his client was reported in all three newspapers: two of the three agreed that he had delivered a forceful defence of Mary Ann Milner. His main lines of defence, according to the newspapers, were that the evidence against her was merely circumstantial and there was no irrefutable proof of her guilt. She was therefore entitled to an acquittal. The report in the *Stamford Mercury*, if accurate, created a sense of desperation in Mr Miller's plea, in that he suggested that the arsenic purchased from Mr Percival had been left to lie around the house and had accidentally ended up in the food consumed by Hannah Jickels. The words used by the newspaper to describe this explanation of the tragedy consisted of barely disguised scepticism: the truth of the matter, according to Mr Miller, was that the arsenic 'by some mysterious and inexplicable mischance got into the food of which the deceased had partaken'.

The idea of accidental food contamination had been successfully argued by Mr Miller in his defence of Mrs Milner in the first indictment: it was rather optimistic to expect the same jury to swallow it a second time.

It didn't.

In his summing up of the case, Lord Justice Rolfe appears to have been measured and detached, presenting the facts of the case and the options open to the Grand Jury. There could be no doubt, he said, that Hannah Jickels had been a victim of arsenic poisoning, and that arsenic had been discovered in the pancake, as demonstrated by the medical evidence. The question for the jury to decide upon was whether the introduction of arsenic into the pancake was deliberately or accidentally done by the prisoner. However, despite Rolfe's reported even-handed address to the jury, with its insistence that it must weigh up the circumstantial against the probable in the light of the evidence, he betrayed his personal prejudices by inventing an explanation for the absence of any motive in the case. It might have been a difficult sticking point for the jury, but his Lordship kindly provided a useful get out clause: 'With respect to the motive, there were many passions which were beyond the reach of human penetration'.

Once the evidence had been reviewed, the judge concluded with the usual judicial formula: if the jury had any doubts whatsoever about the guilt of the prisoner, they must find her not guilty; on the other hand, if they found the evidence conclusive, they must 'fearlessly do their duty to their country and find her guilty'.

The more alert members of the Grand Jury, having heard this, might well have recalled the words of Lord Denman at the opening of the Assize, warning them about verdicts which favoured a prisoner and being responsible for 'the indulgence of passion and a disregard of duty' to the detriment of society.

According to the *Evening Mail*, the jury took about twenty minutes to reach the guilty verdict; the *Stamford Mercury* reported that it took around thirty minutes; whilst the *Lincolnshire Chronicle* preferred a vague and probably more pointed estimate of 'some minutes'.

Once the guilty verdict had been reached, the uncertain narrative of Mary Ann Milner, a young woman suspected of killing three members of her family, could now become an unquestionable story of a diabolical mass murderer, beyond the pale of all human decencies. The identity of Mrs Milner was now ripe for manipulation, reinvention and transformation into a commercial product by the media, ready for popular consumption.

The appetite for such an unsavoury narrative was both stimulated and sanctioned by the final words of Lord Justice Rolfe, reported by the *Evening Mail*, as well as the two Lincolnshire publications. In passing the death sentence, the relieved judge took the opportunity to observe that any other verdict would have made him 'tremble for the security of human life and of the continuance of the system of trial by jury'. The jury had quite rightly found Mary Ann Milner guilty of one murder, but in all probability she had committed many more, apparent from 'the document before him'. He once again skirted around the uncomfortable issue of motivation by suggesting that it was beyond their power to ascertain a reason for such a diabolical deed. In a rhetorical flourish which unconsciously recalled the murder of King Duncan by Macbeth, the facts were so clear that 'the very stones told of her guilt'. The use of the motif of luring the victim to her house under the pretence of hospitality, when recalling Mrs Milner's breakfast invitation to her sister-in-law, perhaps suggests that the reference to Shakespeare's play was more than unconscious black-capped learning. Her 'deeds of blood' left no possibility of mercy this side of the grave: Mrs Milner's only hope was to take advantage of the spiritual instruction she would be offered in gaol before execution and its consequent 'reconciliation with that God whose laws she had violated'.

And that was that, or so it seemed: the story of Mary Ann Milner of Barnetby le Wold, however, was only just beginning.

Suicide of Mary Ann Milner, Night of 29th or Early Morning, 30th July, 1847

Throughout the entire trial, Mrs Milner had not betrayed the slightest emotion nor shed a tear, according to the *Evening Mail*. She maintained the same 'perfectly firm and collected' demeanour, reported by the *Lincolnshire Chronicle*, even as his Lordship was passing the death sentence. The *Stamford Mercury* was more expansive in its account, especially of the moment of condemnation: Mrs Milner, now unquestionably the culprit, remained emotionless – 'not a muscle of her face moved; and with the exception of a slight heaving of the breast, she seemed as placid as she had been throughout the whole of the horrid investigation'. Just in case the reader might experience an unguarded moment of sympathy or admiration for the apparent stoicism of Mary Ann Milner, the newspaper identified a strong sense of the justice and horror pervading the court which 'subverted that feeling usually betrayed on the sentencing of a wretched fellow-creature'.

It was now open season on Mrs Milner, with inconvenient evidence from the judicial proceedings being either omitted, modified or completely contradicted. According to the *Sheffield Independent* of Saturday, 31st July, the condemned prisoner had confessed to six other murders, including three members of another family in the village. Publishing the same claims, the *Lady's Newspaper and Pictorial Times* of the same day claimed to have resolved the vexed issue of motivation for 'the perpetration of these wholesale murders': it was nothing more than avarice, the expectation of financial gain from the burial club. *The Express*, in London, as part of a lengthy article campaigning to restrict the sale of poison, compared Mary Ann Milner's 'quadruple poisoning' with the killing spree of Anna Maria Zwanziger, the German serial killer beheaded in 1811 for multiple murders by arsenic.

The execution date fixed by Lord Justice Rolfe was Friday, 30th July, at noon. By early morning, the partially constructed temporary wooden gallows would have been visible to the public; and William Calcraft, the incompetent career executioner, who had arrived in the city on the previous day from Newgate, would have been pondering with pleasure, no doubt, his next job of work.

The various reports of the public hanging of Mary Ann Milner were unusually short and to the point. The wretched murderess had expiated her dreadful crime on the scaffold, as required by law. The hangman had made the necessary adjustments to the rope, the drop had fallen and after struggling for few seconds, she ceased to exist.

The report was published in various newspapers, either as a free-standing short account or as a part of a larger narrative which supplied sensational background information to the case. The earliest account seems to have been published in *John Bull*, Friday, 30th July, the day of the execution, and replicated across the country.

The reason why the account of Mary Ann Milner's execution was so lacking in detail, beyond the usual tawdry clichés of judicial execution, became clear in early August: it never actually happened. The report in *John Bull*, followed by the *Northampton Mercury*, the *Bucks Gazette*, the *Durham Advertiser* and the *Morning Advertiser,* amongst others, was a complete fiction, probably written in the case of the *John Bull* newspaper article, the day before the execution was scheduled to take place. The fake news of judicial execution in Lincoln was still doing the rounds on the

12th August, courtesy of the *Exeter Flying Post*, which also included the equally unlikely tale of a confession written by Mrs Milner before she was executed.

The misappropriation of the truth was much lamented by the *Lincolnshire Chronicle,* published on the 6th August, in a short piece with the mocking headline 'The Prophetic Globe'. The Lincolnshire newspaper took great exception to *The Globe and Traveller*, a London publication, reporting an event which had never taken place, describing it as 'a regrettable hoax'. Perhaps sensing an opportunity to score a point against metropolitan competitors, the 7th August edition of *The Atlas*, not only drew attention to the error, but also quoted the full shameful text published in *John Bull*.

For a while, there was a media scramble to retract the story, but there was little evidence of an apology to its readers, more a sense of a truculent deflecting of blame: the *Liverpool Mercury*, 6th August, for example, censured officials of the gaol for allowing a report to be circulated that Mary Ann Milner had been privately executed within the walls of the prison. The *Bristol Mercury*, 14th August, on the other hand, made it clear that the blame for their error of the previous week was a London newspaper from which it had copied the report.

Bizarrely, the story of Mrs Milner having been executed was still being reported as fact in the *Daily*

News, 2nd August, 1929, under the strapline 'In the Days of Dickens'.

Once activated, the judicial machinery of Victorian England, especially of capital punishment, was irresistible: that is what made it so such a frightening prospect for those individuals trapped in its workings. Having done or not done something wrong, ordinary men and women who once had lived an unremarkable life somewhere on the edge of insignificance, suddenly became the significant centre of a strangely constructed world of big buildings packed with oppressively grand, brown furniture and equally oppressive self-important strangers, who would otherwise have never been part of their ordinariness.

There was the occasional threat of derailment brought about by an unexpected act of clemency, of course, one of those false notions of mercy and compassion derided by Lord Justice Denman perhaps, but the machine was resilient enough to absorb any such shocks. The accused getting off, even at the last minute, was, after all, part of the design and inner workings of the machine.

What was not part of those inner workings was the accused, without so much as a by-your-leave, re-arranging the time of their own death, becoming both the executioner and the executed, and cancelling all triumphant narratives related to the proper administration of justice.

The suicide of Mary Ann Milner not only exposed the machine's inner workings as inadequate, but also put some of those self-important people, the drivers of the machine, in the dock, to answer a few uncomfortable questions about truthfulness and professional standards.

Inquest on the Suicide of Mary Ann Milner, 31st July, 1847

The inquest into the death of Mrs Milner, held on the morning of Saturday, 31st July, was reported by the *Stamford Mercury* in forensic detail, using the attention-grabbing headline, 'Self-Destruction of Murderess'. It was clearly a story worth expending some effort on its creation: rather than the usual factual preliminaries, which were the staple of inquest reports, the newspaper adopted a more literary approach to the narrative. Rather than being dropped into the dry background of the case, the reader was gently dipped into the sleepy world of Lincoln on the early morning of Friday, 30th July.

Shortly before 8 o'clock, the city had been slowly aroused from 'that overpowering sense of weariness whichever comes from a period of excitement'. The excitement in question was that of the recent fiercely contested local election, which had clearly taken its toll on the citizens of Lincoln, as much as the four candidates. Such torpor was dispelled, however, by the slowly circulating rumour that the woman who was due to be executed at the Castle that day had been found dead in her cell. The gradually emerging uncomfortable truth meant that the hundreds of people who had travelled to the city and had already gathered 'to gaze upon the horrible spectacle of the strangulation of a human being' would be doomed to great inconvenience and disappointment.

The surprisingly sympathetic and graphic description of death by public hanging evoked by the newspaper would have been made even more powerful should the reader have been familiar with the short-drop method of hanging favoured by William Calcraft, which strangled the prisoner slowly, rather than broke their neck instantaneously.

The first witness to give evidence was Henry William Richter, the Prison Chaplain, who had last seen Mrs Milner at about 8 o'clock on the night of Thursday, 30th July. She appeared to be reconciled to her judicial fate, and was described by the Reverend Richter in an expertly crafted phrase of evasive non-commitment, as 'though evincing firmness, she indicated no hardihood.'

What followed was a lengthy account of his conversation with Mary Ann Milner which, if true, provided some interesting new information.

It was not entirely unexpected that the Chaplain claimed that Mrs Milner had said that she had nothing more to confess to him and that she had made her peace with God. Still less unexpected was the claim that the prisoner had expressed 'great gratitude' to Richter for having 'so influenced her mind that she had been brought to a full confession.'

It was the familiar material of ecclesiastical self-congratulation.

In addition to providing a testimonial on the efficacy of Richter as a spiritual advisor, Mrs Milner also expressed great sorrow for her crimes and sympathy for those individuals whom she had 'sent unprepared out of the world'. She also expressed concern for the welfare of her little boy: in a dramatic moment, before finally leaving Mrs Milner, the Chaplain had been called back and was begged to write a letter to her husband 'to give the best account of her he could' and also to ask Mr Milner to take care of the child. The reason for her concern was that her mother and friends were emigrating to America, leaving no one but her husband to look after the child. The Reverend Richter assured Mary Ann Milner that he would do so, as well as write to John White, the parish priest of Barnetby le Wold; in response, and with considerable feeling, Mrs Milner said, 'Pray do'.

Henry Richter continued his deposition by telling the Coroner and the jury that during his visit Mrs

Milner 'betrayed more dejection than at former times', but that did not give him occasion to think that she might commit suicide: her dejection, in his opinion, was more to do with her feelings, than any loss of reason.

His final comment was that he had not ordered Mrs Milner a candle as she could not read well – only imperfectly.

Mrs Emily Johnson, the prison Matron, was allegedly the last person to see Mary Ann Milner alive, having visited her at 9.15 that evening, as part of her daily round. She did not appear to be quite so well as she had been, but the Matron did not observe anything significant in her behaviour nor notice anything different about her cell. When Mrs Johnson last saw her she had been sitting up, but perhaps the Matron was not able to see too much: as she pointed out, there was no candle in the cell. She confirmed that there was no order for her to visit a condemned prisoner more than any other prisoner and that there was no order for anyone to sit up with Mrs Milner on the night before her execution. She had worked as the prison Matron for many years, during which time no one had ever been ordered to sit up with a condemned prisoner.

According to Emily Johnson, she had discovered the body of Mrs Milner at 8.45 on the morning of Friday, 30th July, suspended against a cupboard door. She had immediately alerted the two warders on duty,

Mr Melson and Mr Bescoby. When the deceased was removed, she noticed that her bonnet was tied up: it had not been tied up when she departed from the cell on the previous night. The handkerchief by which she had suspended herself, on the other hand, which Mrs Milner habitually wore round her neck, she was wearing when Mrs Johnson had left the cell.

John Nicholson, the Governor of the gaol, after being informed of what had happened, immediately informed the Coroner, the Sheriff and the Visiting Magistrates. He confirmed Mrs Johnson's evidence that there was no requirement to sit up with a condemned prisoner on the night before execution. He had noticed the handkerchief used by Mr Milner to suspend herself: in his opinion, the knot was 'of such power and strength' that strangulation was inevitable. His opinion was supported by William Calcraft, the public hangman, who had examined the knot and concluded that it was done 'in such a dextrous manner' as to make any chance of it slipping impossible. The upper part of the handkerchief had been attached to a nail which had been attached to a storage closet for books. Mr Nicholson reiterated that there was no rule that a condemned prisoner should be attended the night before execution and therefore prison discipline had not been compromised.

William Melson, the Chief Turnkey and William Bescoby, the officer under him, were called by the

Matron after her discovery that Mrs Milner had hanged herself. They had taken the body down with some difficulty and the Governor had been alerted. Mr Melson had felt the neck of the deceased which was hard 'as if she had been dead for some time'. His observation was confirmed by the prison Surgeon, Ralph Howett, who had been called to the scene by the Governor. There were two chairs near the door of the prison cell, either of which Mrs Milner could have used to jump off to suspend herself.

After a short deliberation, the jury returned a verdict of *felo de se*, and Mrs Milner was buried in the prison precincts, having been found guilty of the crime of committing suicide.

The inquest into the suicide was reported also by the *Lincolnshire Chronicle*. It duplicates much of the material in the *Stamford Mercury* and departs from it only occasionally. The reported time of Henry Richter leaving Mrs Milner in her cell was around 9.30, for example, rather than 8 o'clock, which made him the last person to see her alive, rather than the Matron. It also provided details concerning Mrs Milner having been discovered suspended without shoes or underpetticoat – irrelevant titillating information which no doubt was the root of a least one later report which claimed that she died naked.

The only significant addition to the report in the *Stamford Mercury* related to Henry Richter departing from Mrs Milner for the final time: she had nothing more to say to him, 'beyond some confession which she had made to him in confidence.' The implied respect for the sanctity of private confession was a throwaway remark which is puzzling in the light of later developments published in the *Stamford Mercury*.

The *Prison Journals* of the Gaol Keeper and the Surgeon, both of whom had significant contact with Mrs Milner during her incarceration, were probably examined in camera. The former's record of the last days of Mary Ann Milner were purely administrative and in the main confirmed the chronological account of the prisoner's confessions of her crimes provided by the Reverend Richter. His recording of the time of the discovery of the suicide differed considerably, however, from that of Mrs Johnson, stating that she had been found dead at 7.30 that morning – a difference of over an hour. The body of Mrs Milner was buried on the evening of the inquest, at 9.15, in the castle keep. In addition to these mundane facts, the Keeper also noted in his *Journal* entry for the 28th July that the Reverend White would be writing from Barnetby le Wold and visiting 'the convict Mary Ann Milner under sentence of death this evening from an order from G J W Sibthorpe (*sic*).'

The *Journal* of the Prison Surgeon, Ralph Howett, recorded a good deal of interesting and detailed information about the physical and mental well-being of Mary Ann Milner, as he had in the case of Eliza Joyce, in 1844, which can be placed alongside the accounts heard at the inquest. His earliest observation on Mrs Milner was on the 21st July, the day on which she was condemned to death: she was 'in a nervous and distressed and distressing state.' Her distressed state continued the next day, but gradually over the following days she seemed to regain some composure, improving from 'tolerably tranquil' to 'very calm': she had managed to have some sleep and to eat. By the 29th July, Howett noted, 'her bodily state surprisingly good. Her mind apparently very calm.'

Whilst the descriptions of a condemned woman struggling to maintain her mental equilibrium make uneasy reading, Howett's precise description of his examination of the wrecked body of Mary Ann Milner does even more so. After examining her, he concluded that she must have been dead many hours: her face was a livid purple and was swollen, the tongue protruding and also swollen; the silk handkerchief used to suspend herself had made a livid permanent groove around her neck; her eyes were wide open and staring, and the pupils dilated and considerably irregular.

It was perhaps a mercy that the popular press did not gain access to Howett's report.

On the surface, the judicial machinery driving due process had worked efficiently to bring a satisfactory closure to the case of Mary Ann Milner: no rules had been broken and everyone involved, with the exception of Mrs Milner, had correctly followed official protocols.

However, despite the best efforts of the inquest, there seemed to be a lingering sense of public unease relating to what had happened. In particular, there seemed to be some concern about the involvement, or lack of it, of the Prison Chaplain.

It was an unease anticipated by Henry Richter himself, not only in his evidence to the inquest, but also in a long open letter to the editor of the *Stamford Mercury* which he penned on the 31st July, and was published immediately below the newspaper's report on the inquest.

Essentially, the letter is a detailed account of the various confessions made by Mary Ann Milner to Richter whilst she was in Lincoln gaol. The intention, according to the Chaplain, was to provide the public with a correct version of those confessions, up to the time of her suicide. Why the cleric thought it necessary to do this, in addition to giving evidence at the inquest, cannot be answered with confidence, but may give rise to some unsavoury speculation.

Before presenting the confessional material, Richter reminded the reader of the background to the case. Mary Ann Milner had been indicted for the murder of her mother-in-law and had been acquitted;

she had been indicted for the poisoning of her sister-in-law, had been found guilty and condemned to death; there had also been a third indictment against her for poisoning her brother's daughter.

The Chaplain was quite precise about dates, although incorrect. On the morning of Wednesday, 21st July, Mrs Milner confessed to having poisoned her brother's wife, by inviting her into the house to eat pancake made of batter in which she had put arsenic.

In all respects, this information was already in the public domain, apart from Mrs Milner's admission of guilt.

On the morning of Monday, 26th July, the prisoner confessed to having poisoned the infant daughter of her brother's wife, elaborating on this statement later by saying that she put arsenic in its tea after having brought the child round to the house for that purpose. This confession was also noted in the Gaol Keeper's *Journal* for the same day.

In the evening of the same day, Mrs Milner confessed that she had intended to poison her husband's father by putting arsenic into his rice pudding, but she 'declared solemnly' that she did not intend to poison her mother-in-law, and that she must have accidentally eaten some of the rice pudding that was left over from her father-in-law having eaten it. The same confession was also recorded in the Gaol Keeper's *Journal*, although for the following day.

In retrospect, the confession justified both Mr Miller's line of defence in the first indictment and the jury's decision to acquit, at least on the charge of murder.

There were no more confessions, but there was a lengthy explanation from Mrs Milner of her motives for murdering members of her own family.

Mary Ann Milner's reasons for killing, without any kind of further context, appeared to be either a total fabrication or a despicable and disproportionate response to domestic difficulties. According to Henry Richter, Mrs Milner decided to get rid of her sister-in-law, Hannah Jickels, because she was the root cause of arguments between her husband and herself; further, her sister-in-law 'was continually vexing her and making herself unpleasant'. Her poisoning of Hannah Jickels and her child was a very unpleasant act of revenge, it seems.

In response to being asked about the poisoning of her father and mother-in-law, Mrs Milner told Henry Richter that they did not treat her well either, turning up at the house when they felt like it, 'as though it was their own', taking away what was not theirs to take and doing 'what they liked with no regard to her'. To make matters worse, her husband 'gave money and things' to his parents, leading to an exasperated Mary Ann Milner threatening to leave her husband if he continued to do so.

In the end, her solution to her domestic difficulties had been to poison her husband's father.

The Reverend Richter's startling revelations ended with a lofty statement of philosophical detachment. He did not intend to comment upon what he had heard from Mrs Milner. He would leave it for the public to decide how much credence to give her confessions and therefore reach their own conclusions about her.

The trial of Mary Ann Milner had established that she had the opportunity and the means to administer arsenic, but the question of motive remained elusive; in his over-insistence that the prisoner's motivation was unfathomable, the judge seemed uncomfortable with a crime without any discernible motive. Henry Richter, however, had now triumphantly supplied an explanation of an unfathomable mystery.

Despite the implausibility of such horrific crimes being motivated by petty domestic squabbles, the account of those domestic contexts in which the crime was committed and then discovered, suggested in the trial report of the *Evening Mail*, in particular, gives weight to Mrs Milner's confession. In the witness depositions, there is a strong sense of friends, relations and neighbours, including Mrs Milner herself, moving freely and easily from one house to another on a regular basis. It is a context in which the mutual support of close community could easily slip into an uncomfortable smothering claustrophobia, as well as fuelling personal animosities at having to endure the inconvenience of over-familiar intrusion.

If it was a case of a woman feeling aggrieved at being treated badly by her husband's family, the alleged lack of support for his wife from John Milner would have intensified that sense of being disregarded by others. If thoughts of revenge, the taking of decisive action to right a perceived wrong, were a temporary soothing solution for injured feelings, real or imagined, the taking of brutal revenge with extreme prejudice would have been a fearfully empowering palliative to a woman at breaking point, without any other hope of redress.

The ineffectiveness of the letter to the *Stamford Mercury* in terms of deflecting any public disquiet about the conduct of Richter in relation to the suicide of Mrs Milner, is confirmed by the newspaper running another article on the issue three weeks later, on Friday 20th August. Overtly, it was a discussion of the Secretary of State having ordered that in future no condemned prisoner should be left unwatched. In reality, it was a robust defence of Henry Richter's professional conduct as a Prison Chaplain, veering wildly between common sense, shameless misogyny, apoplectic outrage and feeble apologia.

The source of the disquiet is not revealed, beyond the vague identification of 'some parties', who had clearly taken great exception to what they saw as a dereliction of his duty of care: in the opinion of the aggrieved parties, the Chaplain should not have waited for an order to ensure the safety of Mary Ann Milner.

The first line of defence was that Chaplains were employed to give religious instruction and that to censure Richter for not 'trespassing beyond his clerical duties' the writer deemed harsh. It was especially unfair as neither the Matron nor the prison Governor had chosen to subvert prison discipline by breaking the rules.

Had the Chaplain observed any 'disposition to self-destruction' and not acted upon it by implementing 'a careful watch' he would have been culpable, but even then, he would have been going beyond his duty had he done so, as there were 'regularly authorised persons to attend to the government of the prison.' Having said that, the Chaplain had not observed any problems with the disposition of the prisoner, as he had stated at the inquest. The article further reminded the reader that the Chaplain had noted Mrs Milner's spiritual equilibrium, having confessed and made her peace with the Almighty; she had even expressed her gratitude to the Chaplain for inducing her to make a full confession of guilt. To attach any blame to Mr Richter indicated a complete lack of charity.

It was also an absurdity to condemn a man for not doing what he could not do without infringing the rules of a system laid down by others: if Chaplains were expected to be responsible for the actions of convicts, they should be empowered to override the visitorial directions of magistrates and the subordinate powers of governors and matrons.

At this point, the writer moved away from the constraints of the hierarchical structure of the judicial system to an unrestrained attack upon the character of Mary Ann Milner. Her feigned repentance, even whilst she solemnly prepared for eternity, was a mere repetition of the hypocrisy which had carried her through 'so many revolting scenes of blood and with the appearance of innocence through a conviction'.

In a flurry of rhetorical questions, the article seemed to lose all sense of proportion and decency. The Chaplain was blameless quite simply because he had been contending with the dark forces of evil: 'Is he to be accounted a match for all the Devil-cunning which was the ripened fruit of many years growth?' In a contrived triplet, the writer defined the true nature of Mary Ann Milner, 'She cheated those who had confided in her; she cheated him; and she cheated the hangman'. It was unfortunate that the newspaper had forgotten its proclaimed revulsion at the sight of a human being strangled in public by the hangman, only a few weeks previously.

After seeming to have acquired a unique knowledge of Mrs Milner's damaged childhood, the article raised the theological stakes: a Chaplain cannot be blamed if he repeats the Fall of Man by being deceived by a woman.

Switching similes, the report then moved away from theological commonplaces to the secular cliché of the cleric as physician. If a doctor failed to eradicate a long-standing disease he should not be blamed; nor should a Chaplain who fails to cure 'a long-standing moral and religious disease'.

In the final sections of the article, the writer resumed a slightly more detached approach to his defence of the prison Chaplain. In it, he both quotes and summarises the criticisms which had been levelled at Henry Richter: the vocabulary and ideas, if accurately reported, suggest that the unnamed 'various parties' were religious groups in the area. Regret, it seems, had been expressed that 'a minister of Christ's church should not have spontaneously availed himself of the glorious opportunity to calling this wretched sinner to repentance'. This was easily dealt with by the writer, pointing out that thanks to the exertions of the Chaplain, the prisoner appeared to be fully repentant and grateful for his spiritual support. Somewhat disingenuously, he suggested that Richter having 'left her with her own heart and the Almighty was a far more Christian course than the minister to be constantly with her.' The logic of this piece of special pleading was that remaining by her side in the cell would have been an unwelcome distraction from realising her total dependence upon God.

The 'various parties' had also censured the Chaplain for the very little time spent with the condemned prisoner, amounting to a neglect of his spiritual duties and the loss of an opportunity to have prevented the catastrophe. At these suggestions, the report once again became quite prickly, describing the accusation as 'a paltry shuffle' to shift blame on to the weakest. 'Why should a Chaplain spend all night previous to an execution with a culprit?' the article thundered; 'And had it been done in this case, would it have been an effectual preventative of self-destruction?'

The diatribe ended, perhaps predictably, by quietly agreeing with the Secretary of State, and accepting that all condemned criminals should be watched from the moment of their sentence; equally predictably, but less quietly, it insisted that Richter should not be blamed for the lack of such a provision in the system at the time.

Both at the inquest into her death and by way of an open letter published in the popular press, the prison Chaplain had attempted to frame the narrative of Mary Ann Milner's last weeks of life and his part in them. He had done his duty and had enabled a sinner to be reconciled to God through repentance and confession: he had done all that he could in difficult and challenging circumstances.

An examination of the Reverend Richter's *Journal* of his daily rounds in Lincoln prison, however, indicates that the Chaplain's public construction of reality, was arguably somewhat partial, and lends a degree of support to the concerned reservations of 'other parties' derided by the *Stamford Mercury*.

The document records his visits to see Mrs Milner between Saturday, 3rd July and Thursday, 30th July, inclusive. Of the eighteen visits to speak with her, there is little information noted, day by day, other than the fact that the visit had been made. There are just three exceptions to this virtual blankness. On the 3rd July, he wrote 'visited the woman Milner, charged with poisoning'; on the 19th July, the day before the trial, he wrote the single word 'confessed'; and on the 30th July, the day of her death, Richter briefly noted that he 'came to the prison between 9 and 10 o'clock hearing that the prisoner had committed suicide'. What is most surprising about the contents of the *Journal* is the absence of any reference to Mrs Milner confessing the details of her crimes beyond the cursory reference on the 19th July.

The image created by the sparse entries is one of a lack of interest and a disengagement from Mary Ann Milner, in distinct contrast to the detailed record of his visits to support the condemned Eliza Joyce three years earlier. It is also in contrast to the image of busy concern and support for Mrs Milner created in the

Press and by Henry Richter himself. The lack of any detail easily creates the impression of dull routine and indifference to her welfare. The absence of even a hint of joy in the single word entry recording a confession the day before the trial is surprising given its centrality to the Chaplain's work and in contrast to his celebratory recording of the confession of Eliza Joyce. Most puzzling of all is the underwhelmed recording of Mary Ann Milner's suicide: as an extraordinary event in the daily life of a Prison Chaplain, it might reasonably have been expected to elicit more reaction and comment than the glib reference to having heard about it.

The problem with prison confessions, of course, is that nobody ever hears them other than the person listening. There is therefore a reliance on that individual to recollect correctly and honestly what was said, should it be disclosed. The inquest testimony of Richter and his open letter, both made claim to an honest representation of the truth, the former by virtue of the context, the latter, by virtue of the writer's expressed intention to put before the public a definitive account of what Mary Ann Milner told him in prison. The details emerging from the letter especially were dramatic and sensational, creating a sense of the Chaplain having formed some kind of meaningful relationship with the condemned woman: Henry Richter's prison *Journal*, in the absence of references to her several confessions and the glib recording of her death, create quite the opposite impression.

Mrs Milner's penitential outpouring to Richter which explained her motives for killing resonates with the picture of daily life in Barnetby le Wold evoked at the trial. At the same time, her supposed desperate plea to Richter asking him to write to her husband to ensure that he took care of their child, as well as to acknowledge personal fault to a husband, is oddly similar to that of Mrs Joyce, recorded in Richter's prison *Journal* in 1844. Both incidents capture a narrative of maternal desperation and penitential guilt, as well as of a concerned Chaplain promising to do his best for a woman on the eve of being executed: only one of the stories was recorded in the Chaplain's *Journal*, however. The anguished outcry from Mary Ann Milner that her mother and friends were leaving to make a new life in America also created a dramatic moment of shared confidence with Richter: however, the information in the 1851 Census clearly records that both her father and her mother, Joseph and Sarah Jickels, were still living in the village, on Brick Pit Lane, nearly four years later. It may be that some of Richter's recollections of her last days are as reliable as the report in some newspapers that Mary Ann Milner, a woman who could barely read and write, had written a full confession of her misdeeds which should only be read after her death.

The letter written by Henry Richter, as well as the support expressed in the local press, seemed to restore a reassuring sense of normality for public consumption, in the aftermath of extraordinary events. The robust article published in the *Stamford Mercury*, on the 20th August, seemed to be the last word on the subject.

However, glossy public surfaces often hide uncomfortable underlying realities. An examination of the various documents from the Gaol Session of the 7th October, 1847, suggests that the suicide of Mrs Milner generated private concern and discomfort to the point of dishonest denial.

It is clear that letters were sent out from Lincoln Castle on the day of the discovery of Mary Ann Milner's suicide and that they received immediate attention from the recipients, who expressed some alarm at what they had read.

Lord Brownlow, as Chair of the Gaol Sessions, was immediately informed by Frederick Burton, the Clerk of the Gaol Sessions, concerning the discovery of the body of Mrs Milner. Referring to 'your letter of yesterday's date', Lord Brownlow responded to the news of the suicide with a predictable, but ultimately unhelpful mixture of knee-jerk bluster and threat. His immediate response was to allocate blame on the Gaoler and the Turnkeys for what he described as 'a gross instance of neglect'. Brownlow's supposition was that the Gaoler would be dealt with by the Sherriff and instantly dismissed and that 'the strange dereliction of duty' by the Turnkeys of leaving the prisoner unwatched and not opening her cell until 8 o'clock in the morning, would be the subject of a strict investigation. Brownlow's concern about the opening of the cell was not so much related to the humane supervision of a woman only four hours away from her execution, as an anxiety that it left her little or no time for religious exercises with the Chaplain. His parting shot was to express as fact 'that the brains of prison officers were addled by the City Election', which had taken place the day before, and that they should be 'called to severe account'.

The post scriptum informed Burton that he had written to J W Moore, the Under-Sherriff, expressing similar sentiments.

The uncomfortable duty of breaking the news of Mary Ann Milner's suicide to the Home Secretary, Sir George Grey, was undertaken by Henry Williams, the Deputy Under-Sherriff. In a letter dated 30th July, Williams gave a clear, albeit guarded account, of what had happened, qualified with expressions such as 'It is supposed', 'I am informed' and 'It is conjectured'. It presented a coherent narrative which was later heard at the inquest, although it was vague on some key points of interest, such as the precise time at which Mrs Milner was left alone in her cell ('the usual hour') and the precise time which she was found dead ('this morning'). It also departed from the version of events later heard at the inquest when it claimed that the person who discovered Mrs Milner was the female Turnkey; according to the testimony of the Matron, Emily Johnson, it was she who discovered Mary Ann Milner.

It was a painful duty, but it provided an opportunity to construct a version of events before any investigation was underway. It was also an opportunity to explain and excuse what had happened to the Home Secretary. Unlike Newgate and other prisons, it had never been the custom or practice at Lincoln to keep a watch over a condemned prisoner. Further, he had been informed by both the Governor and the Chaplain that neither had observed anything in the conduct or demeanour of the prisoner 'to excite the slightest suspicion of any intention on her part to commit suicide'.

In order to mollify the situation, Williams made assurances that measures would be put in place to prevent a repetition of a similar occurrence in the future, and that a formal inquest would be organised immediately; the body of the prisoner would then be buried in the prison precincts.

The response from the Government, penned by Sir Denis le Marchant, the Under-Secretary of State for Home Affairs, on behalf of Sir George Grey, on the 31st July , was unambiguous in its concern and displeasure. Enclosing a copy of the letter received from Williams, Marchant wished to communicate to the gaol authorities that the Home Secretary expected an immediate enquiry into the circumstances of Mrs Milner's suicide; more pointedly, he wished to know why the Governor had allowed the prisoner to have the means of suicide 'through the whole of the night, unwatched'.

By way of moving forward on a formal basis, the Under-Secretary of State wrote a second letter, dated 2nd September, this time specifically to the Chair of the Gaol Session, with instructions from Sir George Grey. The letter contained an addition to the rules governing the treatment of prisoners condemned to death which he wished to have presented to the magistrates assembled at the next meeting of the Gaol Session. The letter described the addition of the rule to the existing governance of the Lincolnshire prison as a recommendation, but it was clear what the Home Secretary meant.

The well-attended Gaol Session, chaired by Lord Brownlow, met on Thursday, 7th October, and it was obvious what the main business of the day would address. Frederick Burton, the Clerk of the Gaol Sessions, presented his *General Report* to the Committee and the assembled magistrates, which gave an account of the suicide of Mary Ann Milner and its subsequent developments. In view of the inquest having taken place already and reported in detail by the newspapers, plus the almost immediate involvement of the Home Office, the wording of the document required meticulous accuracy if it was to avoid any contradiction of information already in the public domain. At the same time, it required a good deal of tact, in that whilst the apportioning of responsibility for the 'unfortunate occurrence' was required if the same mistakes were to be avoided, a robust debate had already taken place in the newspapers concerning the involvement of the Reverend Henry Richter in the scandal.

Burton's report described in clear terms the discovery of Mrs Milner's body in her cell and the means by which she had killed herself. The Visiting Magistrates had made 'strict enquiry into the circumstances of the case' and, in compliance with the request of the Secretary of State, new rules had been agreed relating to the twenty-four hour guarding of a condemned prisoner.

At this point, the document drew attention to the rules of the prison at the time, approved by Sir James Graham in November, 1843, which did not contain any directive relating to the constant monitoring of a condemned prisoner. It was therefore the opinion of the Visiting Magistrates that there had been no infringement of the prison rules. However, in view of what had taken place, there should be a change in procedure in line with the Home Office recommendations. What had taken place, according to the investigation of the Visiting Magistrates, was thin on detail, but it did identify two key points in the timeline of the events. The first was that Mrs Milner had been locked in her cell at 8 o'clock at night; the second was that the cell door was re-opened at the same time that morning.

A familiarity with the reported inquest makes it clear that there were several different versions of both of these key points in the timeline. According to the *Stamford Mercury*, the Reverend Richter had last spoken to Mrs Milner at 8 o'clock that evening, but the *Lincolnshire Chronicle* reported that he had said 9.30. Further, the Matron had deposed that she did her final visit to the cell, as part of her normal rounds, at around 9.15. There was a similar variance in relation to the discovery of the body: the Gaol Keeper told the inquest that the body was found at 7.30 in the morning, whilst the Matron said that she had discovered Mrs Milner at 8.45. In addition, Lord Brownlow, fuming in Belton House, had been informed by Burton's letter that the cell door had not been opened until 8 o'clock that morning.

The Report concluded with the note that the Visiting Magistrates were of the opinion, minuted in their meeting, that the conduct of the Matron and the

Gaol Keeper required 'censure and reprehension' for their conduct.

In short, the blame for the suicide of Mrs Milner lay not with a systemic failure, but with two individuals.

In the division of blame, there is no mention of the Prison Chaplain, who by his own admission and as recorded in the notes of his *Prison Journal*, had a good deal to do with Mrs Milner on a daily basis, including her last night in the condemned cell.

When things go wrong in organisations, especially ones constructed around a rigid culture of social, political and personal hierarchies, there often arises a sense of individuals deflecting responsibility away from themselves and on to others, further down the chain of command. Apportioning blame becomes more important than the truth as a convenient narrative is constructed and inconvenient problems are left unspoken or unresolved.

In circumstances in which the constructed version of the truth, seems to be built on unreliable facts, uncertain recollections and deliberately misleading assertion, it is very easy to slip into an alternative narrative to the official one which sees conspiracies at work, when there were none there.

However, in the case of Mary Ann Milner, there is arguably a case to be made and it is an unpleasant one. On the surface, the report of Frederick Burton heard at the Gaol Session, but not made public, seems like a straightforward attempt to summarise the investigation of the Visiting Magistrates which exonerated the prison authorities in that they had followed existing protocols. In terms of the crucial matters of the time at which Mrs Milner's cell was closed and then reopened, there had been a good deal of conflicting evidence voiced at the inquest, especially from the Gaoler and the Matron, but the investigation was clear:

> '…*it appeared on their investigation the unfortunate culprit had been locked up in her room at about 8 at night and that the doors were not again re-opened til about the same hour on the following morning..*'

This seems clear enough, except it isn't.

A close inspection of this part of the original document raises some awkward questions. The first difficulty is that the spaces in which the times have been recorded are oddly disproportionate, compared to the rest of the document, as if the space had been left to fill in later, when the information became available, or agreed upon. This seems to be confirmed by 'the same hour' requiring a superscript 'hour', as if not enough room had been left to insert the whole phrase. The second problem is that the times have been altered by a later hand using a different colour ink. The second alteration is perhaps just a matter of greater clarity in that 'the same hour' is crossed out and replaced with a superscript '8 o'clock'. What is of greater concern is that original insertion of the numeral 8, in reference to the closing of the cell, has been crossed out and replaced with a superscript 'half-past nine'.

The difference between the two versions is a big one, which curiously reflects the conflicting reports of the inquest in the newspapers relating to when the Prison Chaplain left Mrs Milner in her cell. The *Lincolnshire Chronicle* asserted it was 8 o'clock, whilst the *Stamford Mercury* said it was 9.30.

Given that documents can be altered out of the best of intentions, it may be both fanciful and unworthy to think in terms of an alteration of the inconvenient for less than worthy motives. However, the public dissatisfaction with the Chaplain in his professional relationship with Mrs Milner, as well as his need to urgently put his side of the story into the public domain as the definitive truth, creates a sense of disquiet. It is an unease increased by the fact that at the point at which the Reverend Richter was writing his entry relating to the suicide of Mrs Milner in his *Journal*, it is clear that a page has been removed. The thin remainder of the page contains a couple of words, so it was obviously not a blank which had been cut out, for whatever reason.

It is perhaps yet another puzzling and uncomfortable twist in the story of Mary Ann Milner.

References to the husband of Mary Ann Milner, during the course of the reporting of the case are remarkably sparse: he was briefly mentioned in passing by witnesses at the trial, as well as in Richter's letter to the press. Further information is also supplied by two brief entries in the Gaol Keeper's *Journal* of 25th and 26th July which record that John Milner and his child were admitted to visit his wife.

However, this was all to change a week after the suicide of Mrs Milner when it was reported in the *Lincolnshire Chronicle* of Friday, 13th August, and in other newspapers beyond the county, that John Milner, on hearing about the death of his wife, had made an application to a funeral club in Brigg for £10. Unfortunately for Mr Milner, the funeral club had either refused or was unable to make a payment, leading him to threaten legal action.

If true, it was an astonishing story of breath-taking brazenness and a gift to the popular press, which was able to point the moral and draw the lesson. The tragic and awful events which had unfolded in Bartleby le Wold should have given rise to serious moral reflection in the minds of Mary Ann Milner's relatives, rather than an unprincipled rapaciousness and a thirst for filthy lucre.

It was a depressing end to a distressing episode in the history of C19th Lincolnshire, but perhaps no more disheartening than the staggering lack of a sympathetic perspective shown by the *Hull Packet and East Riding Times* newspaper in its reporting of the suicide of Mrs Milner. In a short account, which carried the headline, 'A Double Disappointment', the newspaper lamented the fact that the many sightseers who had arrived in Lincoln to witness the execution of Mary Ann Milner had been thwarted by her strangling herself in prison. Equally disappointing, it seems, was that on the afternoon of the same day, the chairing of Colonel Waldo Sibthorp after winning the local election had to be deferred, as he was indisposed by illness.

However, despite being later compelled through 'a serious indisposition' to decline the chairing altogether, there was a happy ending to the story, in that Colonel Sibthorp generously donated £50 each to three fortunate medical charities in Lincoln.

What the Hull newspaper did not report, of course, was the less than happy ending of Mrs Milner, having suffered an even more serious indisposition than the gallant colonel and also being the unlucky recipient of a less than generous resting place, next to Eliza Joyce.

APPENDIX

Key Players in the Mary Ann Milner Story

BAINBRIDGE, T. Served on the Grand Jury at the trial of Mary Ann Milner, at the Lincoln Assizes.

BAYLES, Slater. Hatter. Served on the Grand Jury at the trial of Mary Ann Milner, at the Lincoln Assizes. Resident of Lincoln.

BESCOBY, William. Prison officer, Lincoln Castle.

BLOW, Samuel. Plumber. Served on the Grand Jury at the trial of Mary Ann Milner, at the Lincoln Assizes. Served on Lincoln Board of Guardians. Shareholder in Lincoln and Lindsey Bank. Resident of Lincoln.

BODENS, C H. Served on the Grand Jury at the trial of Mary Ann Milner, at the Lincoln Assizes.

BONSOR, Samuel. Grocer and Tea-Dealer. Served on the Grand Jury at the trial of Mary Ann Milner, at the Lincoln Assizes. Resident of Lincoln.

BOOTH, William. Cordwainer. Gave evidence at second indictment at the trial of Mary Ann Milner, at the Lincoln Assizes. Resident of Barnetby le Wold.

CALCRAFT, William. Public executioner, brought from Newgate to hang Mary Ann Milner. Paid £10/3/– 'for attending at Lincoln to have executed Mary Ann Milner for murder'.

DENMAN, Right Honourable Thomas. Lord Chief Justice of England, present at Lincoln Summer Assizes. Resident of Middleton Hall, Stoney Middleton, Derbyshire.

DENNISON, Beckett. Counsel for the Prosecution at the trial of Mary Ann Milner, at the Lincoln Assizes.

DYMOKE, John. Wholesale Chemist and Druggist. Served on Grand Jury at the trial of Mary Ann Milner, at the Lincoln Assizes. Resident of Lincoln.

FLINT, J. Served on Grand Jury at the trial of Mary Ann Milner, at the Lincoln Assizes.

GARTON, Thomas. Tobacconist. Served on Grand Jury at the trial of Mary Ann Milner, at the Lincoln Assizes. Resident of Lincoln.

HAVERCROFT, Thomas. Carpenter, gave evidence at

first indictment at the trial of Mary Ann Milner, at the Lincoln Assizes. Resident of Barnetby le Wold.

HITCHINS, James. Coroner at inquest into suicide of Mary Ann Milner.

HOWETT, Dr Ralph. Surgeon of Lincoln Castle prison. Gave evidence at inquest into the suicide of Mary Ann Milner.

HYDE, William Henry. Grocer. Served on Grand Jury at the trial of Mary Ann Milner, at the Lincoln Assizes. Resident of Lincoln.

JICKELS, Ellen. Daughter of Thomas and Hannah Jickels. Resident of Barnetby le Wold.

JICKELS, Hannah. Sister-in-law of Mary Ann Milner, poisoned with arsenic. Resident of Barnetby le Wold.

JICKELS, Joseph. Father of Mary Ann Milner. Resident of Barnet le Wold.

JICKELS, Sarah. Mother of Mary Ann Milner. Resident of Barneby le Wold.

JICKELS, Thomas. Husband of Hannah Jickels. Resident of Barnetby le Wold.

JOHNSON, Emily. Matron of Lincoln Castle prison, gave evidence at inquest into the suicide of Mary Ann Milner.

JOHNSON, F. Served on Grand Jury at the trial of Mary Ann Milner, at the Lincoln Assizes.

JONES, W H. Served on Grand Jury at the trial of Mary Ann Milner, at the Lincoln Assizes.

LEARY, R E. Lincoln publisher of broadside account of trial and conviction of Mary Ann Milner.

MARRIS, George. Coroner at inquest into death of Hannah Jickels and subsequent exhumation of the bodies of Ellen Jickels and Mary Milner. Resident of Spilsby.

MELSOM, William. Chief Turn-Key Lincoln Castle prison. Gave evidence at inquest into the suicide of Mary Ann Milner.

MILLER, _____ . Counsel for the Defence at the trial of Mary Ann Milner, at the Lincoln Assizes. Probably the Sergeant Miller who later presided over many cases on the Midland Circuit with great distinction. Defended Eliza Joyce at the Lincoln Assizes, when accused of attempting to poison her stepson.

MILNER, Elizabeth. Daughter of Mary Milner, gave evidence at first indictment at the trial of Mary Ann Milner, at the Lincoln Assizes. Resident of Barnetby le Wold.

MILNER, Hannah. Daughter of Mary Milner. Resident of Barnet le Wold.

MILNER, John. Husband of Mary Ann Milner. Resident of Barnetby le Wold.

MILNER, Martha. Daughter of Mary Milner, gave evidence at the first indictment at the trial of Mary Ann Milner, at the Lincoln Assizes. Resident of Barnetby le Wold.

MILNER, Mary. Sister-in-law of the deceased Mary Milner, gave evidence at first indictment at the trial of Mary Ann Milner, at the Lincoln Assizes. Resident of Barnetby le Wold.

MILNER, Mary Ann. Convicted of poisoning her sister-in-law, niece, mother-in-law and father-in-law, committed suicide at Lincoln Castle. Resident of Barnetby le Wold.

MOXON, Dr James Burdett. MRCS, Surgeon. Attended William Milner, Mary Milner and Hannah Jickels and gave evidence at first and second indictment at the trial of Mary Ann Milner, at the Lincoln Assizes. Resident of Brigg.

NEWTON, T. Served on Grand Jury, as Foreman, at the trial of Mary Ann Milner, at the Lincoln Assizes.

NICHOLSON, John. Governor of Lincoln Castle prison. Gave evidence at inquest into the suicide of Mary Ann Milner.

PATERSON, Dr Robert Henry. Surgeon. Attended William Milner and Mary Milner and gave evidence at the first and second indictment at the trial of Mary Ann Milner, at the Lincoln Assizes. Resident of Brigg.

PENNELL, Charles. Glass, china and earthenware dealer. Served on Grand Jury at the trial of Mary Ann Milner, at the Lincoln Assizes. Resident of Lincoln.

PILKINGTON, William. Grocer, gave evidence at first and second indictment at the trial of Mary Ann Milner, at the Lincoln Assizes. Resident of Barnetby le Wold.

PLUMTREE, John. Grocer and tea-dealer. Served on Grand Jury at the trial of Mary Ann Milner, at the Lincoln Assizes. Resident of Lincoln.

REEVE, J W. Actuary for Lincoln Savings Bank. Served on Grand Jury at the trial of Mary Ann Milner, at the Lincoln Assizes.

RICHTER, Reverend Henry William. Chaplain of Lincoln Castle prison and Rector of St Paul in the Bail, Lincoln. Gave evidence at inquest on suicide of Mary Ann Milner. Resident of 23 Minster Yard, Lincoln.

ROLFE, Honourable Robert Monsey, sentencing judge at the trial of Mary Ann Milner, at the Lincoln Assizes. Resident of Holwood House, Keston.

SEELY, Robert. Grocer, tea dealer and confectioner. Served on Grand Jury at the trial of Mary Ann Milner, at the Lincoln Assizes. Resident of Lincoln.

SHARP, Jemima. Gave evidence at first and second indictment at the trial of Mary Ann Milner, at the Lincoln Assizes. Resident of Barnetby le Wold.

SPENSER, G. Served on Grand Jury at the trial of Mary Ann Milner, at the Lincoln Assizes.

SHUTTLEWORTH, A. Served on Grand Jury at the trial of Mary Ann Milner, at the Lincoln Assizes

SINGLETON, W. Rope and waterproof manufacturer. Served on Grand Jury at the trial of Mary Ann Milner, at the Lincoln Assizes. Resident of Lincoln.

SLACK, J. Served on Grand Jury at the trial of Mary Ann Milner, at the Lincoln Assizes.

THOMPSON, Elizabeth. Gave evidence at second indictment at the trial of Mary Ann Milner, at the Lincoln Assizes. Resident of Barnetby le Wold.

WATSON, George. Gave evidence at second indictment at the trial of Mary Ann Milner, at the Lincoln Assizes. Resident of Barnetby le Wold.

WILDMAN, Richard. Counsel for the Prosecution at the trial of Mary Ann Milner, at the Lincoln Assizes.

WILKINSON, J S. Served on Grand Jury at the trial of Mary Ann Milner, at the trial of Mary Ann Milner, at the Lincoln Assizes.

WINTER, Elizabeth. Daughter of Mary Winter, gave evidence at second indictment at the trial of Mary Ann Milner, at the Lincoln Assize. Resident of Barnetby le Wold.

WINTER, Mary. Gave evidence at second indictment at the trial of Mary Ann Milner, at the Lincoln Assizes. Resident of Barnetby le Wold.

Chapter Three

Priscilla Biggadike (1833-1868)

Priscilla Biggadike Timeline

13th January, 1833: baptism of Priscilla Whiley, daughter of George and Susannah Whiley of Broadgate, Gedney.

14th February,1853: marriage of Priscilla Whiley, aged 21, and Richard Biggadike, aged twenty-three, both residing at Kirton End.

30th September, 1868: around 6 o'clock in the evening, Richard Biggadike, well-sinker and labourer, living in Stickney, taken ill with symptoms of arsenic poisoning; local surgeon, Dr Peter Maxwell, called to treat him.

1st October, 1868: death of Richard Biggadike, around 6 o'clock in the morning.

2nd October, 1868: post mortem on body of Richard Biggadike carried out by Dr Maxwell, concluding that he had died from the effects of irritant poison. Stomach, intestines and viscera placed in sealed jar and bottles, and given to Superintendent Wright of Spilsby, who witnessed the post mortem.

3rd October, 1868: adjourned inquest into death of Richard Biggadike, held at the Rose and Crown Inn, Stickney, presided over by District Coroner, Dr Walter Clegg. Against the advice of the Coroner, Priscilla Biggadyke makes a statement describing the events surrounding her husband's death, denying that any poison was in the house.

Priscilla Biggadike taken from Stickney to Spilsby House of Correction by Superintendent Wright, on suspicion of murder. Priscilla Biggadike reveals to the superintendent that she had found a suicide note in Richard Biggadike's pocket which she had subsequently burnt.

6th October, 1868: bottles and jars containing stomach, intestines and viscera of Richard Biggadike taken to London by Superintendent Wright and delivered to Dr Alfred Swaine Taylor, Professor of Medical Jurisprudence at Guy's Hospital, for chemical analysis.

15th October, 1868; Priscilla Biggadike requests interview with Mr J Farr Phillips, Governor of Spilsby House of Correction, to make a statement about the death of her husband, which implicates Thomas Proctor in his murder, leading to his arrest.

21st October, 1868: resumed inquest, Priscilla Biggadike and Thomas Proctor found guilty of the wilful murder of Richard Biggadike, followed immediately by the appearance of the accused in front of the Magistrates Bench in the school room at Stickney. Both of the accused remanded in custody at Spilsby House of Correction to await removal to Lincoln Castle.

25th October, 1868: Priscilla Biggadyke and her eight month old child, along with Thomas Proctor, received into Lincoln Castle prison.

1st November, 1868: Rachel, infant child of Priscilla Biggadike, removed to Lincoln Union Workhouse.

10th December, 1868: case against Priscilla Biggadike and Thomas Proctor heard in front of Grand Jury, at Lincoln Assizes, presided over by Sir John Barnard Byles. Grand Jury find a true bill against Priscilla Biggadike, but throw out the bill against Thomas Proctor.

11th December, 1868: trial of Priscilla Biggadike for wilful murder of her husband. Found guilty, but with a recommendation of mercy. Recommendation for clemency ignored by Justice Byles, who sentences Priscilla Biggadike to death.

28th December, 1868: 9 o'clock, Priscilla Biggadike executed at Lincoln Castle; 3 o'clock, formal inquest on the body presided over by District Coroner, Dr George Mitchinson.

29th December, 1868: Priscilla Biggadike buried in the prisoners' graveyard, Lincoln Castle, at 1.15 in the afternoon.

TRIAL AND EXECUTION

PRISCILLA BIGGADIKE,

For the wilful Murder of her Husband on the 1st of October, 1868, who was tried
before the Right Hon. Sir John Barnard BYLES, Knight, on Friday, Dec. 11th.

COUNTY HALL, THE CASTLE, LINCOLN.

She was Executed in private at the South End of the County Hall, Lincoln Castle,
MONDAY morning, DECEMBER 28th, 1868.

THE STICKNEY MURDER.

PRISCILLA BIGGADIKE, widow, 29, was charged with the wilful murder of Richard Biggadike, her husband, at Stickney, on the 1st of October, 1868.

Mr. Bristowe and Mr. Horace Smith appeared on behalf of the prosecution; Mr. Lawrence defended the prisoner.

Mr. Bristowe, at considerable length, detailed to the jury all the principal facts of the case, and the circumstances under which the murder was committed revealed a depth of moral depravity and social degradation we could fain hope has no parallel elsewhere in the county of Lincoln. The following witnesses were examined:—

James Turner said he knew the deceased and he always appeared to enjoy excellent health.

George Ironmonger said: I lodged in the house with deceased. Mrs. Biggadike, Proctor, and I had tea together before deceased came home on Wednesday evening, Sept. 30th. We had two "short cakes," which were made by Mrs. B., who did all the cooking. I went out after tea, and when I returned deceased was just finishing his tea, and seemed quite well. He got up a few minutes after and went to the privy, and I heard him retching, and very sick. After he had returned he went again, and then he said, "I am very bad; I can't live long this how; send for the doctor. I fetched the doctor immediately. Deceased died at six next morning. I was upstairs once during the night.

Peter Maxwell, surgeon, deposed: I was called to the deceased at seven o'clock on Wednesday evening. .... I found him in great pain in bed, sick, and violently purged. He had all the symptoms of poisoning by some irritant poison. I sent him suitable medicines, and saw him again at eleven o'clock, when he was collapsed and rapidly sinking worse. I heard he died early next morning. .... On 2nd October I made a post-mortem examination of the body. The head and chest were perfectly free from disease. I removed the viscera and contents of the stomach, placed them in jars securely sealed, and handed over to Supt. Wright. I believe deceased died from the effects of poison.

Supt. Wright, of Spilsby, deposed: On the 2nd October I received one jar and three bottles, sealed and secured by Dr. Maxwell. On the 6th I delivered them to Dr. Taylor, ... Hospital. I apprehended the prisoner, and then charged her with wilfully murdering her own husband. She .... hard work I should bear all the blame alone."

Dr. Alfred Swaine Taylor stated that he was a Fellow of the College of Physicians, and Professor of Medical Jurisprudence at Guy's Hospital. On Tuesday the 6th of Oct. he received certain jars from Supt. Wright, containing the contents of the stomach of Rd. Biggadike. Dr. Taylor's evidence was very lengthy, full of the usual scientific details, and showed that he had not the slightest doubt that the deceased had died through the administration of arsenic, which was the only conclusion he could draw from the results of his analysis.

Mary Ann Clarke said: I am a widow residing at Stickney, and close to Biggadike's. On the 30th I heard a noise in their house as of many people talking, and went to see what was the matter. Proctor sat against the door, and he said, " Dick's very bad since he got his tea." A short time after the prisoner came to my house with a piece of cake in her hand, and she said, " the doctor says I've put something into the cake which I ought not to have done, but I hav'nt. I heard deceased in his agony say," the Lord have mercy upon me." He died while I was there.

Jane Ironmonger said: I saw deceased in bed very sick and bad. I asked the prisoner if she had sent for his brother, and she said, " No, it does not matter, for they have not been on very good terms lately." I fetched his brother. We found the prisoner and two lodgers in the lower room. I was there when he died. On one occasion I heard the prisoner say she hoped her husband might be brought home dead, and another time she said she wished he might be brought home stiff. She then asked me how the murderers Garniers (of Marsham-le-Fen) got on about their poisoning case. She said they searched the meal and sago.

Thomas Proctor said: On the 30th of September last I lodged at Biggadike's. On that day I went fishing with George Ironmonger, a fellow lodger. We came home together to tea, and afterwards went fishing again. Ironmonger went first, leaving Mrs. Biggadike, and the child in the house. I never put any white powder in's tea cup, neither on that occasion or any other. I had no white powder or poison in my possession. I am a rat-catcher, and keep ferrets, but never keep any poison. When we came home from fishing, Mrs. Biggadike was in the house and her husband. He was taken very ill, and continued so all night. I remained with him until he died. The prisoner prepared our food.

The jury, after a consultation of only a few minutes, returned a verdict of GUILTY, accompanied by a recommendation to mercy, but upon the Judge asking upon what grounds, the foreman of the jury seemed perplexed, and again consulted with his fellows for a short time, and then said that the only ground for such recommendation was that the evidence was entirely circumstantial.

His Lordship then put on the black cap, and amidst the most solemn silence passed the sentence of death upon the unhappy woman. In addressing her his Lordship said : Priscilla Biggadike, although the evidence against you is only circumstantial, yet more satisfactory and conclusive evidence I never heard in my life. You must now prepare for your impending fate, by attending to the religious instruction you will receive, to which, if you had given heed before, you would never have stood in your present unhappy position. The sentence of the court is that you be taken to the place from whence you came, and thence to the place of execution, there to be hanged by the neck till you and may the Lord have mercy upon your soul .... to be buried within the precincts of the .... then walked firmly away from the .... lasted seven hours.

Rigmarole Stories: The Life and Death of Priscilla Biggadike

Introduction

Only weeks after her execution at Lincoln Castle on the 28th December, 1868, having been found guilty of the wilful murder of her husband, Priscilla Biggadike was transformed into an artefact for public delight and instruction.

A brief notice in the *Boston Guardian*, 6th March, 1869, which advertised various travelling entertainments to be seen in Spalding that week, drew the reader's attention to the visit of Payne's Theatre: specifically, it highlighted that amongst its minor attractions could be found a placard announcing that 'Priscilla Biggadyke, the Stickney murderer, had just come from London in waxwork'.

In due course, Mrs Biggadike came back to London, this time on view as one of the macabre attractions in Madame Tussaud's Chamber of Horrors, in the company of Charles Peace, Francois Courvoisier and many other grim wax reminders of human depravity.

In 2011, and no longer a wax effigy, the erstwhile Stickney poisoner returned to Lincoln Castle prison, now transformed into the central character of *Priscilla*

Biggadike: the Musical, part of a BBC celebration of the county's cultural heritage. As well as being performed in the place where Mrs Biggadike lost her life, the show was also staged the following year at the village hall and two local schools in Stickney, the place where the story of her misfortunes first began to unfold. Once reviled as an impenitent husband killer by the Press, Mrs Biggadike was now confidently rehabilitated by the *Lincolnshire Echo* newspaper, as the unfortunate victim of a miscarriage of justice, 'whose tragic tale captured people's imagination'.

The ironic geographical and conceptual symmetries of Mrs Biggadike returning to the scene of the crime and simultaneously having her sentence quashed in the court of popular opinion did not receive comment at the time.

One of the obvious difficulties in unravelling the alleged crime of Priscilla Biggadike is that she denied her culpability, even as she was about to be executed: unlike Eliza Joyce and Mary Ann Milner, there was no confession of guilt, no admission of responsibility. At the foot of the gallows, under intense pressure from the single-minded prison Chaplain to admit her most grievous fault, as well as perhaps from the very human temptation to try out a last-second variation of Pascal's wager to save her soul, Priscilla Biggadike refused to budge. Like Mary Lefley, sixteen years later, her unwavering claim to be innocent of poisoning her husband with arsenic, also viewed by some contemporary commentators as perverse intransigence, denied the welcome certainties of a straightforward narrative of crime and punishment.

Even more problematic for a clear-cut understanding of the case is that it consists of so many tangled knots of different stories wrapped up inside a convoluted narrative, some of them contradictory, some plausible and some of them partially credible inventions which somehow managed to get themselves imperceptibly woven into the narrative fabric of the case as unquestionable truth.

Inquest into the Death of Richard Biggadike, 3rd October, 1868

What is undeniable, is that Richard Biggadike returned home, on the afternoon of 30th September, from his job as a well-sinker and ate a meal consisting of cakes made by his wife, cold mutton and a cup of tea. What is equally undeniable is that soon after he had finished eating, he rapidly became very ill and a doctor had to be called out. By morning, the next day, despite medical attention, Richard Biggadike was dead, having spent all night enduring the distress of violent vomiting and purging.

The *Stamford Mercury* of Friday, 30th October, perhaps sensing a story with the essential juicy ingredients of low-life village immorality and cold-blooded murder, constructed a very lengthy account of what it knew, or thought it knew.

Information from the initial inquest into the death of Richard Biggadike, under the direction of Dr Walter Clegg, did not require much space to report, as it consisted only of the evidence of Dr Peter Maxwell who had been summoned to attend Richard Biggadike as he lay dying, and who had later conducted a post mortem. Dr Maxwell concluded that the deceased had been poisoned, but decided to consult the opinion of Professor Alfred Swaine Taylor of Guy's Hospital, by sending him the stomach, intestines, viscera and 'vomited matter' for chemical analysis.

It is clear, however, from reading the whole of the lengthy report on the case, as it stood, that either the editor or the reporter had decided to omit some of the material heard at the initial inquest, preferring to include it in the retrospective summing up of the Coroner, later on in the article.

As there was apparently little to report from the inquest, due to its adjournment to await the findings of Professor Taylor, the newspaper expended a good deal of print building up the expectations of the reader for a sensational blockbuster.

It started by ruefully pointing out that the murder committed at Stickney was yet another addition to the regrettable annals of crime reported in the parish.

The newspaper reminded the readers of the case of the vicious killing by William Pickett and Henry Carey of William Stevenson, at nearby Sibsey in 1859, who was violently bludgeoned to death and whose body was dumped in a sewer. Whilst the poisoning at Stickney was 'less brutal in its nature', it involved 'a far greater amount of moral depravity': Pickett and Carey had no connection to William Stevenson and their cruel assault on the old man had been fuelled by alcohol. In contrast, there had been 'the closest of human ties' between the victim and 'one of the suspected parties' in the Stickney poisoning case, and there was no doubt that the crime had been 'committed in cold blood'. The report did not specify who the guilty party might be, but the choice between the victim's 'own wife and her paramour' left little room for speculation.

By way of further information, the newspaper noted that the Biggadikes supplemented their income by taking in lodgers, one of whom was a twenty-one year old boatman by the name of George Ironmonger, whilst the other was Thomas Proctor, a rat catcher, aged thirty-one. What the report did not mention, at this point, was that Proctor was the one of the 'suspected parties' in the murder of Richard Biggadike.

Whilst the information was useful in terms of the background to the case, it soon became apparent where the report was going. The house in which Priscilla

Biggadike lived with her husband, three children and the two lodgers was typical of the 'cottages of the rural peasantry' in that it was 'miserably deficient of sleeping accommodation'. The uncomfortable details of the cramped bedroom, in which four adults and three children shared two beds only eighteen inches apart, was not so much a concern for the dignity of the rural poor as an explanation of unpleasant domestic discord. There was an inevitability, according to the newspaper, that Proctor would take advantage of Richard Biggadike leaving early for work in a morning and equally inevitable that violent domestic quarrels would ensue between husband and wife. The virulence and frequency of these quarrels, the report confidently suggested, led to Mrs Biggadike planning the murder of her husband.

Probably without having ever seen the Biggadike house, the *Stamford Mercury* identified it as a key factor in the case, and was supported by the *Lincolnshire Chronicle* in its short report on the inquest published the day after, describing the Biggadike home as 'a wretched hut' which contained only one bedroom. The inadequacy of the living conditions inevitably led to 'an improper intimacy between Mrs Biggadike and one of the lodgers', which in turn led to the plot to murder Mr Biggadike.

Resumed Inquest into the Death of Richard Biggadike, 21st October, 1868

Having set the scene and provided a thumbnail sketch of the initial inquest, the *Stamford Mercury* of Friday, 30th October continued its report with a detailed account of the resumed inquest at the Rose and Crown Inn, Stickney, Professor Taylor having finally completed his investigations.

However, before revealing the scientific details of Taylor's report, the newspaper mentioned that both Thomas Proctor and George Ironmonger, the two lodgers, had given evidence at the first inquest, which the newspaper would now make available to the interested reader, as well as an extended version of Dr Maxwell's testimony. In addition, it was revealed that when giving evidence at the first inquest, Thomas Proctor was 'at large if not unsuspected of complicity in the murder', but since then, circumstances had arisen which had led to him being apprehended and charged. The account of Proctor's deposition was an undifferentiated compound of what was said at both inquests, it seems.

Proctor confirmed that he had lodged with the Biggadike family for four years and that he slept with them in one bedroom, as did George Ironmonger. The deceased had come home from work around 5.45 on Wednesday, 30th September, appearing in good health; Mrs Biggadike and the two lodgers had already eaten. Richard Biggadike ate hot cake, made by Mrs Biggadike, and also a quantity of mutton. A small piece of cake was left over on the table, a part of which Proctor ate and then gave the rest to the children.

Within half an hour or less of finishing his tea, Richard Biggadike became unwell and went to the privy, where he was very sick. A short time after this bout of 'heaving and retching', he returned to the privy to be sick again, at which point he asked his wife to fetch a doctor.

Proctor had sat up with Biggadike all night, only occasionally leaving his side, and recalled him being constantly purged and sick: he had been with him when he died.

As far as he knew, Mrs and Mrs Biggadike lived on good terms and he had never heard them quarrel. He also stated that white mercury had never been in the house. Whilst he kept ferrets (and by implication used them as part of his job as a rat catcher), he never had any poison.

The deposition of George Ironmonger, whilst supplying a few more precise details, supported the account of events heard from Proctor. After eating his tea, he had left the house, returning around 6 o'clock, just as Biggadike was finishing his meal. He became very ill, very quickly, declaring, 'I am very bad, I can't live long like this now, send for a doctor'. It was Ironmonger who went to get medical assistance.

Biggadike was ill throughout the night, although Ironmonger remained downstairs, only going upstairs once, at 3 o'clock in the morning, when Mrs Biggadike and Proctor had called for his help to get the sick man back into bed: in his great pain, he had rolled on to the floor.

Like Proctor, George Ironmonger confirmed that the couple had been on good terms, as far as he knew, and that to his knowledge, there was no poison in the house, as they did not have a problem with mice or any other vermin.

One additional piece of information which Ironmonger gave was that Priscilla Biggadike, at some point, went to the doctor to get the prescribed medicine and whilst doing so she took a piece of the cake which Richard Biggadike had not eaten during tea, in order to show to Dr Maxwell, 'as he did not seem satisfied'.

Dr Peter Maxwell, aged twenty-eight, recent graduate of Edinburgh University, and a relatively inexperienced general practitioner, attended Richard Biggadike at around 7 o'clock on the evening of 30th September. In his opinion, the condition of the patient suggested all the symptoms of having ingested an irritant poison. In response to the obvious question concerning his most recent meal, Mrs Biggadike informed him that her husband had eaten nothing different from anyone else in the house. After having provided 'suitable medicine', Dr Maxwell left the house, returning at 11 o'clock, to discover that Richard Biggadike was in a state of collapse 'and getting rapidly worse'. At that point, the doctor was silent concerning any further medical attention, merely recording that Biggadike had died the morning after.

On the following day, he had carried out a post mortem and concluded, after seeing the patches of inflammation on the intestines and the mucous membrane of the stomach, that death had occurred as a result of poisoning. There were no signs of disease to account for death: however, out of caution or deference to greater experience, Dr Maxwell declined to undertake a chemical analysis.

If Dr Maxwell required the re-assurance of a senior professional, the choice of Alfred Swaine Taylor, Professor of Medical Jurisprudence at Guy's Hospital and the author of several standard textbooks on the subject, seemed an ideal choice. Professor Swaine had also given evidence at numerous high profile murder trials, although his reputation had been somewhat tarnished in 1859, at the trial of Dr Thomas Smethurst for poisoning his wife, when he admitted that his application of the Reinsch test using copper coil contaminated by arsenic, had produced unreliable results.

Professor Taylor's report confirmed Maxwell's supposition about the cause of death, and in addition provided helpful guidance to the Coroner and the jury, concerning some unusual aspects of the case. Death had occurred, 'more rapidly than usual: the average time is eighteen to twenty-four hours: in this case, it was barely twelve hours after the attack'. Further, a portion of the arsenic in the stomach had remained in powder form, which was curious; it had been impossible to identify in what form the arsenic had been ingested, because the chemical always mixed with whatever was in the stomach – in this case, no food was discovered in the stomach other than 'a little starchy substance'.

Elizabeth Fenwick, related by marriage to Richard Biggadike, was a key witness in providing circumstantial evidence of various kinds, which was to be later used at the Lincoln Assizes. The most important part of her deposition was one which contradicted those of Thomas Proctor and George Ironmonger: on the occasion of visiting Mrs Biggadike, about three or four months previously, she had been offered white mercury to deal with a possible problem with mice. Mrs Fenwick was happy to accept the substance, although her husband, Edwin Fenwick, refused the offer as it might endanger his children. Her second piece of evidence was more recent, in that it related to an conversation on the day after the death of Richard Biggadike. Whilst at the house, she overheard Thomas Proctor and Priscilla

Biggadike talking whilst they were outside, Proctor warning her to be careful what she said, to which Mrs Biggadike had answered somewhat abruptly, 'Do yah think I'm a fool, don't tell me more than I know'. Her response to Proctor was equalled in its uncompromising tone when confronted by Elizabeth Fenwick's assertion that people were saying that Mrs Biggadike had poisoned her husband. Her forthright dismissal of the rumour seemed to confirm the opinion of several later witnesses that Mrs Biggadike was a plain speaking woman, not averse to using intemperate language, 'Yes, I know they do – it was that Dr Maxwell, but I'll give the devil it'.

Mary Ann Clarke, a young widow living about fifty yards from where the Biggadike family resided, told the inquest jury that about 7 o'clock on the evening of 30th September, she heard voices coming from the house. Quite naturally, she went to see what was happening and was met at the door by Thomas Proctor who informed her that Richard Biggadike had 'took very bad since he ate his tea'. At that point, Dr Maxwell was coming down the stairs and so Mrs Clarke discreetly walked away. At 6.15 the next morning Proctor had called on Mary Ann Clarke, to tell her that Richard Biggadike was dying, and to ask her to come to the house. On arrival, she went upstairs and picked up a teacup from the floor, asking Mrs Biggadike what it was doing there. According to Mrs

Biggadike, her husband had thrown it at her; further, during the course of his illness he had kicked her off the end of the bed and thrown his arm backwards and knocked her down.

The anecdotes seemed to have little value in working out the facts of the case and it is hardly surprising that the evidence of Mary Ann Clarke was not highlighted in the Coroner's summary. The only significant information she supplied, perhaps, was that Thomas Proctor was not with Richard Biggadike when he died, as he had claimed.

Jane Ironmonger, the grandmother of George Ironmonger and a woman of miscellaneous opinions, lived next door to the Biggadike family and clearly saw herself as something of an authority on the domestic life of Priscilla and Richard Biggadike. She immediately established that the couple were on bad terms and that they frequently rowed. By way of proof that domestic life next door was turbulent, she claimed that Priscilla Biggadike had once said that she hoped her husband would be brought home dead; and on another occasion, she said that she hoped that he would be brought home stiff.

On Monday, 28th September, just two days before Richard Biggadike was taken ill, she had been visited by Mrs Biggadike. Their conversation, Mrs Ironmonger recalled, was on the subject of poisoning: first, in relation to a dog which the couple had owned and which had died the previous winter after being poisoned; secondly, concerning the case of the Garners, living at nearby Mareham-le-Fen, who had been indicted for poisoning a few years earlier at the Lincoln Assizes. Mrs Biggadike informed her that the Garners were transported for life and that the doctors and police had been unable to find any trace of poison in the food consumed by the victims.

Her final statement recorded by the newspaper was that Richard Biggadike could neither read nor write.

The evidence of the women at times seemed to amount to very little more than suggestive anecdote. The testimony of Mr John Farr Phillips, Governor of the Spilsby House of Correction, however, carried much more weight, not only because of his social position, but because Mrs Biggadike had insisted on making a formal statement to him concerning the death of her husband. Quite correctly, the Governor had cautioned Mrs Biggadike that whatever she said to him would be written down and possibly used against her in court. However, she had remained determined, despite his advice.

On the 15th October, Mrs Biggadike produced a statement which almost certainly led to the arrest of her lodger, Thomas Proctor.

According to her statement, reproduced in full by the *Stamford Mercury*, Priscilla Biggadike had seen

Thomas Proctor drop a white powder into a teacup, followed by a quantity of milk. At the time, her husband was washing himself in the dairy, but later came into the house, sat down and poured out his tea into the cup. About half an hour later, her husband became ill and went out of doors to be sick; after being sick a second time, he went to bed and asked her to get a doctor. It took the doctor about an hour to arrive at the house. Mrs Biggadike went to see the doctor about a quarter of an hour after he had left the house, in order to get her husband's medicine. Dr Maxwell gave her some medicine with instructions to give him two tablespoons every half an hour; she was also told to apply a mustard plaster on his stomach. She saw the doctor later, at 11 o'clock, but after that, not at all.

Needing to go to the privy herself, she had asked Proctor to go upstairs to and sit with her husband, which he did. On returning up the stairs, she saw Proctor putting some white powder into a medicine bottle with a spoon, after which he went downstairs and left her with her husband. Once Proctor was out of the bedroom, she poured some of the medicine into a cup and gave it to her husband; she also tasted it herself. The result was that she felt very sick an hour afterwards and was ill for two days. The incident with the medicine took place around 2 o'clock in the morning.

Mrs Biggadike insisted in her statement that a copy should be sent to the Coroner, and further, that she would like to be present at the resumed inquest 'to state her case before them as it is the truth'. The document was signed with her mark, although the newspaper oddly gave her the name Biggleswade.

It was an astonishing story which created future difficulties for Mrs Biggadike and for anyone having to defend her in court.

It was all the more astonishing in that it came only two weeks after Mrs Biggadike had revealed to Superintendent Wright, the arresting officer who escorted her to the Spilsby House of Correction, a very different story which was even more improbable.

On being apprehended, she had been cautioned very strongly not to incriminate herself by saying something which might be used against her. Either unable or unwilling to restrain herself, Mrs Biggadike had said to the Superintendent, 'It's hard work I should bear all the blame: I am innocent'. The police officer seemed to ignore what she had said and appeared to try and distract her with some small talk about having made good time from Stickney to Spilsby, as the last train had not yet arrived at the railway station. At which point, Mrs Biggadike, launched into an incredible story to explain her husband's death to the Superintendent. She had apparently found a piece of paper in her husband's pocket which was essentially a suicide note, explaining that he was deep in debt. In response, the bemused policeman commented that he had been informed that her husband could neither read nor write. He also, not surprisingly, asked Mrs Biggadike what she had done with the piece of paper. Her response was that she had burnt it. As with her later statement on the 15th October concerning her husband's death, Mrs Biggadike was quite insistent that the adjourned inquest should hear the story.

Superintendent Wright's final words recorded that on apprehending Thomas Proctor and charging him with murder, he had claimed to be innocent and knew nothing more than what he had stated at the initial inquest.

The summing up by the District Coroner, Walter Clegg, for the benefit of the jury, was not an easy one: as with many cases of poisoning, the evidence heard in court was purely circumstantial, with all its attendant difficulties; but those difficulties had been given greater complexity by Mrs Biggadike's conflicting statements.

He began on safe ground: the adjournment of the inquest for nearly three weeks had been a long one, but had provided certainty concerning the cause of death. Based upon the post mortem by Dr Maxwell and the expert deposition of Professor Taylor, there was no doubt that Richard Biggadike had been poisoned by arsenic. The questions for

ATTIRED IN DEEPEST MOURNING

the jury, were how and by whom was the poison administered?

Before unpicking the legal intricacies of the case, the Coroner simplified matters for the jury by declaring that accidental poisoning and suicide were not options for consideration. In the interest of balance, perhaps, even in the face of such an improbable fiction, Dr Clegg did highlight the discovery of a suicide note by Mrs Biggadike, adding to the reported evidence of Superintendent Wright that she had explained away the difficulty of an illiterate man writing a suicide note by suggesting that someone must have written it for him. How much credence should be given to the story he left in the capable hands of the jury.

The Coroner reminded the jury that both the widow of Richard Biggadike and the lodger, Thomas Proctor, were in custody charged with murder, but they must consider them as separate cases. He also instructed them that Mrs Biggadike's statement made to the Governor of the Spilsby House of Correction, implicating Thomas Proctor in the crime, was inadmissible evidence against him.

Dr Clegg's exposition of the evidence against the wife of the deceased was clear and to the point. The poison which had killed Richard Biggadike could be traced back to his last meal and that meal had been provided by his wife. A question which had to be addressed was whether Mrs Biggadike had arsenic in her possession. This was not an easy question to resolve as there were different versions of the answer to consider. Speaking as a witness at the first inquest, she had 'solemnly declared that she did not know what such a poison as white mercury was, and that no poison of any sort was in her house'. This statement had been contradicted by the words of Elizabeth Fenwick to whom Priscilla Biggadike had offered white mercury to kill mice, only three or four months previously. It had also been indirectly contradicted by Priscilla Biggadike's own statement that she had seen Proctor drop a white powder into a tea cup and a medicine bottle which had made her ill and had killed her husband. Dr Clegg reminded the jury, but without pressing the point, that Mrs Biggadike had allegedly watched Proctor drop white powder into a tea cup, but had not interfered; and further, that she had administered medicine to her husband which she knew, by her own admission, contained a suspect white powder.

In terms of a motive, the jury was required to focus upon the deposition from Mrs Ironmonger, that the couple often had violent quarrels and that Mrs Biggadike had expressed the wish that her husband might be brought home dead. These were harsh words, said Dr Clegg, but which required caution in their interpretation. The jury should not attach too much importance to words spoken in the heat of passion, quite simply because in our daily lives, 'we never pass along the streets without hearing threats and imprecations which, if carried out, would involve the destruction of life and limb, but there is no real intention , on the part of those using them to carry such threats into effect'. However, the deposition from Mrs Ironmonger did indicate that there was a degree of disharmony between man and wife, and that this should be taken seriously.

The evidence against Thomas Proctor was less clear and Dr Clegg once again emphasised that the accusation against him by Mrs Biggadike was not legally acceptable and, in addition, it was uncorroborated. What he did say, however, was that the reported conversation between Mrs Biggadike and Thomas Proctor overheard by Elizabeth Fenwick was evidence 'which tends to direct very serious suspicion to Proctor', and, 'would seem to bear but one explanation'.

The jury took only a few minutes of deliberation to declare that Priscilla Biggadike and Thomas Proctor were guilty. Both were immediately taken to the Stickney village schoolroom to be charged in front of the two presiding magistrates, the Reverend R D Rawnsley and the Reverend T H Lister: the process was overseen by Captain Philip Bicknell, Chief Constable of Lincolnshire.

The hearing lasted five hours and consisted mainly of the evidence heard at the resumed inquest that morning. There were, however, some additional pieces of information presented by Superintendent Wright and Mr Phillips, which supplemented their original deposition, as well as further anecdotal evidence from two new witnesses, Susan Evrington and Mildred Conyers.

Before reporting the fresh evidence, the *Stamford Mercury* took the opportunity to recreate a sorry scene of human misfortune in the schoolroom. Both prisoners looked downcast, but given the seriousness of the situation did not appear to be too deeply affected: of the two, Mrs Biggadike appeared to be least troubled.

At this point, the writer of the report slipped from reportage into the creation of a sub-literary fantasy world. The village schoolroom was 'crowded almost to suffocation' by the local villagers eager to observe the proceedings. Mrs Biggadike, though by no means pretty, was 'tolerably good looking', but Proctor, on the other hand, had 'a repulsive countenance'. The equation of facial ugliness with villainy seemed to be a favourite rhetorical device of the *Lincolnshire Chronicle*, as the same words had been used to describe the Sibsey murderers William Pickett and Henry Carey in 1859: even more telling, Carey also had 'an expression and low forehead which are thought to distinguish murderers': the description of criminal atavism in Lincolnshire would not have been out of place in the text books of the Italian criminologist, Cesare Lombroso.

The pantomime villain sketch of Thomas Proctor contrasted with the touchingly sentimental scene of Mrs Biggadike breastfeeding an infant of six or seven months, whose innocent prattling served to highlight the painful position of its mother. Such was the sadness of the piteous scene, those villagers who had been lucky enough to squeeze into the packed schoolroom, could scarcely refrain from weeping.

The scene in the schoolroom was not described in the *Lincolnshire Chronicle*, whose coverage of the appearance of Mrs Biggadike and Thomas Proctor in front of the Magistrates was relatively brief, compared to that of the *Stamford Mercury*. However, the *Boston Guardian* of Saturday, 31st October, more than made up for the omission with an absurd invention of its own, straight out of the pages of Victor Hugo. According to the report, Proctor was 'the most uncouth looking individual in the district' with a countenance which was 'very repugnant'; in addition, he had 'a high back and his legs appear to have a serious malformation'. The newspaper's rhetorical intent to turn Thomas Proctor into a repulsive monster had its counterpart in the reporter's assessment of the situation as an 'inhuman outrage', which had caused 'great excitement in the district' to such an extent that 'every man, woman and child are discoursing on the indelicate particularities connected with the crime'.

It wasn't the last time that the *Boston Guardian* was to pedal sensationalised fictions about the Biggadike case: nearly twenty years later when covering the story of Mary Lefley, the newspaper shamelessly re-invented details of the crime scene, as well as listing the two Stickney women alongside some of the most infamous female poisoners in history.

Further doubts about Priscilla Biggadike having found a suicide note were increased by Superintendent Wright when he gave fresh evidence. He had made enquiries amongst the village tradesmen concerning the claim that Richard Biggadike was heavily in debt, but had not discovered any evidence to support the claim. Mr Phillips introduced further doubts about the reliability and credibility of Thomas Proctor, but without revealing precise details: he merely told the hearing that the prisoner had made a statement to him which amounted to 'a rigmarole story' with no relevance to the case.

Two women who had not given evidence at the resumed inquest made appearances which also seemed to make little difference. Susan Evrington claimed to have heard Mrs Biggadike say that she could not abide her husband: it amounted to a very little little, but found its way into the Assize trial at Lincoln, and Miss Evrington had her moment in the limelight in front of a full house. Mildred Conyers was a little more loquacious, recounting a meeting at her house with Thomas Proctor, on Tuesday, 6th October. In confidence, Proctor had told her that he had something on his mind 'which would make any man's blood run cold'. The ominous and enigmatic words were followed by a distressed Proctor holding his head in his hands, bursting into tears and lamenting the fact that 'he had lost his best friend'. To any sceptic in the room hearing the story, it might have seemed a transparent and unconvincing performance from a badly produced amateur melodrama.

The remaining new evidence, as reported by the *Stamford Mercury*, emerged from questions fired by the two prisoners at various acquaintances in an attempt to obtain their support.

Mary Ann Clarke was asked by Mrs Biggadike to confirm that she had been sick and ill: no, you were not, was the reply. She was then asked by Proctor to confirm that he was in the bedroom when Richard Biggadike died: no, you were not, was the reply. Undeterred, Proctor asked the same question to Jane Ironmonger, but got the same answer.

At this point, the two prisoners were asked if they had anything else to say in answer to the charge? Mrs Biggadike stepped forward and said that Elizabeth Fenwick and her husband had told lies, and that she was innocent. She ended by saying rather forlornly that she had no witnesses to call in her defence. In contrast, Thomas Proctor was not going down without a fight. He asserted that he had done nothing wrong and that Mrs Biggadike had told lies about him. In a direct address to the Bench, he expressed his trust in their judgement as to whether he could possibly have had anything to do with the murder when he was 'nowhere near the house when Biggadike was getting his tea'.

Proctor moved towards the climax of his self-justification by bringing George Ironmonger forward to answer questions from both himself and Mrs Biggadike. The latter asked only one question of Ironmonger which was whether or not he was in the house when Proctor confessed to the murder: he was not. Thomas Proctor asked his fellow lodger if he had seen him take something out of his pocket and drop it in Richard Biggadike's cup: he had not. Ironmonger was then asked if he had ever seen Proctor do anything wrong: no. Ironmonger was a man of few words, but as far as Proctor was concerned, they had been the right ones. Unfortunately, George Ironmonger did not produce the goods when asked by Proctor if he had been in the house when Richard Biggadike was eating his tea: he was out fishing at the time and therefore was unable to say. After such a strong start to proving his case, he failed to get corroboration for his assertion to the magistrates that he was out of the house when Biggadike was eating his tea. Proctor's final witness, Mr Thomas Waite, 'a labourer of advanced years', was even less helpful to him, as his evidence was dismissed by the Bench as immaterial: given Mr Waite was around 83 years old at the time, it was probably the right decision.

The final act in the village drama, before the prisoners were scheduled to stand trial at the Lincoln December Assizes, was Mrs Biggadike asking for bail: refused.

Trial of Priscilla Biggadike for Wilful Murder: Part One: 10th December, 1868

The trial of Priscilla Biggadike and James Proctor was reported extensively by both the *Lincolnshire Echo* and the *Stamford Mercury*. The witnesses called to give evidence, apart from a Stickney joiner by the name of Henry Turner, were the same as those heard at the hearing in front of the magistrates. However, in a couple of cases, the witness produced significant new evidence, which had either not been heard before or had not been previously reported in the newspapers.

In a sense, the most important contributor to the judicial process, at least during the first day of the proceedings, was the judge, Lord Justice John Barnard Byles, a man familiar with the difficulties of poisoning cases, having presided over the sensational trial of the former Spalding nurse, Catherine Wilson, who was hanged in 1862.

Press reports of the opening remarks of an Assize judge tended to consist of a brief synopsis of the cases which the Grand Jury would be required to consider and occasional guidance on their relative importance. Sometimes, when the judge thought it necessary to vigorously expound his views on the current state of law and order in its crusade against 'vice, profaneness and immorality', the press helpfully provided details of the salient points. The report on the prefatory observations on the business of the day, which focused exclusively on the indictments against Biggadike and Proctor, was extraordinary in its comprehensiveness. There had been no lecture on the failings of the justice system, as were seen in the trials of Eliza Joyce and Mary Ann Milner, but rather, a minute, point by point review of the evidence against the prisoners, interlaced with reminders to the Grand Jury of the seriousness of the task ahead of them. Perhaps because Judge Byles chose to comment upon so many particulars of the evidence, the newspaper report created a sense that the judge was not so much advising the Grand Jury, as directing it towards a convenient conclusion.

The names on the Grand Jury, mainly drawn from established county families and powerful landed gentry, had a familiar look about them:

- Sir Charles H J Anderson (foreman)
- Henry Hynman Allenby
- Colonel Weston Cracroft-Amcotts MP
- John Bromhead
- Richard Ellison
- William Robert Emeris
- John Lewis Fytche
- George Henry Haigh
- Edward Heneage
- George Eden Jarvis
- Alexander Samuel Leslie Melville
- Charles H Massingberd-Munday
- Colonel Charles Thomas John Moore
- Edward Peacock
- John Welby Preston
- John Hassard Short
- Arthur Trollope

After formally opening the trial at the Crown Court at 11 o'clock, on Thursday, 10th December, Mr Justice Byles got down to business, losing no time in alerting the Grand Jury to a key issue for their deliberation. The case involved the most serious of charges and that would probably be the responsibility of the court to consider in due course. However, there was one aspect of the case which was solely within the jurisdiction of the Grand Jury: despite the complications of his polished circumlocutory style, it was obvious that

Judge Byles was highlighting the key responsibility of the Grand Jury to decide whether or not to a find a true bill against Thomas Proctor – obliquely referred to as 'one of the prisoners'.

The judge had examined the various depositions with 'great attention and a great deal of anxiety' and so was able to present to them the facts of the case, as they appeared to him, although he was willing to be corrected 'by their fuller information'.

The facts of the case listed by Judge Byles, on the whole, were explicitly linked to particular circumstantial evidence prejudicial to Mrs Biggadike, and so arguably were mere conclusions drawn from uncertain evidence, rather than indisputable facts. Further, the very choice of the so-called facts, legitimised by the status of the judge, despite his assurance of being open to persuasion, was effectively building a case for the Prosecution.

The list of facts started innocuously enough with a description of Richard Biggadike being perfectly healthy up to the time of his death, a fact verified by various witnesses, including two doctors. He had also been married for some time and had a family of three children. At this point, the definition of fact acquired a worryingly blurred flexibility: Richard Biggadike was not the father of three children, only 'the supposed father'. Judge Byles next pointed out that Biggadike and his wife had not lived happily together and quarrelled 'frequently, loudly and passionately', a fact which would be supported by 'abundant evidence', he said, but without mentioning the possible unreliability of the sources of that evidence. In an attempt to create a sense of fairness and balance in his exposition of the facts, Judge Byles did caution against attaching too much weight to language used in the heat of the moment, something which Walter Clegg had also highlighted, but much more forcefully, in his summary at the resumed inquest.

What followed from Byles amounted to an accumulation of evidence to support the supposed fact of Richard Biggadike not being the father of one of his children, rather than an objective list of key points for consideration by the Grand Jury. He referred to a quarrel in which Richard Biggadike had said that the infant seated on his wife's lap was not his child, to which Mrs Biggadike had given an evasive response, thus confirming that the husband doubted his wife's fidelity and 'she knew that he did'. Further confirmation of serious marital difficulties, according to Justice Byles, was evident from another quarrel in which Richard Biggadike claimed that his wife had bought a dress, but not with his money: 'From this it was fair to presume that he supposed the money came from someone else, in a way which it ought not'. The most important evidence according to Justice Byles, however, was that provided by witnesses concerning Mrs Biggadike having wished to see her husband dead: the judge pointed out to the Grand Jury that these witnesses would be brought before them and they would have the opportunity to judge their credibility. It was a statement of impartiality, but the cat was already out of the bag: without too much difficulty, Judge Byles had arguably established a motive for murder, rooted in Priscilla Biggadike's supposed infidelity and contempt for her husband.

Having provided a coherent narrative concerning the state of the relationship between the Biggadikes, Judge Byles moved on to the vexed question of the possession of arsenic by the accused, always a key issue in any poison trial. In terms of absolute factual accuracy, Justice Byles used the cautious expression, 'It would appear', when drawing attention to the evidence that Mrs Biggadike had offered a quantity of white mercury to a witness in order to deal with an infestation of mice. The subject of Mrs Biggadike having possession of poison received no further elaboration other than a strange and largely irrelevant suggestion that when she described the substance on offer as white mercury, she may have meant corrosive sublimate. In a rare moment of humility, Judge Byles admitted that he was unable to say what Mrs Biggadike really meant. However, he was clear that she could not have meant arsenic: having said that, it was probable that neither Mrs

Biggadike nor the Grand Jury nor himself, could distinguish the difference between white mercury, corrosive sublimate and arsenic, based only upon external appearance.

Judge Byles next drew attention to Mrs Biggadike having had a conversation with her next door neighbour on the subject of poison. She had spoken about an incident involving the poisoning of a dog in the neighbourhood and the difficulty of identifying poison in dog food. Either the press had misreported what was said by the judge or Justice Byles was mistaken: according to newspaper reports on the adjourned inquest, the conversation between the witness and Mrs Biggadike moved on from the story about dog poisoning to a discussion about the recent case at Mareham le Fen involving John and Elizabeth Garner, accused of poisoning the mother and the first wife of John Garner. What Justice Byles did get right, however, was that the alleged conversation took place a couple of days before the death of Richard Biggadike and also that he had mentioned it to them already: his Lordship had clearly thought it worth repeating.

What his Lordship also thought worth mentioning was that whilst it was clear that Mrs Biggadike was at home with her husband when he was eating his tea, it was uncertain that this was the case with Thomas Proctor: he too may have been there during the whole of the time when Richard Biggadike was eating and drinking, but it was possible that he was only there for part of the time, towards the end of the fatal meal. The evidence against Proctor was neither clear nor consistent, Judge Byles noted, although he thought he should remind the Grand Jury that they did have the clarity and certainty of 'the female prisoner' having prepared the food and drink consumed by her husband. In some detail, although occasionally incorrect in its chronology, Judge Byles also reminded the Grand Jury of the horrors which Richard Biggadike endured after the administration of 'a very large' quantity of arsenic. It hardly needed saying by his Lordship, but he said it anyway: 'Suspicion fell upon the prisoner.'

The final part of judge's seemingly interminable remarks to the Grand Jury consisted of a review of the evidence against both of the accused. The statements were often followed by judicial caveats, which left the Grand Jury with a good deal to reflect upon: more than for Mrs Biggadike, however, the caveats surrounding the evidence against Thomas Proctor were perhaps a lot more helpful in simplifying their deliberations.

Judge Byles reminded the Grand Jury that the marital relationship was under strain to the extent that the wife had expressed a wish that he was dead. Further, it was a fact that there was poison in the house and it had been put into the husband's last meal. At this point, his Lordship appeared to provide some wriggle room for the Grand Jury: the poison may have been administered on purpose, 'by some felon', but arguably it may have been taken accidentally or knowingly by the deceased himself. What followed made the wriggle room shrink somewhat, however, as Judge Byles went through the claim by Mrs Biggadike that she had found a suicide note and casting doubt on its truthfulness by describing it as possibly 'the commencement of a fabrication by her of exculpatory evidence'. In his surprisingly liberal continuation, Judge Byles suggested that too much weight ought not to be placed on such statements, as even the innocent might make such statements 'with the terrors of the law hanging over them.' Unfortunately for Mrs Biggadike, the even hand of justice, at this point, went limp, caused by the unarguable assertion from his Lordship that the Grand Jury would judge the story of a suicide note as 'manifestly false'. They would therefore have great difficulty in believing Mrs Biggadike's second story about seeing Thomas Proctor drop white powder into her husband's teacup. His Lordship also tersely reminded the Grand Jury that even if Mrs Biggadike's story was true, it would not absolve her from the crime: in the eyes of the law, to observe the commission of a crime without trying to prevent it was in effect to assent to it, and therefore that person would be just as guilty as the perpetrator of the crime.

Judge Byles admitted that the evidence against Mrs Biggadike was entirely circumstantial: it seemed a reasonable note of caution to the Grand Jury in deciding whether or not to find a true bill against her. However, he reassured the gentlemen of the jury that 'circumstantial evidence, when the facts were well-established, was necessary in a case like this, and experience showed it to be satisfactory in its results.'

The evidence against Thomas Proctor was not as extensive as that against Priscilla Biggadike, Byles observed; there was evidence to consider, but his Lordship helpfully also noted either its inadmissibility or its unreliability. Just in case the Grand Jury had been swayed into believing Mrs Biggadike's second story, he reminded them that it could not be used as evidence in court against Thomas Proctor, and any petit jury would be told as much, should a true bill be found against him.

In his witness statement at the inquest, Proctor had said that he was unaware of any poison in the house and that he never used poison in his work as a rat catcher: this contradiction of other evidence could be explained by him simply not knowing about the existence of the poison in the house, said the judge. Further, Proctor's enigmatic conversation with Mildred Conyers, also reported at the inquest, in which he appeared to be sharing a distressing guilty secret might easily be interpreted as Proctor having witnessed the crime or merely having found out about it later. The strongest evidence against Thomas Proctor, according to Walter Clegg in his summing up, had been the conversation reported by Elizabeth Fenwick, in which he seemed to be warning Mrs Biggadike about the indiscretion of talking too much. In response to this evidence, Justice Byles told the Grand Jury that recollections of conversations by a witness were 'the least satisfactory evidence that could be offered.' It was a reasonable observation by his Lordship, but not one which seemed to have been applied equally to the various conversations that had allegedly taken place between Mrs Biggadike and her neighbours.

In his opening remarks, Lord Justice Byles had reminded the Grand Jury that the finding of a true bill, or not, was an overwhelming responsibility as 'the administration or the failure of justice might depend on the mode in which they discharged the important functions which the law entrusted to them.' In his closing remarks, he was more plain speaking: if the Grand Jury found a true bill against Thomas Proctor, based on insufficient evidence, he would be acquitted by a petit jury and would have immunity from any future prosecution. If there was any doubt about sufficient evidence, the Grand Jury should throw out the bill, on the understanding that they, as magistrates, had the power to have a police watch placed on Proctor; and further, to have him re-arrested and tried on the same charge, in the event of compelling new evidence coming to light.

Spoken in a spirit of pragmatic good sense and followed by his Lordship's earnest assurances that he had not advised them in this matter, he declared that he was content to leave the matter in the capable hands of the Grand Jury.

It probably came as no surprise, that a true bill was found against Mrs Biggadike and the bill against Thomas Proctor was thrown out.

Trial of Priscilla Biggadike for Wilful Murder: Part Two: 11th December, 1868

There were two accounts of the second day of the trial of Priscilla Biggadike published in the *Lincolnshire Chronicle*. The first, and shorter one, was essentially a potted version, following the lengthy report on the first day, published on Saturday, 12th December; the longer one, taking up nearly an entire page of densely packed newsprint, was published on Friday, 18th December. A similar long version of the second day of the trial was also published by the *Stamford Mercury* on the same day, with various omissions and minor variants.

The shorter version in the *Lincolnshire Chronicle* is interesting in that it refers, in passing, to the conclusion of the first day, recording that a true bill had been found against Mrs Biggadike, but 'at the suggestion of his Lordship', the bill against Thomas Proctor had been dismissed. It may have been just a casual journalistic remark, but it captured the sense that despite the protestations of the learned judge to the contrary, the Grand Jury had without doubt been strongly directed into making the decision. The outcome certainly had advantages, and not just to Thomas Proctor: it simplified the case against Priscilla Biggadike and it freed up Proctor to testify against her.

Justice Byles took his seat at 10 o'clock and the proceedings occupied the entire day. The trial jury, predominantly wealthy farmers from around the county, was listed as follows:

- Joseph Avery, Crowland
- John Brownlow, Martin
- Frederick Cooke, Alford
- Thomas Cooley, Moulton
- Henry Dudding, Panton
- Thomas Emmerson, Haxey
- John Jesson, Fleet
- George Gott, Gedney
- John Richard Nainby, Barnetby-le-Beck
- Richard Oldfield, Sturton and Bransby
- George Storey, Stow
- John Wakefield, Beesby in the Marsh

The two Counsels on the day were Samuel Botelier Bristowe and John Compton Lawrance, both rising stars of the Midland Circuit, and both in later years to have distinguished legal careers.

The trial was opened by Mr Bristowe for the Prosecution, who gave a lengthy synopsis of the case for the benefit of the jury. On the whole, it was a measured account, presenting the death of Richard Biggadike and its aftermath in clear, factual terms, free from distracting rhetorical tricks. It was clearly his intention to introduce himself to the jury as an eminently fair and reasonable man in search of the truth. His reference to the improbability of suicide, for example, was explained on purely logical grounds, without any dismissive reference to Mrs Biggadike's improbable story: Richard Biggadike had been a man in good health and spirits, and on becoming ill, he had requested a doctor: strong reasons not to suppose suicide.

Similarly, when considering the question of who might have administered the poison, he pointed out that only two people were in the house on the afternoon of 30th September: Mrs Biggadike and Thomas Proctor. The latter, 'if he was rightly informed', went out fishing for a short time, leaving Mrs Biggadike alone in the house whilst her husband was eating his tea. His cautionary note concerning the truthfulness of Proctor's own account of his movements was further emphasised by Mr Bristowe when he reminded the jury that Proctor himself had been formerly indicted of the crime along with Mrs Biggadike, and would only be appearing in the witness box due to the discretion exercised by the Grand Jury.

In an apparent spirit of fair play, Mr Bristowe also pointed out to the jury that it was almost impossible to obtain clear and positive evidence concerning the administration of poison, and that they should therefore focus upon the surrounding evidence. By this, he meant 'the conduct of the woman' and 'how she acted under the circumstances of the terrible illness from which her husband was suffering'. It was a clever ploy by the Prosecution, detaching the main line of argument from a reliance on any questionable evidence provided by Thomas Proctor.

In a slow, but undisguised turning of the screw, Mr Bristowe then put his cards on the table concerning how he was going to proceed against Mrs Biggadike. He would show that she did not demonstrate any distress in response to her husband's condition and that for a time she had left him alone upstairs, as he lay dying. He would also question the integrity of Mrs Biggadike by examining various statements made by her which were inconsistent, as well as proving that some aspects of her behaviour were 'highly suspicious'.

Finally, he briefly addressed the issue of the motivation of the accused and the opportunity she had to carry out 'this horrible act'. He would call several witnesses to hear their testimony about marital disharmony, including a declaration from the accused that she had wished him dead. Despite having 'no distinct and positive proof that the woman was in possession of arsenic', he would present evidence that she had offered to give some to a neighbour two or three months earlier. It was familiar territory from the inquest, but Mr Bristowe introduced new material to shore up a possible weakness in the case for the Prosecution: it was true that no arsenic had been found after the death of Richard Biggadike, but as the house had not been searched until three days later, there had been abundant opportunity to dispose of any incriminating evidence. Unsurprisingly, Mr Bristowe, in his quest for the truth, made no reference to the musings of Justice Byles on the differences between arsenic, white mercury and corrosive sublimate, and their implications for the case against Mrs Biggadike.

The first witness to be called was Stickney joiner, Henry Turner, who had known Richard Biggadike for several years. Turner had last seen him at work on the 30th September and he appeared to be in good health; he had left work around 5.30 that evening. Mr Turner confirmed that Biggadike could neither read nor write.

Under cross-examination by the Counsel for the Defence, John Compton Lawrance, Henry Turner said that Biggadike was a man of few words and was generally in good spirits.

The testimony of George Ironmonger was largely a repetition of his deposition at the inquest, although he did provide further details relating to the movements of Thomas Proctor, not all of them very clear. He and Proctor had been out fishing before returning to the house 'at about half past four or five' to eat his tea prepared, as usual, by Mrs Biggadike. After eating their meal, both he and Proctor went out fishing again, although he had left first and was only joined about half an hour later by Proctor. They set off back to the house together, but he had got there first on account of Proctor being slightly lame: on arrival, Richard Biggadike was in the privy and when he came back into the house he was coughing and 'seemed full of pain'. After a further distressing visit to the privy, Biggadike asked Ironmonger to fetch the doctor as he would be quicker than Mrs Biggadike, which he did.

During the course of Richard Biggadike being ill, he saw him only once, as he had deposed at the inquest, and was not with him when he had died, as he had gone off to work.

In response to questioning, Ironmonger confirmed that neither he nor Priscilla Biggadike were ill that evening, although he observed that 'she seemed down'. He did not see Mrs Biggadike prepare the cakes as meals were always waiting for him when he arrived home from work. He also confirmed that Richard Biggadike was illiterate.

The cross-examination by the Defence was obviously trying to establish clear time lines. Both Proctor and himself were at tea for about a quarter of an hour, before going fishing at a place about two hundred yards away from the house. Richard Biggadike was not in the house when he left, but food was waiting for him on the table. He confirmed that Mrs Biggadike was her usual self, but repeating his earlier vague description of her being 'a bit down'. He also said that he had never heard the couple fall out, although they occasionally 'had a few words'.

Ironmonger was re-examined by Mr Bristowe and it was established that he was a boatman, often away from home a month at a time: when not out at sea, he lodged with the Biggadikes. Whilst not pressed, it would seem that the Counsel for the Prosecution may have been probing the security of Ironmonger's statement about never having heard the couple fall out, if he was away at sea for long periods of time.

With reference to the cake left on the table, Ironmonger agreed that it was the same cake that he had been eating earlier.

The next witness was Dr Peter Maxwell who had attended Richard Biggadike and had carried out a post mortem. Inevitably, there was little to add to the medical evidence heard at the initial and resumed inquests. His only additions were interesting, but perhaps rather less significant than Dr Maxwell seemed to think. He went into detail concerning the collecting and storage of the vomit produced by Richard Biggadike whilst upstairs in bed. He had seen the vomit in a chamber pot and had asked Mrs Biggadike for a bottle into which he could pour it. At first, she thought she did not have one, but then went downstairs and produced a bottle. Clearly dissatisfied about the cleanliness of the bottle, he asked her to wash it, which she did; the newly washed bottle contained an old cork, but as far as he could tell, the bottle was now clean. When he returned at 11 o'clock that night, he had found Richard Biggadike vomiting large quantities of blood and in a much worse state than when he had left him earlier in the evening. He had then proceeded to once again empty the contents of the chamber pot into a second bottle, also provided by Mrs Biggadike. He took both bottles of vomit home with him and the next day sent for Sergeant Berry, the Stickney policeman.

During the cross-examination by the Counsel for the Defence, Dr Maxwell said that his suspicions had been aroused when he had first asked Mrs Biggadike for a bottle, although he did not explain why. Equally unsatisfactory was Dr Maxwell's confirmation that Mrs Biggadike had brought a piece of cake to his surgery when she came to collect the prescribed medicine: he had refused to take it, but did not give a reason why he had refused to take it. There was a sense that there was little love lost between Dr Maxwell and Mrs Biggadike, perhaps confirmed by her claim that when he had first arrived at the house he was drunk and had taken an hour to get there.

The deposition by Superintendent Wright of Spilsby was memorable not so much for what he said, as most of it had been heard before at the Coroner's inquest, but more for the objection made by Mr Lawrance to part of that evidence being heard in the Assize court and the response of Mr Justice Byles to that objection.

Superintendent Wright had been absolutely scrupulous in the performance of his police duties: he had witnessed the post mortem performed by Dr Maxwell; he had delivered a stone jar and three bottles to Professor Taylor in London, in exactly the same condition in which he had received them from Dr Maxwell; at the end of Coroner's inquest in Stickney, he had apprehended Mrs Biggadike on the serious charge of wilful murder and had cautioned her not to say anything which might be used in evidence against her; and after having been tried at the Magistrates' Court, he had escorted Mrs Biggadike to Spilsby Prison.

The deposition was going smoothly until Superintendent Wright began to tell the court about his conversation with Priscilla Biggadike on reaching Spilsby which was to lead to her claim of having discovered a suicide note.

Mr Lawrance cut the witness off in full flow and objected to the Superintendent repeating what had been said to him on the grounds that Mrs Biggadike had not been cautioned a second time before she spoke. It was a desperate and rather obvious attempt to derail damning evidence against his client. His Lordship would have none of it, however: the first caution at the end of the inquest was sufficient and even that had not been absolutely necessary. In his judgement the woman's statement was admissible.

Supported by the judge, the Superintendent confidently recounted the episode and even remembered to include Mrs Biggadike's strange claim that someone had written it on behalf of her husband, a detail which Dr Clegg had mentioned in his summing up. Perhaps in a moment of unexpected recollection, or buoyed up by the trust of his Lordship, the Superintendent elaborated upon an incident only briefly touched upon in his deposition at the inquest. After having heard about the supposed discovery of the suicide note, the Superintendent was asked by Mrs Biggadike to make sure that her story would be heard. His recounting of the incident acquired a fresh dramatic intensity from the addition of new details: as he was entering the prison, specifically between the inner and outer gates, Mrs Biggadike had grabbed his arm to get his assurance that he would 'tell the gentlemen' about the suicide note.

It was a moment of pathos which the *Stamford Mercury* chose not to publish.

The Superintendent ended his deposition by returning to the more mundane business of routine enquiries in Stickney concerning Richard Biggadike's debt, which had supposedly led to his suicide: he had found no evidence of such debt, at least in the village.

The chemical analysis of the internal organs of Richard Biggadike by Professor Swaine Taylor was once again reported in detail by the *Lincolnshire Chronicle*, although the *Stamford Mercury* limited its report to a short paragraph. In terms of the needs of the jury, the key points made by the expert toxicologist were that Richard Biggadike had been given a large quantity of arsenic and that he 'must have suffered acute pain' very quickly. In passing, Professor Taylor mentioned that arsenic was frequently called white mercury, with the added complication that there were also two different substances called white mercury: white precipitate powder and corrosive sublimate. The fine discrimination was perhaps a useful antidote to the self-confessed limited understanding of his Lordship on the subject.

The cross-examination by Mr Lawrance, also omitted by the *Stamford Mercury*, pressed Professor

Taylor concerning whether the arsenic had been administered in solid or in liquid form. The response, whilst cautious, was that given the absence of any great quantity of food in the stomach and the rapid development of symptoms, he was inclined to favour an explanation of liquid form introduced by the drinking of tea. Mr Lawrance also seemed to have sought clarity on the time taken by arsenic to work on the human digestive system: the answer was not definitive in that in most circumstances the symptoms would appear after about half-an-hour, but he had known cases in which symptoms had taken as long as nine hours to become apparent. The line of questioning by Lawrance was perhaps trying to establish, at least, the possibility of shifting the time frame of the narrative away from tea time at the Biggadike house, to an earlier fatal consumption of arsenic.

Mr Bristowe had seen where the question and answer might be leading, it seems, as he made a decisive intervention: from Taylor's response it is clear that he had been asked if Biggadike's death, within twelve hours of being poisoned, was consistent with the condition of the organs. The answer had been in the affirmative and perhaps even more conclusively, their appearance was not consistent with the poison 'having laid dormant for some time.'

In the interest of further clarification of the facts, Judge Byles asked a supplementary question, concerning the quantity of arsenic used to kill Richard Biggadike: had the Professor formed any idea from examining the contents of the stomach and intestines, and well as from the statements he had heard, concerning how much arsenic had been used? Taylor would not be drawn absolutely on the matter, as the chemistry alone could not provide a definitive answer: all he would say was that the quantity was a large one, by which he meant thirty to forty grains: a teaspoonful would contain around one hundred and thirty grains. The Professor made no reference to the unspecified statements he had supposedly heard, mentioned by His Lordship.

Mary Ann Clarke, a close neighbour of the Biggadikes, had spoken at the adjourned inquest and had also been called to answer questions from the two accused in front of the magistrates. After prefacing her deposition with the additional credentials that she had known the Biggadikes for five years and that she knew them very well, Mrs Clarke repeated her story of going over to the Biggadike house at around 7.15 in the evening of 30th September. Now appearing on a bigger stage, however, Mrs Clarke seemed to remember things which were considerably more important than what was heard in Stickney. She said that around 8.30 that same evening Priscilla Biggadike paid her a visit, to show her a piece of cake, claiming that 'the doctor says I have put something in that I ought not to have done, that I put some poison in it.' Mrs Clarke told the court that Mrs Biggadike neither confirmed nor denied the accusation by Dr Maxwell.

After having accompanied her to the doctor, Mrs Clarke also returned to the Biggadike house, went upstairs, and discovered the pitiful scene of Richard Biggadike bleeding from the mouth and nose, saying 'Lord have mercy on me.'

Mrs Clarke then repeated her story from the inquest concerning having been called over to the house the following morning, as Richard Biggadike was on the point of death, although her time frame altered from 6.15 to 5.55. Once again, Mrs Clarke's memory had improved, managing to recall events in greater detail and more sharply. On entering the bedroom, Richard Biggadike appeared to be on the point of death: he was flat on his back, his feet and legs were hanging out of bed and he was unable to move. Mrs Ironmonger and Mrs Biggadike were in the bedroom at the time, and once Richard Biggadike had died, she assisted Mrs Ironmonger in laying him out.

After repeating the conversation which she had allegedly had with Mrs Biggadike about the teacup, she remembered things far more important and prejudicial to her. Following this conversation, Mrs Biggadike had told her that her husband had instructed her not to bring either the baby or its chair upstairs, as he did not want them. Mrs Clarke also added that Mrs Biggadike was not crying and did not fret until she and Mrs Ironmonger fretted. When they had later had breakfast together and were talking, Mrs Biggadike 'appeared in her usual spirits'.

After a brief cross-examination from the Defence Counsel establishing that Mrs Clarke lived about fifty yards away from the Biggadike family, Justice Byles made another intervention, by ordering that a portion of Mrs Clarke's deposition from the magistrates' court should be read out. The section in question related to what Mrs Biggadike had allegedly said in response to the accusation of Dr Maxwell that she had put poison in her husband's food. The reading repeated exactly what Mrs Clarke had just said, but with one exception. In her later statement she had said that Mrs Biggadike had neither confirmed nor denied the accusation: the reading out of the earlier deposition made it clear that Mrs Biggadike had denied putting poison in the food. To make it absolutely clear to the jury, Byles pressed Mrs Clarke to confirm the truth of what the court had just heard read out, which she did.

The reason for the intervention of the judge is unclear: on the one hand, it may have pointed to the unreliability of a prosecution witness; on the other hand, it may have suggested that Mrs Biggadike was possibly less than truthful when she contradicted the doctor.

The final words of Mrs Clarke, under cross-examination from Mr Lawrance, did little to resolve the ambiguity: she had been 'on intimate terms' with Mr and Mrs Biggadike and yet rather oddly, she was unable to say 'how they lived their lives together.'

Like Mary Ann Clarke, Jane Ironmonger, also a witness at the resumed inquest and called to answer questions in front of the magistrates, went out of her way to make it known that she had been acquainted with Mrs and Mrs Biggadike for a long time, in her case for seven years. She also lived in the adjoining house to them, a fact which was especially advantageous in overhearing conversations through a boarded partition, it later turned out.

As with Mary Ann Clarke, the memory of Jane Ironmonger had improved since her last courtroom visit. At 9 o'clock, on the night of the fatal poisoning, she had visited Richard Biggadike and found him very sick: her visit had not been mentioned before. After going home, she returned at 11 o'clock and saw Mrs Biggadike upstairs with her husband. Perhaps sensing that Biggadike was close to death, Mrs Ironmonger asked his wife if she had sent for his brother, who lived in the village. She replied that it didn't matter as they had not been on good terms with the brother. At this point, Mrs Ironmonger had taken matters into her own hands, put on her bonnet and shawl, and went to fetch the brother herself. She returned with him and his wife about a quarter of an hour later.

In a significant recollection, she remembered reaching the house and finding Mrs Biggadike seated downstairs with the two lodgers, whilst her husband was very sick upstairs. Richard Biggadike spoke with some difficulty to his brother, as he was complaining of being thirsty and wanting a cup of cold tea. Mrs Biggadike brought him the tea, at which point, Mrs Ironmonger departed. She returned the next morning and was with Richard Biggadike when he died.

After confirming that Mrs Biggadike showed no symptoms of being ill nor having complained of being ill, she repeated her previous evidence concerning her conversation with her about the poisoned dog and the poison case against the Garners in Mareham le Fen. She also recalled the words of Mrs Biggadike hoping her husband would come home dead. What she also said, not mentioned in her first account at the inquest, was that the words of Mrs Biggadike were not part of a conversation she had with her, but rather, something overheard through the board partition between the two houses: 'I could hear every word they said', Mrs Ironmonger asserted triumphantly.

Mrs Ironmonger's testimony was queried by Mr Lawrance, during which she declared that Mrs Biggadike was 'a rather noisy woman and is in the habit of using strong language'. Mrs Biggadike's loudness was hardly a character endorsement, but given that Mrs Ironmonger herself had earlier mentioned that Richard Biggadike was 'very hard of hearing' and that George Ironmonger had earlier testified that he was 'rather deaf', there may have been a reasonable explanation for it, at least in one sense of the word 'noisy'.

His Lordship once again intervened in the proceedings, asking Mrs Ironmonger a question, or questions, which produced the answer that the couple had been on bad terms lately, and that when Mrs Biggadike had wished her husband might be brought home dead, she was 'in a great passion.'

As with the previous intervention by Judge Byles, the significance of the outcome was uncertain and ambiguous in terms of taking the case forward. It re-emphasised the discord in the relationship between the couple, a significant factor in identifying motive, as well as the intemperate language of Mrs Biggadike. At the same time, it might have suggested to the jury, as it had to both Walter Clegg and Judge Byles himself, that words spoken in anger were not necessarily a reliable indication of intent to harm.

Susan Evrington, who had known Mr and Mrs Biggadike for three or four years, had made a cameo appearance in front of the magistrates with a testimony which amounted to little more than tittle-tattle relating to how much Mrs Biggadike disliked her husband. Her reappearance produced a more expansive version, supported by references to time and place, which was a significant contribution to the construction of the criminal identity of Priscilla Biggadike as an outrageously brazen and amoral woman.

In essence, her evidence was a record of an extended conversation in which Miss Evrington had delved into the private life of Priscilla Biggadike, by way of pretended sympathies, impertinent leading questions and shameless prying; if true, the responses of Mrs Biggadike were at best, unguarded, at worst, ill-judged.

She had opened the conversation by expressing her great sorrow at hearing that the couple had been 'unfriendly together lately': in particular, she had heard that they had met up in Boston and had a fall out over money. Miss Evrington had also heard that when they got home from Boston, Mr Biggadike had thrown his wife out of the house. Mrs Biggadike had sharply refuted the story, quite simply because she would never go to Boston, or anywhere else, to meet her husband. Susan Evrington had expressed her surprise at this assertion as she thought Richard Biggadike a good-looking man and, she hoped, 'a kind, good husband and father'. In her reply, Mrs Biggadike was unambiguously frank, telling Miss Evrington that she could not abide her husband.

At the time, Mrs Biggadike was suckling her child, prompting Miss Evrington to ask if Mr Biggadike made a big fuss over the baby. In retrospect, it wasn't so much a pleasant enquiry, as the teeing up of some juicy gossip: Mrs Biggadike apparently obliged by telling her that her husband had on several occasions, when drunk, claimed that the child was not his; in response she had said, 'It's no matter whose else it is; I know it's mine'.

The brief cross-examination of the witness revealed very little other than Richard Biggadike being in good health and spirits at the time of his death, and that she had never seen him drunk.

At the resumed inquest, Eliza Fenwick had testified that Priscilla Biggadike, about four months before her husband's death, had poison in the house. She had also provided further vital circumstantial evidence when she told the inquest about the surreptitious conversation which she had overheard between Mrs Biggadike and Thomas Proctor. At the Assize trial she repeated her previous depositions and, like Susan Evrington and Jane Ironmonger, was also able to recall further information to put before the court. It was less convincing in terms of its usefulness to the jury than her earlier statements, but it added further evidence to support the story of Mrs Biggadike having an extra-marital relationship: as with all her other witness statements it grew out of a conversation.

That conversation took place about four weeks before the death of Richard Biggadike, concerning a new dress which Mrs Biggadike had been keen to show Mrs Fenwick. Whilst she was admiring the dress, Richard Biggadike passed the comment that it had not been bought with his money; to which Mrs Biggadike gave a now familiar blunt, but oddly elusive retort, which confirmed that the dress had indeed not been bought with his money. The matter seemed to end with Richard Biggadike uttering an obscure comment of his own: 'But he's a fine man when he gets dressed up in his black cloth.'

In his cross-examination of Mrs Fenwick, Lawrance focused upon all aspects of her evidence. His initial questioning established that there had been a conversation about white mercury, but it was confirmed that she had never actually seen any. He clearly asked her about her understanding of what Richard Biggadike had said at the end of the conversation about the new dress: Mrs Fenwick had no idea what he meant – it was probably a response shared by the jury.

Under further cross-examination little more emerged: Mrs Fenwick confirmed that the overheard conversation was outside the house and that Mrs Biggadike's contemptuous dismissal of Dr Maxwell had taken place immediately after that conversation.

Mr Bristowe for some reason asked Mrs Fenwick to clarify her exact relationship with the deceased: her sister had married Richard Biggadike's brother.

At this point, Justice Byles made it clear that he thought Mrs Fenwick had omitted material relating Dr Maxwell's supposed accusation which she had deposed at the Magistrate's Court: specifically, material connected to Mrs Biggadike's denial of its truth. It was a curious mirror image of the earlier intervention by his Lordship when Mary Ann Clarke was on the witness stand: she too had left out the crucial denial. It may have been a very odd coincidence , but to an alert jury, it might have looked like the inept collusion of two hostile witnesses.

The taking of the stand by John Farr Phillips, for the most part, was a routine repetition of Mrs Biggadike's interview with him during her incarceration in the Spilsby House of Correction, in which she claimed to have seen Proctor putting white powder in a tea cup and medicine bottle. The text of her statement had been read out at the adjourned inquest and had been transcribed by the *Stamford Mercury* of the 30th October; the same transcription has been used by the newspaper in its report of the 18th December on the Assize trial. However, it appears that a contentious detail had been omitted in the press transcriptions and had certainly not been mentioned in the Coroner's or Magistrates' court. The omitted detail was included in the transcription of Mrs Biggadike's statement in the *Lincolnshire Chronicle* of the 18th December, and was for the first time examined in court: it was therefore clearly not an invention of the press nor a careless journalistic error. In her statement to Mr Phillips, Mrs Biggadike had said that Dr Maxwell took an hour to get to the house and when he did eventually arrive, 'he was quite intoxicated'.

Dr Maxwell was recalled to the stand to explain his version of events in response to Mrs Biggadike's assertions. The doctor, not surprisingly, denied being drunk and also pointed out that his house was only five or six minutes' walk from the Biggadike home; further, he had set off ten minutes after being summoned. In a continuation of the defence of his professionalism, Dr Maxwell said that he had prescribed the same medicine as he always did for an inflammation of the stomach: there was no arsenic in it nor anything of an inflammatory nature. Not surprisingly, the *Stamford Mercury* did not report the recalling of Dr Maxwell to the witness stand.

The final deposition was from Thomas Proctor, now released by the Grand Jury to give evidence against Priscilla Biggadike. The evidence from Proctor was a predictable mash up of previous narratives which focused upon him being away from the house fishing with George Ironmonger, whilst Richard Biggadike was eating his tea, and his attentiveness to him after he became very ill. He also claimed to have been at his side when he died – something contradicted by Mary Ann Clarke and Jane Ironmonger. Proctor also went out of his way to remind the jury that it was Mrs Biggadike who always prepared the meals and that it was Richard Biggadike's usual routine to eat his tea alone.

It was also obvious that Mr Bristowe in his cross-examination of Proctor was going out of his way to remind the jury that Mrs Biggadike's incriminating statement about what she had supposedly seen Proctor do with a white powder was untrue. For the most part, it was a series of questions relating to his ownership of poison and the use of poison, which allowed him to answer with a simple yes or no. Just in case the jury did not grasp the picture, he also ensured that Proctor testified that he did not witness Mrs Biggadike being sick during the course of the evening in question.

The cross-examination by the Counsel for the Defence steered well-clear of Mrs Biggadike's statement and instead focused upon Proctor's account of how long he was out of the house when he left to go fishing the second time with Ironmonger.

On this point, Judge Byles followed up with his own short cross-examination of Proctor to get absolute clarity on the essential point. Had Richard Biggadike got home for tea when he left the house? No. Had he finished his tea by the time he had got back from fishing? Yes.

At this point, the Counsel for the Prosecution announced its intention to have read out in court the statement made by Mrs Biggadike at the first inquest made in front of Dr Clegg, the Coroner. Mr Lawrance, who was clearly uneasy about statements made by Mrs Biggadike, immediately objected on the grounds of the inadmissibility of a statement made by a prisoner on a murder charge before a Coroner, citing the case of the King v Chittey as the legal precedent for this objection. What followed was a series of lively exchanges between the judge and two counsels, involving various niceties of Case Law, resulting in the crushing defeat of Mr Lawrance.

Mr Bristowe was allowed to call Dr Clegg to read the statement made by Mrs Biggadike at the first inquest on the 3rd October.

Before doing so, Dr Clegg provided the court with essential details concerning the circumstances which had led to it. Mrs Biggadike had not only given the statement freely, but had insisted upon doing so despite the Coroner's formal caution that such evidence would have to be made under oath. He had written down everything that Priscilla Biggadike had told him, refraining from asking more questions 'than was absolutely necessary'. The written statement had been returned with the other documents from the Coroner's depositions. What he held in his hand was the original document as he had not made a copy of it. It had not been signed by Mrs Biggadike because she had demurred and he had not pressed her on the issue. Dr Clegg made it clear that in awkward circumstances he had been absolutely scrupulous and fair towards Mrs Biggadike, as well as having followed legal procedures.

The statement, claiming to tell all that Mrs Biggadike knew about her husband's death, was read out verbatim to the court by the Coroner. It was a straightforward point by point account of the events of Wednesday, 30th September. Mrs Biggadike had made baked three cakes in the frying pan for tea, two of which were consumed by herself, the two lodgers and her children, at 5 o'clock. A third cake, made from the same dough, had been left for her husband to eat once he got home. He had got home about 6 o'clock and took this tea alone, eating half of the cake and some cold mutton, along with a cup of tea. Both herself and Proctor were present in the house whilst her husband ate his meal.

A short time after finishing his meal, her husband became ill, being sick and purging himself twice before asking to see a doctor. He went to bed and the doctor attended him. Mrs Biggadike was with her sick husband all night and 'waited on him til he died'. She was sure that no poison got into the cake accidentally as there was no poison in the house to her knowledge.

When she went to the doctor's house to collect the

medicine, she took a piece of cake which her husband had left to show him, claiming that 'I took it for his satisfaction, for I thought he did not seem satisfied'. The doctor did not examine it, so she took it home, where she and her children ate it the next day.

It was now the turn of the two Counsels to remind the jury of the key points for consideration before arriving at a verdict.

Mr Bristowe had opened the case with a balanced exposition, free from emotive rhetoric; his closing remarks adopted the same reasonable and measured approach. He reminded the jury that Mrs Biggadike had prepared her husband's evening meal and had herself denied the possibility that poison had been accidentally introduced into the food. He also suggested to them that the possibility of suicide, based upon the evidence which they had heard, was impossible. The only remaining conclusion was that someone had administered the poison: it was for this reason that he had placed Thomas Proctor in the witness box to give him the opportunity to clear his name after being implicated in the crime by the statement of Mrs Biggadike.

He then drew the attention of the jury to the 'demeanour' of the accused, as described by various witnesses. Did that demeanour suggest that she had been living on amicable terms with her husband or did it suggest something very different?

In terms of establishing a motive, Mr Bristowe admitted that in many other similar cases a clearer and stronger motive had been proved, but the jury in this case must weigh up the evidence available to them and draw their own conclusions. Specifically, they must decide whether or not the witness statements had been pressed unduly hard against the prisoner, or not. Reduced to simple terms, if the jury thought that if the couple had been living on bad terms, there was a motive for murder: whether it was a sufficient motive, the jury had to decide.

His most important remarks, he told the jury, would consider the different statements made by Mrs Biggadike, which he considered to be 'of a most serious and damaging sort against her'. Mr Bristowe began his list of such statements with fairly unconvincing ones which were hardly compelling as a case against the accused. He first drew the attention of the jury to Mrs Biggadike's account of taking a piece of cake to Dr Maxwell, before he had made any reference to the possibility of poisoning, in order to convince him that the cake which she had made contained nothing sinister. The second statement, and even less convincing as clinching evidence against Mrs Biggadike, was her discussing the Garner poisoning case with a neighbour. It soon became clear, however, that Mr Bristowe was slowly working towards the most critical statements made by the accused. He reminded the jury that even before she was in custody, Mrs Biggadike had made a statement to the Coroner 'when the matter was full and fresh in her mind', which contained no reference to the discovery of a suicide note, mentioned soon afterwards to the Superintendent of police. The logical conclusion was that the two statements were inconsistent and, even more damning, the truth could not be found in either of them.

It did not require the sharpest legal mind in the room to work out what was coming next from the Counsel for the Prosecution. On remand in Spilsby House of Correction, Mrs Biggadike had made 'another and totally different statement' in which she claimed to have seen Thomas Proctor drop white powder in her husband's tea and, later, into his medicine bottle. If this was true, Mr Bristowe insisted, the prisoner would not have forgotten to mention it to the Coroner. Allowing himself a pointed rhetorical question, the Prosecution Counsel asked the jury, 'Did they not think the prisoner had manufactured this story in order to throw the whole blame upon Proctor, who had no motive for getting rid of the deceased?'. In the final analysis, the jury must satisfy themselves that none of the statements by the prisoner was true and that 'all were more or less false'.

In his final statement, Mr Bristowe generously sympathised with his colleague, the Counsel for the

Defence, having such a grave responsibility to defend the prisoner. However, he was comforted by the fact the jury would have the advantage of hearing a careful and accurate examination of the evidence from his Lordship before coming to their verdict.

Such a prospect was perhaps cold comfort to both Mr Lawrance and Mrs Biggadike.

In his closing address to the Jury, Mr Lawrance presented the case for an acquittal of Mrs Biggadike with acute analytical skill and a shrewd awareness of the weaknesses of the Prosecution case. However, the formal statements made by Mrs Biggadike, contradictory, fanciful and sometimes bizarre, all made against well-intentioned advice, were always going to be problematic.

His opening remarks set the tone for the entire speech. It was essentially a reasoned, polite and polished presentation, carefully responding to the key points made by the Prosecution. It was a text book performance which perhaps required more than text book precision to save Mrs Biggadike from the hangman.

Taking his cue from his learned colleague, Mr Lawrance acknowledged the 'solemn duty devolved upon him', but like his learned colleague, he took great comfort from the knowledge that he would be followed by his Lordship, who would 'supply any omissions he might make'. In the same manner of cosy formal politeness, he thanked the Counsel for the Prosecution who, 'in that spirit of fairness which always characterised him', had reminded the jury of the need to dismiss what they had heard about the case outside the courtroom. It was a standard, formal caution to a jury, of course, but one which was worth highlighting, given that over three months had elapsed since the crime had been committed.

Once he had moved beyond the formulaic niceties, Mr Lawrance started his defence of Mrs Biggadike on the front foot, pointing out that the Prosecution case was built upon a notable absence of hard fact. The accused supposedly kept poison in the house, and yet none had ever been seen or found. In cases such as the present one, he pointed out, it was generally true that the poisoner either dealt in poison or traces were found in their possession: neither was true of the prisoner.

Any clear, hard evidence of a motive for the crime was similarly absent. The jury had heard several witness statements that Mrs Biggadike and her husband lived on bad terms, but this was hardly sufficient reason to commit the crime of murder. The evidence of such witnesses as Jane Ironmonger and Susan Evrington were flimsy reports of 'idle words', spoken by a woman with a hot-temper and in the habit of using unguarded language. It was clear, suggested Mr Lawrance, that since the death of her husband, every word spoken by Mrs Biggadike 'had been raked up against her' to suggest that she intended to murder her husband, none of which had 'any possible weight'. The polite formalities of courtroom discourse were probably a constraint on Mr Lawrance, but what he meant was that village gossip and hearsay should be treated with thoroughgoing scepticism, if not complete contempt.

Mr Lawrance then moved on to the statements made by Mrs Biggadike, but chose to leave the most problematic of these until last.

He started with a quick victory. The Prosecution had stated in its presentation of the evidence that in her conversation with Dr Maxwell, Mrs Biggadike had been the first to mention the possibility of poisoning. This was true, but misleading: she was the first to explicitly mention it, but 'she was led to do so by the conduct of the medical man'. Dr Maxwell had voiced the opinion that he thought Richard Biggadike had eaten something which had disagreed with him and asked his wife what her husband had eaten for tea. Both the statement and the question had suggested to the prisoner that he was suspicious that 'all was not right' – a feeling which was strengthened when she was asked for a bottle in which to put the vomit. The implications of the conversation put Mrs Biggadike on the defensive to the extent that she quite naturally took a piece of cake to the surgery for the doctor to retain and have analysed, neither of which he did, to her great surprise.

He then moved on to undermine the credibility of two key witnesses: his reason for doing so was a matter of court record and so he was on unarguable grounds. Both Eliza Fenwick and Mary Ann Clarke had given evidence against Mrs Biggadike, but both had also deliberately suppressed evidence which altered their original testimony against the prisoner. Lawrance, in passing, mentioned that it was the learned judge who had ascertained for the benefit of the court the irregularity of the testimonies against Mrs Biggadike.

Probably the most reliable evidence heard in the entire trial was that from Professor Taylor in his analysis of the stomach and viscera of Richard Biggadike: he was an eminent scientist and his testimony dealt in hard fact. It was not surprising, therefore, that Lawrance turned to the science to undermine the Prosecution case. He pointed to two 'unusual circumstances' which had been noted by Professor Taylor: Richard Biggadike had shown symptoms of arsenic poisoning very rapidly and he had died within twelve hours of ingesting the fatal substance. Based upon the comments heard from the medical man, Lawrance contended that the supposition on which the Prosecution had built its case, that Richard Biggadike had ingested poison at tea-time, was open to question: it was equally probable that he had taken it earlier on in the day. It was a suggestion which received additional support from the notable absence of poison in the house and from the lack of proof that Mrs Biggadike administered the poison. It was a theoretical possibility, rather than a probability, for the jury to consider, but Mr Lawrance may have overplayed his hand when, in a moment of unusual ironic levity, he suggested that Richard Biggadike's death had 'ensued in the shortest time ever known'.

Mr Lawrance had now reached the point where the three statements of Priscilla Biggadike required his best legal ingenuity to either explain them away or to dismiss their significance: in the main, he chose the latter approach. Whilst the statements were unarguably inconsistent, they did not provide any evidence that the prisoner had poisoned her husband. The first statement, made to Dr Clegg, was simply a straightforward account of events which implicated no one. The second statement made to Superintendent Wright and the third statement made to Mr Phillips, were glossed over by Lawrance who admitted that they were inconsistent, but insisted that inconsistency did not prove guilt. The explanation for the inconsistency of the prisoner's statement was a very human one of a woman acting 'under the influence of the terror which she must naturally have felt in order to clear herself'. It was also an explanation which was a familiar one, having been voiced by Judge Byles in his address to the Grand Jury, only the day before. Mr Lawrance went further, however, by asking the jury if it was credible that a woman capable of planning a cold-blooded murder would tell people a series of different stories, rather than construct a single consistent one.

In his final pleading, there was more than a hint that Mr Lawrance was running out of cogent explanations of, or excuses for, the inconsistency of the statements. In a final rhetorical flourish, he wished the jury to consider that they were dealing with 'a weak woman' who, under suspicion of murder, realised that things were getting worse and had therefore resorted to 'wild and rash statements' in the hope of clearing her name.

It did not have the feel of a triumphant clinching argument.

Both Mr Bristowe and Mr Lawrance had expressed confidence in the imminent summary of the case by his Lordship, before leaving the jury to their deliberations. In a similar spirit of professional etiquette, Judge Byles congratulated Mr Lawrance for his able defence of the prisoner and also for reminding the jury that the case was one which involved a defining moment in the life of the prisoner. However, he wished to also remind the jury that 'if murders of this kind were not punished, it involved the lives of the whole community'.

Before reviewing the evidence, Judge Byles further pointed out that in this kind of case, 'a secret crime', the jury should not expect to have direct evidence in order to reach a verdict, and so would be entirely reliant on the indirect evidence of the circumstantial. In such cases, his Lordship told them, it was his custom to condense his summary into 'a narrow compass', but in the best interests of both the prisoner and the public he would consider the evidence in detail. After doing so, the case would be entirely in the hands of the jury: it was a liberal gesture which, if the reporting of the detailed summary was accurate, was somewhat disingenuous.

The report in the *Lincolnshire Chronicle* omitted the detailed revisiting of the circumstantial evidence by his Lordship; however, the *Stamford Mercury* chose to include it.

This summary was interesting in its concept of fairness to the prisoner, in that its main points of focus, as reported by the newspaper, seemed to be upon undermining the arguments of the Counsel for the Defence. A large part of the summing up, for example, was spent on arguing that Dr Maxwell, on the evening of his visit had spoken prudently and acted impeccably. His suspicions had been aroused about the death of Richard Biggadike and this had been noticed by his wife: it had therefore been in her interests to invent a story that the doctor had arrived at the house intoxicated. It was hardly central to determining whether or not Mrs Biggadike had poisoned her husband, but it implied that she would resort to lies to get herself out of a difficult situation. Similarly, the time spent by Judge Byles on the issue of whether or not Thomas Proctor was the lover of Priscilla Biggadike was both tangential and irrelevant to proving guilt or innocence, but served to remind the jury of the kind of wife Priscilla Biggadike might have been.

Any illusion of balance vanished when Judge Byles assessed the truth of Mrs Biggadikes' statements: the first one she claimed contained 'all she knew', but it didn't; the statement about a suicide note soon after was 'a very strange story'; and the witnessing of Thomas Proctor dropping white powder into a teacup and medicine bottle was 'a most extraordinary story'. In summary, the Jury should view them as 'the fabrication of exculpation evidence, which an innocent person may make, but which a guilty one is more likely to attempt'.

In his final words to the Grand Jury, his Lordship had insisted that he would not, and had not, in any way tried to influence them in their decision making. Even more disingenuously the *Stamford Mercury* quoted Judge Byles as begging the jury to be guided by nothing he had said: he was clearly confident of a convenient outcome.

In his address to the trial jury, he admitted that his observations had 'pressed hardly – possibly too hardly, against the prisoner'. It was an easy admission to make, especially when it had been pointed out that should the jury conclude that Mrs Biggadike had told the truth, she would still not be absolved from the crime, having been by her own admission a passive bystander, as Proctor administered poison to her husband.

In a moment of relief, Judge Byles told the jury that, 'he thanked God that the responsibility rested with them and not with him' for the fate of the prisoner. He may even have believed his own words.

The jury, after only a short consultation, found Mrs Biggadike guilty, but recommended that mercy should be shown to her. There is a strong sense that this was not the outcome which his Lordship had expected, asking the Foreman of the Jury, 'On what grounds?' It was equally clear that the question was not the outcome which the Foreman had expected, as he turned round to other jurors for some guidance on what to say in response to the challenge. After various 'whispering and prompting', the Foreman replied in either desperation or in all innocence that the verdict had been reached, 'only because it was circumstantial evidence'. The inadequate reply carried no weight in terms of grounds for clemency and drew the withering contempt of the reporter in the *Montrose Standard*, published on the 18th December, who declared that, 'The sooner criminals are tried for their lives by rational beings instead of idiots the better'.

Despite the assertion by Judge Byles that the final word on the matter of Mrs Biggadike's fate lay with the jury, he was compelled to ignore the recommendation for mercy without further comment, simply asking for a confirmation that the guilty decision was unanimous.

Perhaps to make the point, in his passing of the death sentence, Judge Byles told Mrs Biggadike that whilst she had been convicted on purely circumstantial evidence, he had never heard 'more satisfactory and conclusive evidence': in an unfortunate lapse of memory, his Lordship seemed to have forgotten all about the second trial of the serial killer, Catherine Wilson, whom he had sentenced to death in 1862.

In addition to expressing his satisfaction that the correct verdict had been reached, Justice Byles advised Mrs Biggadike that in her preparation for death, she should avail herself of religious instruction, something which had she done before, she would never have found herself 'stood in this unhappy condition'.

Both reports of the trial in the Lincolnshire newspapers concluded with a short human interest story which focused upon Mrs Biggadike and her reactions to what was happening in the court. On the whole, it was an account which evoked a variety of images, some of them sympathetic, some questionable, some of them convincingly evocative in their poignant detail.

The description of Priscilla Biggadike as a woman who would be 'considered good looking' was a commonplace of courtroom journalism, although it was qualified by the precise observation of her having 'a smallness of eyes which gave one an impression of great determination'. What followed in its dismal evocation of miserable poverty, was perhaps closer to the truth than the cliché which had opened the piece. She was described as a small, thick-set woman who was 'meanly attired, and her straw bonnet was very dirty, and had evidently seen much service.'

Apart from her court appearances, Mrs Biggadike had spent the previous eighty-six days incarcerated in either the Spilsby House of Correction or Lincoln Castle prison, having endured both physical and mental hardship, as well as tending her infant child: it was hardly surprising that she should look so bedraggled and downtrodden.

The suggestion of Mrs Biggadike's great determination was probably journalistic invention intended to justify the subsequent description of her as she entered the court, with 'utmost composure' and answering the charge against her 'in a firm and determined tone'. During the course of the proceedings, Mrs Biggadike's indifferent fortitude in the face of a possible death sentence had been surprising, in that she 'she appeared to be less interested in what was going on than many of the spectators'. Even as the Judge was summing up the case, she 'remained unmoved' and when the Foreman of the Jury announced his guilty verdict, she 'remained unshaken'.

The rhetorical construction of Mrs Biggadike was engaging, but perhaps undermined by other less comfortable explanations of her demeanour. A woman of limited education and experience of life outside the enclosed agricultural communities of Gedney and Stickney, was always going to struggle to follow, hour on hour, the legal intricacies of a murder trial, as well as the technicalities of forensic toxicology. Even in the best of health, which it later emerged she wasn't, coming to terms with a situation of linguistic impotence and utter powerlessness would have worn down the most resilient of women into bemused passivity, as opposed to surly indifference.

According to the newspapers, the drama of the scene developed a stage further when Mr Collison, the Clerk of Arraigns, whilst performing his formal duty of delivering the allocutus by asking the condemned if there was any reason why the death sentence shouldn't be passed, unexpectedly broke down. At that point, allegedly touched by the sympathy of the Clerk, Mrs Biggadike put her head in her hands and burst into tears.

Despite being in a state of extreme agitation as Justice Byles pronounced sentence, the prisoner was reported as being able to leave the dock without requiring assistance.

Execution of Priscilla Biggadike: 9 o'clock, 28th December, 1868

The date for the execution of Priscilla Biggadike was set for 9 o'clock on Monday, 28th December, in the grounds of Lincoln Castle: it was to be the first judicial execution of a woman to take place in private, out of the sight of morbidly curious spectators. It was also out of the sight of most reporters, as access to the execution had been limited by the Visiting Magistrates to just three representatives of the Press, and was strictly monitored by way of a pre-registered pass, which had to be presented between 8.30 and 8.45 on the morning of the execution. The three reporters, all resident in Lincoln, were Thomas Fox, sub-editor of the *Lincoln Gazette* and *Lincolnshire Times*, which was incorporated into the *Lincolnshire Chronicle*; George Brown, correspondent for the *Stamford Mercury*, as well as a news and advertising agent and James Brooks, reporter for the *Lincoln Gazette* and *Lincolnshire Times*. They also later attended the inquest on the body of Mrs Biggadike and were signatories to the witness document, along with Mr T F Burton, (Deputy Sheriff of Lincolnshire, on behalf of Mr J Wilson Fox, the Sheriff), Mr James Foster (Governor), Reverend H W Richter (Chaplain) and Dr Walter Clegg (JP and County Coroner).

Either because the newspaper was enabled to use first hand reports of the execution or because it took place away from public gaze, the *Lincolnshire Chronicle* took the opportunity to provide its readers with a formidably detailed account of Mrs Biggadike's time in prison, as well as her final hours. Its privileged position in terms of a vehicle for the truth was not lost on the newspaper, which was to include a short section scolding rumourmongers in the city who had circulated lurid stories about what took place behind closed doors, and which were 'totally devoid of the truth'.

However, any assumption that it would have total control of the narrative of the Stickney murderess, by way of its contacts within the prison system and its reporter having witnessed the execution, later turned out to be rather naive.

The late edition of the *Lincolnshire Chronicle* of Friday, 18th December, had supplemented its report of the trial with the information that on Monday,

14th December, Mrs Biggadike had been told of her scheduled execution day by the Governor of Lincoln Castle. In response, according to the report, Mrs Biggadike had replied, 'Is that all the time allowed me?' The entry in the *Prison Journal* of the Governor for that day confirms the story, more or less, in that James Foster records her as having replied to the news with the words, 'Is that all that is left for me?' What he also wrote was that Mrs Biggadike 'appears very much distressed', information to which, it seems, the newspaper did not have access, or chose not to include.

The newspaper's report of Friday, 25th December, the weekend before the execution of Mrs Biggadike was due to take place, was used to build up anticipation for the full story which would be published in due course. Thomas Askern of York had been appointed as her executioner, but 'the unfortunate woman', up to Wednesday, 23rd December, had appeared to be 'utterly callous and indifferent to her position'; further, she had not been visited by any of her relatives. The latter was true at the time and that information could have come from a number of different sources in the prison. However, the outraged assertion that Mrs Biggadike was both 'callous and indifferent' to her situation can only have come from one source and that was the Prison Chaplain, whose *Prison Journal* entries as the day of execution drew near focused increasingly upon her frustrating refusal to confess her guilt. The Reverend Richter's comments contrast markedly with those of the Prison Surgeon and the Governor, recorded on the 23rd December: Edward Farr Broadbent, who provided medical care for the condemned prisoner, noted that she was 'much depressed', whilst James Foster wrote that Mrs Biggadike was 'very much depressed' and 'hasn't taken any food this morning'.

The *Stamford Mercury* of Friday 25th December, in its own prequel to the execution, was more forthright than the Lincoln newspaper in its antipathy towards Mrs Biggadike, describing her as 'unmoved as ever': she had 'made no confession whatever; nor judging from her present obduracy is it expected she ever will'. The newspaper also reported that Mrs Biggadike had not received any visitors, but extended the story by mentioning that her friends had been contacted, but none had been to see her, 'nor does it appear that they intend to do so'. The final sour disapproval of Mrs Biggadike was that she had neither seen her children nor had she made any request to see them. It was the unkindest cut of all in that her youngest child, Rachel, whom she had been suckling in prison cells since her arrest, had been taken away from her on the 31st October and placed in the Lincoln Union Workhouse; whilst her two older children, Alice, aged eight, and Emma, aged four, had earlier been removed to the Spilsby Union Workhouse.

The half-facts and perverse misinformation produced by both newspapers did not auger well for the accuracy of their reporting of a private execution, whose account could not easily be challenged. That the newspapers were unable to control the Biggadike narrative absolutely became evident, however, even before the morning of the 28th December.

In its report of the 25th December, the *Lincolnshire Chronicle* itself drew attention to a letter written to the editor of the *Star* newspaper by Thomas Beggs, Honorary Secretary of Society for the Abolition of Capital Punishment, who had wished to raise the case of Priscilla Biggadike. The synopsis of the letter made it clear that the polemical intent of Beggs was to use the life and imminent death of Mrs Biggadike as an exemplum of the inevitability of crime when human beings live life on 'the degraded level of brutes'. In the process of arguing his highly emotive case for mercy, Beggs created his own narrative of the Stickney murder, which was a mixture of fact, sensational fiction and social commentary on the lives of the rural poor. The explanation of the murder was to be found in the wretched conditions in which the husband, wife, lodgers and children had lived, all sleeping in one room: when people live such lives it completely negates all 'moral and rational conduct', he claimed. No punishment, no matter how terrible, would ever deter 'such abject creatures' from crime quite simply because the future to them was 'always vague and remote'. The outrage of Thomas Beggs was admirable in its concern for the welfare of his fellow human-beings, although his potted history of events in Stickney was somewhat skewed towards a sordid tale of domestic violence: 'The jealousy of Biggadike produced violent quarrels and ill-usage of his wife, who to get rid of him put poison in a cake.'

The letter had also been reported earlier by the *Nottingham Journal* of 23rd December, which noted that it had been sent to the Home Office on behalf of Mrs Biggadike. It was similarly reported by the *Liverpool Weekly Courier,* on the 26th December, but the newspaper was somewhat dismissive of its arguments, as 'somewhat narrow and very peculiar'.

The report on the execution of Mrs Biggadike and the subsequent formal inquest was published in the *Lincolnshire Chronicle* on 1st January 1869, and was a sombre start to the new year. Inevitably, the apparently first-hand account was duplicated and modified by other newspapers, as the story travelled beyond Lincolnshire.

Quite rightly, the opening of the report struck a contrite note, remarking that the newspaper should not weary its readers with the details of Mrs Biggadike's 'shocking crime', as they were by now well-known. Unfortunately, the newspaper decided that its theoretical well-informed reader was still not well-informed enough and proceeded to retell the story, despite its stated good intentions. Except that the retold story was no longer the same narrative, but rather a breath-taking fantasy cobbled together from alarming hearsay, novelistic reworkings of pious platitudes culled from the Prison Chaplain and shameless fabrications which are completely contradicted by the sober day-to-day accounts of Mrs Biggadike by the prison staff, found in their *Journals*.

The familiar account of the problematic lack of space in the Biggadike house and the domestic difficulties between a married couple was transformed into the seedy stuff of Penny Dreadfuls. Immorality 'took possession of the cottage' where 'strong in her guilty passion', the wife had 'morbidly brooded over her miserable condition'. She 'saw but one obstacle to her future happiness' and he, in turn, was removed. The motif of violent conflict between husband and wife, as a result of infidelity, involving 'bitter words and angry blows', was oddly reminiscent of the inventions of Thomas Beggs which the newspaper had cited in the previous week.

If Beggs had been the inspiration, Henry Richter, the Prison Chaplain, without doubt supplied the raw material for what followed.

As a preliminary, the *Lincolnshire Chronicle* reminded its readers that in its report of the trial, the conduct of Mrs Biggadike had been closely observed:

throughout the day she had remained unmoved, 'presenting a bold front to those witnesses whose evidence told against her'. A re-reading of the report confirms that the adjective 'unmoved' was used to describe Mrs Biggadike, but there was certainly no reference to any kind of overt hostile attitude towards witnesses. However, the sense of implacable threat chimed well with the newly created disturbing image of a woman capable of murdering her own husband in cold blood to satisfy her wicked passion.

Despite having had a good deal of time and opportunity to 'seek for mercy for her great and deadly sin' by confessing her guilt, Mrs Biggadike had remained obdurate. Regardless of the daily prayers, exhortations and reasoning of the Chaplain, she appeared to take little interest in her spiritual progress, beyond an alleged polite expression of satisfaction with the religious consolation which she had been offered by the Reverend Richter. The sole glimmer of hope, it seems, was that Mrs Biggadike had only absented herself once from chapel, even though she had persisted in her declarations of innocence.

At this point, the well-informed reader might have suddenly realised the extent of his or her ignorance, having now been provided with the real inside story of the daily life of a condemned prisoner and her spiritual mentor. If what the *Lincolnshire Chronicle* reported was true, the hitherto deluded well-informed reader might well have felt a great debt of gratitude to the newspaper. Unfortunately, the narrative was only a very partial version of reality and had serious defects in its level of factual accuracy.

According to the entries in Henry Richter's *Prison Journal*, between the 25th October, the day of her being received into Lincoln Castle, and the 28th December, the day of her execution, Mrs Biggadike was absent from chapel nine times, mainly in the first half of November, either through serious illness or having to tend her infant. There is no mention by the Reverend Richter of Mrs Biggadike expressing any gratitude for his spiritual ministrations, only a peeved annoyance that whatever he said to her was consistently met with the same responses: she denied having done the deed, refuted having used the expressions about her husband attributed to her in court and persisted in the claim that Thomas Proctor was the guilty party. The lack of any celebration of spiritual progress in Henry Richter's *Journal* is also valuable evidence in disbelieving other post-execution fictions, most notably those reported in *Lloyd's Weekly Newspaper*, 3rd January, 1869, insisting that Mrs Biggadike read religious books provided by the Chaplain, wrote a letter expressing thanks for his 'attention and advice' and was in constant prayer from 4 o'clock on the morning of her death.

To be fair to the Reverend Richter, by his own account, he had done everything in his power to force a confession of guilt out of Mrs Biggadike. After her condemnation at the Assizes on the 12th December, he had visited her on most days, occasionally twice a day, to advise her on the parlous state of her soul; and he had delivered several services in the chapel which made specific references to her.

It is perhaps indicative of the desperation of the Chaplain that he wrote to the Reverend George Coltman, rector of St Luke's in Stickney, on the 17th December, 'requesting him to use his interest in her', which was probably shorthand for obtaining a confession. As well as an act of desperation, it was also one of naïve optimism: the Reverend Coltman may have inhabited the same Lincolnshire village as Mrs Biggadike, but their worlds could not have been more different. As well as being the parish priest of Stickney, the Reverend gentleman was also the perpetual curate of Hagnaby, where Lord Justice Thomas Coltman was lord of the manor, patron of the church and owner of the soil. He had also been a magistrate since 1845, sometimes sitting alongside the Reverend Rawnsley and Reverend Lister, at various Petty sessions. The most recent world of the Reverend George Coltman had been defined by fundraising lecture tours, talking about 'A visit to the Holy Land and Jerusalem, with some notices of Jaffa, Cairo and Alexandria', and by various pressing business matters connected with his post of Deputy-Provincial Grand Master of the Lincolnshire

Masonic Lodge. His no-nonsense approach to law and order, as well as to the office of magistrate, he had been happy to share with the world at the sale of the Hagnaby sheep flock, where he defined the true English spirit as one of respect for the 'constituted authorities of their country', and that if magistrates did hard things, it was because the law demanded they should.

The likelihood of the Reverend George Coltman MA taking a concerned interest in a woman found guilty by the constituted authorities of murdering her husband and who had attempted, in passing, to ruin the professional reputation of his friend, Dr Peter Maxwell, was non-existent.

The response of the Reverend Coltman, which Henry Richter read out to Mrs Biggadike, on Monday, 21st December, probably whilst she was lying prostrate in the prison infirmary, offered little comfort, to either the Chaplain or Mrs Biggadike. Seemingly shaped by the inflexibility of his role as a magistrate, rather than by the charity of a Church of England cleric, he dismissed his parishioner as a lost soul who had assisted in the murder and had attempted to conceal it: there was nothing more to say.

To a large extent, the Reverend Richter's record of his attempts to save the soul of Priscilla Biggadike, albeit without the slightest hint of any success, creates a picture of enormous personal and professional frustration. It was this deep sense of failure which was to impair his judgement and lead him into later difficulties, even more problematic perhaps than those which he had faced after the suicide of Mary Ann Milner.

Having established, at least to his own satisfaction, that Priscilla Biggadike's rejection of any spiritual advice had put her beyond the pale, the writer of the report in the *Lincolnshire Chronicle* was inspired to create a vision of irredeemable hard-necked criminality, constructed out of bits and pieces of simplistic theology and chapbook gothic. 'Never did she willingly glance into that dark and uncertain future which commences when the soul and body is severed', he informed the reader. Even worse: 'In her stolid ignorance, the mysterious future – that black unknown land which lies beyond the world – would seem to have had for her no terror'.

Flights of journalistic fancy, however, come in many different shapes and sizes. Having taken his readers through the dark landscapes of the soul, the reporter seemed to return to the more tangible factual reality of Lincoln gaol, claiming that shortly before her execution, Mrs Biggadike had written a letter to the employers of George Ironmonger, imploring him to seek forgiveness for his sins and to mourn her sad end. She also expressed the hope that he would not despise the children whom she would be leaving behind. Undeterred by the annoying inconvenience of the authorities who, 'for certain reasons', refused to publish the letter, the newspaper expanded the story. On Saturday, the 26th December, Ironmonger had presented himself at Lincoln Castle and had begged permission to visit the prisoner, but he had been refused entry.

It was a story which stretched credibility to breaking point. Mrs Biggadike was almost certainly barely literate and George Ironmonger, based upon his court appearances, created the impression that he was a reluctant participant in the whole unpleasant business, even claiming he wouldn't even recognise poison if he saw it. George Ironmonger seemed a man more interested in fishing than in the apparent sentimental delicacies of women.

Credibility, however, was hardly an issue for the *Stamford Mercury*, as it made its own contribution the extraordinary story. In an extended variant of the *Lincolnshire Chronicle's* narrative, the newspaper reported that George Ironmonger had applied for permission to visit Mrs Biggadike, but had been refused because she had 'expressed no desire to see him'. In addition to this surprising information, the employers of Ironmonger had supposedly replied to Mrs Biggadike's letter and she, in turn, had dictated a response, in which she said that she had made her peace with God, although without mentioning her crime.

In much of the *Lincolnshire Chronicle* report, there is a sense that the newspaper had managed to get hold of small pieces of information and had then modified them into a more convenient shape. This certainly seems to be the case with what followed on from the tall story of George Ironmonger turning up in Lincoln on Boxing Day. Mrs Biggadike did receive visitors that day, something which was formally recorded in the *Prison Journal* of the Governor, the Surgeon and the Chaplain. It was not surprising that the Reverend Richter took the visit as an opportunity to press Mrs Biggadike 'to make a full and truthful confession to them'. It seems that he made no progress, as he recorded yet another fruitless visit to obtain a confession later that evening in his *Journal*. The Surgeon briefly noted that Mrs Biggadike was 'much depressed' after the visit. The Governor did not record any reactions from the prisoner to the visit, although he did list the visitors as George Whiley, Susan Whiley, Rachel Taylor and Ann Reed, identifying them as her brother and sisters. The Surgeon merely identified the visitors as Mrs Biggadike's friends, whilst the Reverend Richter recorded them as being her friends and relations.

It would seem that the reporter had been briefed by the Governor on the facts of the matter, as the newspaper also referred to the visitors as her brother and sisters, and also mentioned in passing that they had stayed two and a half hours, as did the Governor's *Journal.*

It also seems likely that the newspaper had spoken to the Chaplain, as the description of the visit focused entirely upon the possibility of Mrs Biggadike being moved to confess her crime to the visitors. In human terms, the final goodbyes of a prisoner less than forty-eight hours before execution was a poignant situation which might reasonably have evoked sensitivity and compassion. Astonishingly, the reporter took a quite different direction, presenting the family visit as further evidence of Mrs Biggadike's selfish perversity. It had been a difficult meeting for the visitors as 'all the distress and agony of the interview seems to have been borne by them'. They had exhorted Mrs Biggadike to confess her guilt, 'of which they had little doubt'; but their earnest entreaties to make a declaration of her crime only had the effect of rousing her 'into passionate excitement.'

There was no further elaboration of the meeting, other than to mention that Mrs Biggadike's children had not been seen since her conviction.

What the newspaper did not seem to know, and it certainly was never mentioned in any other publication, was that after her visitors had left, Mrs Biggadike requested an interview with a Visiting Magistrate. She was visited by the Reverend George Frederick Apthorp(e), at 2.30 that afternoon: the

Governor's *Journal* notes the request, but does not record the outcome of the visit, other than by referring to the *Visiting Justice's Book*. Apthorp(e), however, did dutifully make a note of his visit: Mrs Biggadike had asked if anything could be done to spare her life, as she was innocent of the crime of poisoning her husband, but he had told her 'there was not the least chance of a reprieve and nothing could be done for her.'

It seemed a moment of crushed hope and blunt finality for Priscilla Biggadike.

The transformation of factual details culled from inside Lincoln Castle concerning Mrs Biggadike into convenient prejudicial fictions did not show provincial journalism in a good light: all kind feelings of a shared humanity seemed to be lost in a preference for transient sensationalism rather than the truth.

In one final extended anecdote, before moving on to the actual execution of Mrs Biggadike, the newspaper reported that 'it is believed that the miserable woman fully intended to commit suicide, but the opportunity never presented itself.' It was a dramatic claim, but one which had only a flimsy basis in fact. The Governor in his *Journal* noted that on Sunday, 20th December, Mrs Biggadike had attempted to conceal one of her father's handkerchiefs on going to bed. He had reported the incident to the Matron who gave her a caution, but nothing more was said, it seems; the Matron did not even think it worth recording in her *Journal*. To the well-informed reader, it might have recalled the dreadful suicide of Mary Ann Milner in her cell, and the newspaper was certainly quite explicit that the handkerchief, like a garter which had also been allegedly removed from Mrs Biggadike, had been confiscated to prevent her strangling herself.

The seriousness of the claim was perhaps undermined by the crass ludicrousness of the final section of the report which claimed that Mrs Biggadike had implored a female warder to swap clothes to give her an opportunity to escape. The anecdote read more like a rejected episode from *The Count of Monte Cristo* than the serious factual reporting of life and death in a Lincoln gaol.

It was clear from the outset that the account of the last hours of Mrs Biggadike's life, between the hours of 7 and 9 o'clock of Monday, 28th December, was going to concentrate upon the Prison Chaplain as much as upon the condemned prisoner. Up to the very last seconds, the unfolding drama was defined in terms of a struggle between the 'hardness of heart and determinate will of the unfortunate woman' and 'the intense pain with which Mr Richter heard this determination.'

The day began at 7 o'clock, with the visit of the Chaplain to Mrs Biggadike's cell, urging her 'to apply for mercy at that source which was alone open to her,' as she had no hope left in this world. Mrs Biggadike remained determined, however, to 'carry her terrible secret with her to the grave.' The entry in the Reverend Richter's *Journal* reflects the correctness of the newspaper account, albeit more prosaically, noting that he had tried to engage her in 'earnest prayer and exhortation to penitence and confession.' Her response was simply to deny having had anything to do with her husband's death. The only real difference from the newspaper account was one related to the time-frame: in Richter's account he spoke to her half an hour before her execution, rather than earlier that morning.

The departure of the Chaplain from the cell left Mrs Biggadike with the Matron and an assistant (possibly Hannah/Elizabeth Dowse, her allocated warder on entering Lincoln Prison) who 'as they have ever done since her conviction, endeavoured to instil greater and better feelings into her breast'. This apparent kindliness in such brutal circumstances was touching, but to some extent the accuracy of the report was limited due to the reporter not having been allowed to see what was happening in the condemned cell, even though he had turned up at 8.30, in the hope of at least witnessing the pinioning process. The truth of what was probably only optimistic speculation is also limited by the Matron's account of her dealings with Mrs Biggadike in her *Prison Journal*. The entries are brisk, business-like records of essential transactions, such as the distribution of gruel, tea when she was particularly ill and a glass of brandy before bedtime, on the instruction of the Surgeon. There is little or no sense of the prisoner as a human being which might have been expected, for example, on the day when her infant child was taken away from her. There are no entries in the *Journal* between Wednesday, 22nd and Monday, 28th, December. The only entry for the day of the hanging consists of a single word: 'Executed'. Whilst Mrs Dowse was not required to keep a daily journal, her supposed attentiveness to Mrs Biggadike's well-being was recorded only once, by the Prison Surgeon, to whom she had reported the prisoner's 'palpitations of the heart'.

The reporter's resigned comment that the attempt to instil 'greater and better feelings' into Mrs Biggadike 'was to no avail', may have been coded language for a failure to elicit the remorse and guilt necessary for a confession.

Because the reporter had not been able to watch Askern pinion Mrs Biggadike, he had to resort to the familiar useful journalistic formula of being informed, rather than witnessing first-hand: the prisoner had undergone the painful process 'with remarkable fortitude' and 'had quickly recovered from a slight faintness that momentarily overcame her'. Similarly, the reporter had also been informed that the Governor had asked Mrs Biggadike if she admitted to the justice of her sentence. According to his informant, the Governor could not hear her reply, but one of the warders had asserted that she had replied in the affirmative. To his credit, or preferring not to miss an opportunity to denigrate the character of Mrs Biggadike, the reporter expressed a considerable degree of scepticism.

The *Lincolnshire Chronicle* reporter seemed to enjoy building up the tension of his piece, as he announced a break in 'our sad narrative for one moment'. Quite simply, he wanted to remind the reader that Parliament had wisely decreed that all hangings were to take place in private to prevent 'the unseemly conduct of the spectators of exhibitions of this kind'. In a further slowing down of the narrative, which had the additional benefit of emphasising the privileged reliability of viewing the scene at close quarters, he went on to describe in precise detail the scaffold on which Priscilla Biggadike was to expiate her crime. It had been erected in a secluded part of the Castle grounds, at the South-East side of the Crown Court and against the Southern boundary wall of the Debtor's Yard. The platform was around 9 feet high and the distance from the prison door was about 160 yards. The exactness of the description probably confirmed to the reader that here was a man who knew what he was talking about and who could be trusted with a narrative.

The sad procession left the entrance of the East side of the prison at 8.45 precisely, in strict ritualistic order, including the three representatives of the press who, with one or two unnamed officials, brought up the rear.

Despite being behind Mrs Biggadike and two warders, the reporter seemed to have been able to get a clear view of her face, which was pallid, her features and expression firmly set; she was resolutely trying to overcome 'the terrors of her position', but was unable to suppress her piteous moans as she moved inexorably towards the scaffold.

If close proximity had validated the factual descriptions of time, height and distance provided by the reporter, it may have also authenticated his clumsy attempts to recreate the pathos of a life on the edge of non-existence.

The wan face of Mrs Biggadike contrasted painfully with her black serge dress and her white, muslin cap. The clear, bright December morning no longer held any charm for her; the beautiful Service for the Dead, spoken by the Chaplain, was now a thing of terror, either unheard or unheeded. What thoughts, he asked, were 'crowding into that poor distracted brain' during these last few moments of a life approaching its end?

The description of the procession, now half way to the place of execution, was resumed with the reporting of words supposedly spoken by Mrs Biggadike, frequently quoted and misquoted in modern accounts of her life and death. According to the report, she lifted her eyes towards the Head Warder at her side and said in a piteous tone, ' I hope my troubles are ended.' His response was a 'kind look of commiseration'. After a few steps more she asked, 'Have we much further to go?' To which she received the laconic reply, 'Not much further'.

Stripped of any emotive poetics, the unsensational ordinariness of the reported words spoken by Mrs Biggadike and the very human unease of the prison officer, struggling to respond, may well suggest the truth of them.

In this section of the report, despite its intended sympathy for a woman about to lose her life on the scaffold, the reader is never allowed to forget that she was a convicted murderer. This is nowhere more apparent than in the chilling description of reaching the platform. The place the procession had now reached was no longer the location of a temporary 9 foot wooden structure, 160 yards from the prison door, but 'the fatal spot where stern justice demanded its sacrifice'. The final word, with its disturbing associations with cruel pre-Christian rituals, was ill-judged. It was also unfortunate, in that it was immediately followed by a lengthy account of a representative of the established church, the Reverend Richter, delivering what can only be described as a hectoring diatribe on the subjects of Repentance, Confession and Sin. It was essentially an arrogant and insensitive continuation of the criminal trial of a convicted prisoner and of what she had been compelled to hear on a daily basis for more than two months in Lincoln gaol.

The entry in the Chaplain's *Journal* for the 28th December refers to his final failed attempt to extract a confession of guilt from Mrs Biggadike. He had 'solemnly put the question to her in the presence of the Deputy Sheriff, the Governor and others present: 'Do you deny the crime for which you are about to suffer?' The bland, business-like version reads more like a dishonest act of sanitisation than the keeping of a true record of what took place: for once, the press record of events captured reality, rather than inventing it. It was a reality which, in due course, would lead to expressions of outrage about the improper conduct of the Reverend Richter from abolitionists and also from within the religious establishment itself.

At the foot of the drop, Priscilla Biggadike was seated on a chair, whilst the Chaplain delivered his final admonitions: the provision of a chair might have been seen as an act of kindness, but the image had more sinister connotations for one later London commentator, who compared what took place to the Spanish Inquisition.

It was a remarkable comparison, even in the context of a polemic against the brutalities of capital punishment, but one which was difficult to ignore. The overweening persistence and length of the Reverend Richter's lecture to a woman only minutes away from being hanged, crossed the line between disappointed clerical duty and an uncomprehending outrage at her continued declarations of innocence. The emphasis upon himself as 'a Minister of Christ', who had the power to absolve Mrs Biggadike of all her sins and to assure her of the mercy of God, felt like the bitter exposition of a personal grievance, rather than a deeply felt sense of ministerial failure.

The *Lincolnshire Chronicle* reporter remained sympathetic to the frustrations of the Chaplain, however, who whilst imploring Mrs Biggadike to admit her guilt, 'appeared to suffer deep grief and trouble.' In response to his pleading, he had been met with the unwanted word 'yes' from the prisoner, when asked if she intended to persist in her claims to be innocent; and with only silence to his final 'earnest appeal' for her to admit the truth. Based on his observation of her manner, the reporter hinted to the reader that even so close to death, Mrs Biggadike entertained thoughts of a reprieve: it seemed a somewhat fanciful claim.

Once Mrs Biggadike had ascended the steps of the scaffold and was placed on the trap door, the final few harrowing moments of the life of Priscilla Biggadike were briskly reported. Askern bound her feet, put the cap over her face and fixed the rope round her neck. The two warders stood to one side and the executioner 'descended the platform to complete his terrible office', leaving Mrs Biggadike alone for a few seconds, before the bolt was drawn.

The sparseness of the account effectively created a sense of summary justice at work. However, the reporter could not resist feeding the taste of the Victorian reader for hearing the final words supposedly spoken by a criminal about to die. Standing alone on the trapdoor, 'any hope of mercy fled from her', the moaning of Mrs Biggadike became 'piteous in the extreme'. At the point of execution, she cried out 'in an agonising tone' that all her troubles were over; as if speaking to Askern, she also cried out, 'Shame that you're going to hang me'; and finally, on the stroke of 9 o'clock, she declared, 'Surely it's ended now.'

The dying words were moving and were recycled in many later accounts, some in significantly altered versions.

For melodramatic intensity, the report could not be faulted, but as a reliable account of Mrs Biggadike's last moments of life, it is perhaps questionable. She was without doubt in appalling distress and the last thing on her mind, if there was anything coherent left in her mind, would have been a clearly articulated accusation directed towards the executioner. The reference to her troubles being over, was a repetition of an earlier quotation, uttered at a point perhaps more likely to have produced the melancholic comment. Her final words, in their impeccable theatrical timing, as the clock was about to strike 9 o'clock and the funereal cathedral bell had just ceased to toll, were the stuff of sensationalist fiction.

The truth of the matter is further clouded by conflicting versions of what was said, and when, from the other local reporters. The report in the *Stamford Mercury*, Friday, 1st January, 1869, claimed that Mrs Biggadike had spoken her last words whilst Askern was binding her feet, in a series of continuous declarations: 'My troubles are nearly over; surely my troubles are ended; surely you won't hang me'. The third report, published in the *Grantham Journal*, on Saturday, 2nd January, repeated the words of the *Stamford Mercury*, but gave the outcry a more satisfactory shape and a greater emotional intensity, by using the words 'Oh surely' at the beginning of the first declaration and removing the word 'nearly'.

The sense of the mangled unreliability of newspaper reports, when they drew upon each other, is evident from the coverage of the supposed last words of Mrs Biggadike in the *Sleaford Gazette*, published on the same day as the *Grantham Journal*. According to this version of events, the words of Priscilla Biggadike had been spoken as the white cap had been drawn over her face by Askern. The reported words were obviously a recycling of other published accounts, but reshaped into a new version with a different impact: 'All my troubles are over. Shame! You're not going to hang me! Surely my troubles are over.'

A similar variety of perception was also evident in the various accounts of the appalling experience of Mrs Biggadike after she had dropped only a few inches. The *Lincolnshire Chronicle*, noting that Mrs Biggadike did not utter any cry to Heaven for mercy, told its readers that the body struggled for a few moments, followed by gurgling sounds which continued for about three minutes, and then there was 'profound silence'. The *Stamford Mercury's* account was more dramatic, mentioning that Mrs Biggadike gave a loud shriek, followed by four minutes of gurgling sounds, before life was 'quite extinct'. The *Grantham Journal*, drawing upon the short report in the *Lincoln Gazette*, spared the sensitivities of its readers, reporting only a 'slight shriek' and a 'slight gurgling in the throat' for a few seconds, before 'all was over.'

Choosing to rely more upon the report of the execution in *The Times*, published on Tuesday 29th December, the *Sleaford Gazette* gave a more generalised version, in which Mrs Biggadike appeared to suffer a great deal 'before her strong vital powers succumbed': but then again, like *The Times*, it also reported somewhat improbably, that she had shaken hands with the Chaplain and the Governor before mounting the scaffold platform.

Inquest on the Body of Priscilla Biggadike, 3 o'clock, 28th December, 1868

The final words of the *Lincolnshire Chronicle* report assured the reader that despite the death of Mrs Biggadike being protracted, she would not have suffered any pain as the spinal column would have been shattered by the first shock. It was perhaps a surprising detail to include, in that it preceded an account of the legal requirement, under the terms of the *Capital Punishment Amendment Act* of 1868, to hold a formal inquest on an executed prisoner's body, which the three press representatives attended as formal witnesses. On the other hand, what transpired during the course of the inquest in relation to the methods used by the executioner, indicate that there had been a sense of unease about what had been witnessed on the scaffold: the report in the *Grantham Journal* even suggesting that there had been considerable alarm amongst the witnesses, at the time, that a terrible blunder had been made by Askern.

Askern had tied the knot in a novel fashion, underneath the chin, so that death had not been instantaneous: it was a concern which also caused some disquiet amongst the inquest jury. It was also an issue which quickly fed into macabre rumours circulating in the city of blood-curdling shrieks and of a twenty minute death struggle by the prisoner.

The report on the inquest created a sense of the rigorous implementation of legal requirements: it was the first ever inquest after the private execution of a woman and, in a sense, the newspaper was reporting on its own part in a correct judicial process.

The inquest was held in the Debtor's Court and presided over by the County Coroner, Dr George Mitchinson, who opened proceedings with an insistent formal clarification of the business in hand. Essentially, it was the legal obligation of the inquest to establish whether or not the execution had been carried out 'with proper decency and humanity' and to prove that the person hanged that day 'was the same that was tried for the murder of her husband'. There was only a small number of people present at the execution 'and the public would therefore wish to know that it had been carried out in a proper manner.'

The precise and careful wording to the point of pedantry by Dr Mitchinson was indicative of the underlying uncertainties and anxieties surrounding the correct administration of private executions. The concept seemed a straightforward common-sense solution to prevent the degrading scenes which often accompanied public executions, as well as to curb the volume of sensational newspaper stories. However, issues relating to uniformity of implementation, the freedom of the press, the democratic right of the public to know and the relative powers and responsibilities of the High Sheriff and the Home Secretary to veto the presence of reporters, could be problematic and contentious issues.

More than ten years later, such difficulties were still arising, most memorably in a particularly prickly parliamentary debate in 1880, between the Home Secretary, Richard Assheton Cross, and John Bright MP, after the High Sherriff of Lancashire had refused press access to the execution of Patrick Kearns and Hugh Burns, in Kirkdale Prison, Liverpool.

Before any witnesses were heard, the jury viewed the body of Mrs Biggadike which was lying in a cell. The reporter's description was appropriately bland and matter of fact, although not particularly helpful: 'The face and hands were quite white, the features well set, and there appeared to be no distortion whatever'.

The first witness was James Foster, the Governor, who gave a brief summary of dates relevant to the incarceration of Mrs Biggadike in Lincoln Castle and confirmed that he had witnessed her execution. According to Mr Foster, there was 'no unnecessary roughness' and he thought that it had been carried out 'to the best of the ability of the executioner'. The

Stamford Mercury report gave a slightly different version of the Governor's words, but amounting to the same sense of restrained dissatisfaction: the execution had been carried out, 'as far as the person engaged was able to do it; but it might have been done more humanely'.

The assessment of the skill of Thomas Askern by the Governor, at best, seemed like damnation by faint praise; at worst, an evasion of a potentially difficult conversation.

Edward Farr Broadbent, the Prison Surgeon, testified that the prisoner had been in his care and that he had seen her every day. He had viewed the body and was able to confirm that it was the same person whom he had treated. Having witnessed the execution, he was confident that the prisoner had died from strangulation and in his opinion the execution was carried out with 'decency, humanity and an average amount of skill'. The bland assessment of Askern mirrored that of the Governor, but as a medical man he clearly thought it necessary to provide more detail about the methods of the hangman. The adjustment of the knot under the chin was something which he had not seen before and it inevitably meant that the deceased breathed for some minutes after the drop. In conversation, the executioner had agreed that the procedure meant that Mrs Biggadyke would remain breathing, but because the head was thrown backwards onto the spine, all sensation would have been destroyed.

Broadbent estimated that Mrs Biggadike had taken three and a half minutes to die and agreed that all sensation might have been destroyed: however, he seemed concerned that Askern's method did not prevent continued breathing.

The version of Broadbent's testimony published in the *Stamford Mercury* was in broad agreement with that reported in the *Lincolnshire Chronicle*, but with the additional uncomfortable comment, made in response to a question from a juryman, that the hanging of Mrs Biggadike was 'a horrid sight to see'.

It was a recollection which was reflected later that evening when the Surgeon noted in his *Prison Journal*: 'Witnessed execution. Her death was somewhat lingering'.

A concerned member of the jury also asked if the executioner was justified in the way he had adjusted the rope. The reply from Mitchinson, reported by the *Lincolnshire Chronicle*, answered the question, but did not fully confront the issue: he merely offered the comment that the officers would not have been justified in interfering 'as to the mode of carrying out the sentence'.

The identity of the body was also confirmed by Police Sergeant James Berry, who was stationed at

Stickney, and who had known Mrs Biggadike before she was committed.

Dr Mitchinson's final remarks before asking the Jury to retire and reach a verdict, merely reminded them that the inquest had been called according to an Act of Parliament: they were required to decide if the execution had been properly carried out and that the person executed was the right one. He did not think that they required any further evidence to decide upon the matter.

The jury unanimously agreed that due process had taken place, in accordance with the law.

All that remained was the signing and despatching of official documents to the proper authorities. This consisted of the death certificate issued by Edward Farr Broadbent, the declaration of the witnesses to the execution, including the three representatives of the press, and finally, the verdict of the inquisition record, signed by George Mitchinson and all members of the Jury.

The members of the jury were named as following:

- John Farrow (Foreman)
- Charles Ashlin Allison
- Thomas Butler
- John Cooling
- Thomas Fatchett
- John Gell

- William Hemstock
- Jarvis Perkins
- John Pettener
- Zachariah Priestley
- Charles Smith
- George Taylor

As part of the required transparency of private execution, the details of the paperwork related to the inquest were published in the *Stamford Mercury* on the 1st January, 1869.

The services of Thomas Askern were never required again in Lincoln, but he was probably happy with the £8/14/= which he received for his 'average amount of skill' in October, 1869; he was probably even happier that he had not been called in front of the inquest jury in order to explain his understanding of the complex relationship between proper decency, humanity and a woman dangling on a rope, still breathing, for nearly four minutes.

The melancholy story of the Stickney poisoner, after more than three months, had now terminated, according to the *Stamford Mercury*.

The body of Mrs Biggadike was buried at 1.15 in the Castle Keep, the day after the inquest, according to the *Prison Journal* of the Governor. All administrative procedures had been strictly observed, including the 'extra attendance of the convict Biggadike under sentence of death', at a cost of £2/2/6, as required following the procedural changes after the suicide of Mary Ann Milner.

Thomas Proctor, lodger, rat catcher and alleged paramour, seemed to disappear, although he was to return later in a fictional death-bed confession, leading to an equally fictional posthumous pardon for Mrs Biggadike. George Ironmonger, lodger, boatman and also alleged paramour, on the 11th April, 1870, married the widow, Mary Ann Clarke, a key witness for the Prosecution against Mrs Biggadike, leaving Stickney to live in Hundleby, near Spilsby, to work as an agricultural labourer. His grandmother, Jane Ironmonger, also an important contributor to the conviction of Priscilla Biggadike, remained in the village with her daughter Eliza, both paupers, but they acquired a new next door neighbour to observe at close quarters: the cramped house where Richard Biggadike had died was subsequently occupied by his brother James, an agricultural labourer, and his wife Rebecca, along with their three children.

However, despite official closure of the case, the return of Stickney village life to quiet normality and the confident assertion of finality by the *Stamford Mercury* reporter, the execution of Mrs Biggadike soon started to take on new meanings and go in surprising directions.

Aftermath

The *Stamford Mercury* of Friday, 8th January, 1869, published a letter to the editor, anonymously signed as 'Observer', titled 'The Recent Execution at Lincoln'. The opening sentence suggested that the writer of the letter was possibly an abolitionist, when he referred to 'feelings of commiseration in the breasts of many', in response to the execution of 'the unfortunate woman'. It quickly became clear, however, that the issue of the lengthy letter was not capital punishment, but rather, the deplorable living conditions of the Biggadike family, and by extension, the rural poor in general. What was not so clear was that the identity of the letter writer was John Paradise, the editor of the *Stamford Mercury*, who from time to time wrote letters to himself, signed 'Observer'.

The house on West Fen Road, Stickney, had been a constant element of the Biggadike story, not just as the crime scene, but also as an explanation for the crime having taken place: described variously in the Press as being a miserable hovel, the living conditions had been seen as an inevitable breeding ground for moral degeneracy. But the writer of the letter was more concerned with the social and economic realities of rural Lincolnshire than murder by poison or the concept of moral respectability.

Essentially, the letter was a call for the closer

supervision of lodger occupation, by legislation if necessary: what landlord, he asked, permitted lodgers to cohabit with a family in a two-roomed house? It very soon became clear that the landlord he had in mind was the unscrupulous farmer who, either as owner or tenant, hired men and their families and housed them in cottages, with the stipulation that they should take in one or two single men as lodgers, who in turn would be employed on the farm. The letter ended with an extended plea to landlords to invest the kind of money which they expended on their animals and farm buildings in better living conditions for the impoverished workers.

The issue of the Biggadike house had shifted from one of moral probity to the appropriate management of rural workers and buildings.

If 'Observer' was hoping for a response to his concerns about rural malpractices, he was not disappointed: within a week he had received a reply, published in the *Stamford Mercury* of Friday 15th January, from no less a person than Hardy Woolley of Moulton, near Spalding. Woolley was somewhat of a local celebrity, who during the course of his life was a Postmaster, Registration, Vaccination and Sanitary Officer for the Moulton District, as well as an occasional contributor to the *Lincolnshire Chronicle*.

Woolley acknowledged that the Biggadike case had 'awakened anxious feelings' and sympathised with the concerns of 'Observer' about a landlord permitting a family to accommodate two lodgers whilst living in a two room house. At this point, Woolley launched into full-blown lecture, kindly meant, which drew upon his detailed knowledge of recent legislation, in particular, the *Nuisances Removal Act*, which had empowered local authorities to deal robustly with 'any house, or part of a house, so overcrowded as to be dangerous or prejudicial to the inmates'. In Hardy Woolley's bold declarations on improving the lot of agricultural labourers – 'the most ignorant and helpless of the population' – 'Observer' had found a kindred spirit. His vision, despite having met with 'odium and ungracious opposition', was, and would continue to be, the banishing of poverty, along with all its associated pain and misery. It was heady rhetoric and there was still more to come, as the letter ended with biblical images of plague and pestilence, should nothing be done to improve the lot of 'our helpless poor'.

The relevance of both letters to the catastrophic events which had taken place in an overcrowded cottage in Stickney, leading to the death of two people and the miserable incarceration of three orphaned children in the workhouse, was all too evident.

The concerns expressed in the letters were deeply felt, informed by an awareness of the unacceptable human cost of rural poverty; at the same time, both were also rational and level-headed in their approach, despite the underlying reformist outrage. The same could not be said about a number of articles which appeared in various newspapers, also in response to having read about the execution of Mrs Biggadike: specifically, her treatment at the foot of the scaffold by the Reverend Henry Richter. All of them had a different agenda, but most of them were incensed at what had taken place. For the second time, Henry Richter found himself in the eye of a storm concerning a condemned female prisoner in Lincoln: in the case of Mrs Milner, it was a matter of what the Prison Chaplain had not done; in the case of Mrs Biggadike, it was more a matter of what he had done.

An early warning of what was to come was published in an anonymous letter to the editor of the *Morning Advertiser*, on Friday, 1st January, 1869, headed 'Ecclesiastical Matters'. On the face of it, the letter seemed to be light-hearted clerical banter, almost whimsical, poking fun at Archibald Tait, the Archbishop of Canterbury and the Oxford theologian, Dr Edward Pusey, over what they had said in public on various religious issues. The third cleric to be taken to task in the letter was the Reverend Richter concerning his remarks at the execution of Priscilla Biggadike: quoting the final few sentences of his speech to Mrs Biggadike, the writer of the letter claimed that the words of the Prison Chaplain had left him lost in puzzled conjecture and forced him to ask the question, 'which was the most powerful in the opinion of the Reverend H W R Richter at that moment, the Almighty or himself?'

The following day, the Chaplain found himself under fire from two provincial newspapers which did not pull their punches. Whilst the letter in the *Morning Advertiser* had focused upon the theological implications of the language used by Henry Richter to Mrs Biggadike, the reports in the *Staffordshire Sentinel and Commercial and General Advertiser* and the *Manchester Times* were more concerned about its inhumanity.

On the surface, the Staffordshire newspaper's contextualisation of what the Chaplain said to Mrs Biggadike did not point an accusatory finger, although its choice of words required little elaboration. The Reverend Richter had urged her to confess with 'well-meant, but extreme pertinacity', and when she had refused, he 'threatened' to withdraw the possibility of him absolving her.

The article politely declined to comment upon the concept of the forgiveness of sin by a priest, but insisted that the obtaining of a confession through the use of terror, in such circumstances – in any circumstances – was abhorrent: 'every consideration of propriety and humanity rises in protest.' The liberal roots of the newspaper certainly rose up in protest: the language used to a woman *in extremis*, who had consistently declared her innocence and was enduring 'moments of supreme agony', amounted to torture. Even in the event of her being guilty as convicted, 'it was deeply horrible'.

The accusation that the Prison Chaplain's fixation on obtaining a confession amounted to torture was to be taken up and expanded by other newspapers.

The *Manchester Times* approached the story from a different perspective, but arrived at the same conclusion. The opening of the article was a bleak one which lamented that 'once again in England a woman has been suspended from the gallows', finding it 'the most disgraceful event of the year which has just concluded'. The position of the newspaper was unambiguous: in line with public opinion on the matter, it thought the hanging of a woman 'repugnant' and felt that it had a 'deeper demoralising effect than the perpetration of murder itself'.

If the Chaplain had been reading the *Manchester Times* that day, he may well have felt uneasy at this point, having the previous week tacitly supported the justness of hanging a woman.

Having made plain its ideological position on the death penalty for women, the writer drew the reader's attention to an incident at a recent execution in Lincoln 'which deserves our reprobation'. The plain speaking continued with a reference to 'the conduct of the Prison Chaplain towards the wretched woman'. In his treatment of the prisoner, he had transgressed the boundaries of discretion in a way which was 'most indecorous'. More specifically, even though the woman had consistently protested her innocence, he should have been acting as a 'spiritual consoler', rather than getting involved in 'an unseemly wrangle with her' at the foot of the scaffold. Even though Mrs Biggadike was convicted on clear evidence, the Chaplain had made a serious mistake in trying the exhort an admission of guilt in the way that he did.

On Saturday, 2nd January, Henry Richter had faced the wrath of outraged media liberalism; on Sunday, 3rd January, he was confronted by potent radical populism. *Reynolds's Newspaper*, a London publication costing only one penny and enjoying increased circulation, had got hold of the story of the hanging of Mrs Biggadike; more to the point, it had got wind of the growing media unease about the Prison Chaplain's treatment of her at the scaffold.

The direct, spare headline of the article clearly intended to buttonhole the reader: 'Was she a murderess?' Any assumption, however, that the newspaper intended to conduct a considered and balanced case review was quickly dispelled. Priscilla Biggadike, the woman in question, who had been hanged at Lincoln Castle, was 'poor, ignorant, and had no friends to defend her with zeal and to supplicate for her the mercy of the Crown'. She had been executed purely on circumstantial evidence, plus a dubious miscellany of 'little facts said to be inconsistent with innocence, and consistent with guilt'.

Once the emotive groundwork had been prepared, the article provided a factual overview of the troubled life of Mrs Biggadike, taken from evidence heard at the trial and reported at great length in the media. The writer provided its readers with sufficient particulars to construct a coherent narrative framework and so enable them to understand more clearly what was to follow. Inevitably, the plain facts also included salacious details of the domestic arrangements which had allegedly given rise to jealousy and which had created a house where 'misery reigned'.

The writer completed this section of the article by alerting the readers to the crucial fact that Mrs Biggadike had refused to confess her guilt in prison to the Chaplain.

With an air of quiet confidentially, the article then announced an imminent denouement. 'We come to the last scene of all – to the scene of the last hour, when the Chaplain came to play his part'.

However, before unmasking the villain and his unspeakable deeds, the writer chose to ramp up the tension even further. In a convenient chronological rearrangement, he described the prisoner having been pinioned and then fainting; even though she recovered, she 'heard little of the service of the dead, being recited over a living being'. In a variant of the words reported in the Lincolnshire newspapers, but removed from the specific context in which they were uttered, Mrs Biggadike had hoped that her 'troubles were now all over', and further, 'she asked plaintively, shall we be much longer?'

Maintaining the theatrical imagery, the article described Mrs Biggadike reaching the drop as being 'detained on the threshold of death in order that a little melodramatic scene might be enacted'. Further, it was a scene 'which we believe is without parallel, and which we hope will never be matched'.

The media noose was now tightening round the neck of Henry Richter.

As a prelude to revealing the dreadful details of the conversation which had taken place in the shadow of the scaffold, the outraged writer demanded to know why a convicted prisoner should be 'teased and tortured to confess' at the point of death. It was an address, according to the newspaper, which could and should have been stopped by the Prison Governor and the Under-Sherriff, had they applied 'more firmness and humanity'.

What followed was a word for word pastiche of the Reverend Richter's address to Priscilla Biggadike, taken mainly from the *Lincolnshire Chronicle*, interspersed with a barbed commentary on it. The comments were unambiguous in their sickened exegesis. The Chaplain had demanded a confession to the sin of murder, 'the very sin which the poor tortured and pinioned convict had just solemnly and firmly denied she had been privy to, in thought, word and deed'. The Chaplain, 'as a Minister of Christ' had promised Mrs Biggadike forgiveness of her sins if she confessed, a declaration which was not only 'very cruel', but represented little more than priestly arrogance in its assumption of the power to grant an absolute pardon.

The 'poor woman' persisted in saying that she had nothing to do with the death of her husband, but 'still the Chaplain would not let her go to her death'. Instead, he pressed her with 'a little more torture', by reminding Mrs Biggadike of her children, her friends and her relatives, who might be consoled if she confessed.

Unable to obtain a confession, the Chaplain duly washed his hands of her, but not before reminding Priscilla Biggadike that if she had made a declaration of her sins, he would have absolved her, something which he was 'entitled to do'. The expression of entitlement, interestingly, is highlighted in the text by way of italicisation. It was clearly a difficult point in the reporting and reception of this part of the story in the media, in that the version published in the *Lincolnshire Chronicle* and the *Stamford Mercury*, had Henry Richter allegedly saying, 'authorised to do', whilst other newspapers published on the 1st and 2nd of January, had reported the more assertive 'entitled to do'. Some newspapers like the *Grantham Journal*, perhaps anticipating possible future difficulties, cautiously omitted the Chaplain's claim altogether.

The construction of the Lincoln Prison Chaplain's identity as a representative of clerical hubris seemed to subside temporarily when the article switched attention to Mrs Biggadike standing face to face with Thomas Askern, her executioner. There was no description of the execution, but rather an astonishing claim that the hangman was 'the most humane person present'. Rather than a serious character endorsement, it was in all probability an indirect continuation of the depiction of Henry Richter, by way of the most grimly ironic contrast.

Irony soon turned to speculative excoriation, as the writer imagined Mrs Biggadike turning on the Chaplain to ask him 'if he felt entitled, as a gentleman and a Christian, to assume her guilt as a certainty', when twelve sworn men had wavered in their judgement when recommending mercy.

At this point, the writer shifted to the broader issue represented by the Biggadike case, with which he had opened the article. The justice system only served the rich and powerful in society, not such 'poor, ignorant, perhaps immoral' women as Mrs Biggadike, who 'had no friends to plead on her behalf'. It was not to such as she that the Home Secretary would extend mercy.

Had she been the wife of a gentleman , or a member of the ruling class, the writer claimed, scientific evidence would have been produced to prove insanity at the time of the deed. To make the point, he reminded the reader of the recent case of the middle-class murderer, George Victor Townley, who was reprieved by the Home Office, on grounds of his mental health, and the less well-off bricklayer, Samuel Wright, who had been hanged for a similar crime of passion. The conclusion was clear: 'There is one law: there are two modes of administering it – one for the rich and one for the poor.'

If he had been reading the article, Henry Richter may well have been thinking that the worse was now over and that the polemical rhetoric of *Reynolds's Newspaper* would continue along a broad political path.

Unfortunately for the Prison Chaplain, the pause in the merciless personal criticism was short lived. In an ambiguous tone, located somewhere between mock resignation and tongue-in-cheek consolation, the writer expressed relief that at least there was a law which, 'may protect poor criminals from impertinence and the vanity of priests claiming the power of remission of sins'.

The article ended in a surprising fashion, in that it unexpectedly turned its attention very briefly to the 'barbarism' of overcrowding permitted by Lincolnshire farmers and landlords, in terms which anticipated the two letters on the issue later published in the *Stamford Mercury*. The reporter did not explore the relationship between rural poverty and crime, but merely used the uncomfortable social reality to suggest that if Mrs Biggadike was guilty, she was not the only one. 'Let him that is without sin in this matter of overcrowding cast the first stone', the writer raged – but only after the Chaplain.

Oddly, despite the Reverend Richter being savagely mauled by the *Reynolds's Newspaper,* he was never once mentioned by name.

The article directly underneath the story of Priscilla Biggadike was an equally scathing attack upon the lamentable 'annual feeding of pauperism' on Christmas Day in the workhouse by 'the pompous purse-proud millionaire'. It may just have been a sad and curious coincidence, but the day before, the *Lincolnshire Chronicle* had published a self-satisfied report on the Christmas Day dinner at the Lincoln Union workhouse, describing it as 'a feast so acceptable and rare'. Even the babies were not forgotten, it proudly informed its readers, 'and amongst them the poor child of Priscilla Biggadike was decorated with a pretty bunch of trinkets'. The infant in question was Rachel Biggadike who was taken from her mother whilst in Lincoln Prison: little Rachel died in the Spilsby Union workhouse, aged two years nine months.

The week had ended badly for Henry Richter and matters did not improve at the beginning of the next, with the publication in the *Uxbridge and West Drayton Gazetteer* of a two page feature article on the implications of the execution of Mrs Biggadike.

The story of the crime and its prosecution, ending in the execution of Mrs Biggadike, was familiar territory, in which the newspaper, despite its apparent repugnance at the hanging of women, had little sympathy for her. The evidence against her was clear and, despite her being a woman, there had been no attempt to seek mitigation. She had been in spiritual conference with the Chaplain, but had refused to admit her culpability, despite his 'assiduous attention'.

The outlook was promising for the Reverend Richter at this point, but the pausing of the narrative at the provision of a chair for Mrs Biggadike at the foot of the gallows, followed by the publication of the full text of his by now controversial address to her, including his unfortunate reference to entitlement, was less than good news. The censure of the *Staffordshire Sentinel and Commercial and General Advertiser* and the *Manchester Times* had been argued on the basis of indiscretion and an ill-judged and over-zealous desire to obtain a confession: the polemical fury of the *Reynolds's Newspaper* had been fired up by concepts of social justice; but the article in the *Uxbridge and West Drayton Gazetteer* went in a quite different direction.

The battleground was more precise and closer to home: what the Reverend Richter had said, in terms of Christian teaching, was just plain wrong. It was a problem exacerbated by the fact that the Chaplain's speech, as part of the 'dismal tragedy', had, or would be, read by millions. The extended description of Priscilla Biggadike as 'the hardened woman' who had rejected all his best endeavours and who had 'persisted in a lie in the very face of the gallows' was probably intended to soften the challenge, as was the reassurance that the newspaper was not denying 'the dogma of the power of the priestly absolution'. However, the writer was absolutely clear that what the Chaplain had said contradicted the doctrines of the Church of England and ultimately, the Bible. In the view of the newspaper, the idea that a priest could absolve all sin on the basis of a verbal confession 'extorted in the last minutes of life', lacked Scriptural authority and could only encourage 'a most dangerous delusion'. In addition, the Chaplain was taken to task for suggesting to Mrs Biggadike that God's forgiveness of her crime was assured, which the newspaper thought to be 'an encouragement to sin that grace may abound.'

It was unlikely that Mrs Biggadike had ever had the time, inclination or opportunity to read John Bunyan.

The story of Priscilla Biggadike seemed to have had a grotesque fascination for the newspaper, as immediately below the censuring of the Prison

Chaplain, appeared an equally strident article on the living conditions of the Biggadike family. Unlike the two letters published in the *Stamford Mercury*, or the diatribe unleashed in the *Reynolds's Newspaper*, there was no sense of sympathy for the misfortunes of others, only blame and contempt: the disgusting truth was that the taking in of two lodgers had been prompted by a 'fatal greed' and 'contempt for the decencies of civilised life'. There were questions to be answered by landlords and agents, but the point was feebly made and read more like a rhetorical preparation for its grandiose axiomatic declaration: 'It is impossible for human beings to live as Christians if they are housed as hogs'.

The lack of a credible understanding of rural deprivation and its relationship to crime was confirmed by the suggestion that if only they had not taken in lodgers, Mr and Mrs Biggadike 'might now have been spending a pleasant Christmas-time in the little home of their united family'.

The writer clearly had had the time, inclination and opportunity to read Dickens.

The extensive article, taken from the *London Review*, and published by the *Richmond and Ripon Chronicle*, on Saturday, 9th January, 1867, would probably have made the most uncomfortable reading of all for the Prison Chaplain. Its sensational and lurid headline, 'The Torture of Criminals', set the tone and defined a good deal of the content, most of it connected with the execution of Mrs Biggadike. It was not the first newspaper article to use the word 'torture' to describe her treatment, but that was said in passing, rather than made the central premise of an article.

It opened with a broadside on the execution of felons, both in public and in private, as barbaric, on the one hand, and deeply flawed on the other. The removal of execution from the public domain was apparently applauded as a step forward in the progress of civilisation: but with a sense of mocking irony lurking beneath the surface, the writer also wished to celebrate the fact that public strangulation was no longer used to amuse a rabble of thieves and ruffians, and that a man made in God's image would no longer be 'killed before their eyes with brute force brutality'. Public opinion had pronounced that such a spectacle did not have the efficacy of being a deterrent and had replaced it with 'the greater mystery, solemnity and consequent terror to evil-doers of the private execution'.

The gentle, covert irony then turned into scathing scepticism about the good intentions of private executions: 'What has become of the promised mystery and privacy?' it asked, when half a dozen correspondents of the Press are present at the execution and produce half a dozen different accounts of the last moments of the condemned. The sometimes divergent accounts of the Biggadike story in the *Lincolnshire Chronicle*, *Stamford Mercury*, *Lincoln Gazette* and *Grantham Journal*, perhaps proved the point. Controlled irony then gave way to unvarnished sarcasm, as the article ridiculed the trivialisation found in reports which provided information about what the prisoner had eaten for breakfast, how they had passed the night, what they said to the chaplain and what was said to him, how he walked to the drop and whether he was firm or had to be supported. Every particular that 'a diseased curiosity can wish for' was supplied for a penny, the reporter observed, with undisguised distaste.

The onslaught suddenly subsided, however, with a moment of calm reflection, when the writer conceded that there were sometimes cases of private execution which required a full report, rather than the Press simply announcing that the execution had been carried out. One such exceptional case was that of Priscilla Biggadike at Lincoln, on the previous Monday.

For the benefit of the reader unfamiliar with the story, the writer gave an overview of the crime followed by information about the judicial process of trial and conviction. The facts of the case had been taken from the *Lincolnshire Chronicle*, but also included various asides, which hinted at a degree of sympathy for Mrs Biggadike.

Priscilla Biggadike had 'lived the life of a dog' in an overcrowded two-roomed house: the comparison seemed a shockingly blunt one, but was intended to establish that 'unlike the most sagacious retriever', human beings have a capacity for suffering. The writer also wished to establish, but without underestimating the foulness of the crime, that the 'shadow of uneasiness upon the minds of the jury' raised 'the bare possibility of the woman's innocence'.

The procession to the scaffold was treated cursorily, although pausing at the brief conversation between Mrs Biggadike and the warder, at which point, the writer was moved to exclaim, 'Poor wretch! So much worse or better than a dog by her capacity to suffer death in every moment's anticipation! Her troubles were not yet to end'.

It might have been expected that this ominous note was about to take the reader to the final scene with the hangman. Instead, the reader was taken to the foot of the scaffold, at the moment in which the Prison Chaplain finished his reading of the Burial Service, and began his final attempt to get Mrs Biggadike to admit that she was guilty. Her refusal was followed, according to the article 'by a refinement of cruelty almost incredible'.

Should the Reverend Richter had been reading the article, the alarm bells would probably have started to ring – very loudly. So far, he had scarcely been mentioned in the narrative, other than in terms of carrying out formalities, and that Mrs Biggadike appeared to take no notice of his reading of the Burial Service. He was now not so much in a bright spotlight, as under a relentless searchlight.

The article drew attention to the fact that a chair had been placed at the foot of the scaffold for Mrs Biggadike, followed by an almost verbatim transcription of the Reverend Richter's speech to her, as found in the *Lincolnshire Chronicle*.

At this point, an apologist for the Prison Chaplain might well have suggested, like some of the earlier newspaper reports, that he was doing a difficult job in an unenviably extreme situation, and that his worthy intention had been, in the final analysis, to save the soul of Priscilla Biggadike from eternal damnation. The article, however, headed off any such apology with a set-piece of powerful emotive rhetoric which left the reader in no doubt about the horrors which Mrs Biggadike had endured and which the Prison Chaplain did little to alleviate: it was the stuff of abolitionist dreams, or nightmares.

The reader was not so much invited as compelled to empathise with 'the wretched woman' who had for weeks on end faced the prospect of death in her prison cell, comforted only by a chaplain 'bent on obtaining a confession'. Meanwhile, hour on hour passed by 'with inflexible regularity', in the full knowledge that she was moving towards 'deliberate, cold-blooded strangulation'.

'Trussed like a fowl', she had been marched to the foot of the scaffold, 'to the tune of the burial service', where seated, she was lectured in the hope that the sight of the rope, 'and the whole vile apparatus', might induce a confession.

There was no confession, and so she was hanged, 'unaneled and unshriven'.

For a moment, it seemed that the article had managed to find some sympathy for the Prison Chaplain after its tirade, when it accepted that he only did what he had felt to be 'a most painful duty'. The sympathy lasted no longer than a full stop: the article sardonically added that this had also been the case of 'the Inquisition of old', and that, 'in the meantime, civilisation had advanced somewhat'.

If there was any doubt about the position of the writer of the article concerning capital punishment, it would have been resolved by what followed. Whilst finding it difficult not to slip into further ironic cynicism, the writer considered the commonplace justifications of capital punishment and found them wanting, although he did concede that the argument either way required more data.

It seemed a welcome respite for the Reverend Richter, but worse was about to come, as the article shifted away from abstract rational discourse on the subject of capital punishment to a merciless verbal assault on the professional competence of a Prison Chaplain. Prefaced by the hope that 'such an ingenuity of torture as that of Priscilla Biggadike' would never arise again, the writer launched his attack with a volley of searching questions concerning the judgment and behaviour of Henry Richter. Had he been motivated by inner doubts about Mrs Biggadike's guilt and therefore chose to obtain a confession to absolve himself from sending an innocent woman to the gallows? Or was it more a matter of the pressure of such doubts driving him beyond all common sense and humanity? Or was it an extraordinary example of being motivated by 'a narrow and repulsive theology, measuring the mercy of God by that of man?'

Whatever the explanation, the judgment of the Prison Chaplain was so much at fault that 'he must never again undertake a duty so painful and so likely to unnerve him as that of ministering to a condemned criminal'.

In an age of deference to the clergy and the hearty toasting of their good health with mighty hurrahs, it was perhaps a public toasting which the Reverend Richter would rather not have had to experience.

After being lambasted by the *London Review* for acts reminiscent of the Spanish Inquisition and on the day before being accused of 'priestly arrogance' by the rabidly anti-Catholic *Christian Times*, in addition to the earlier scorn and mockery of his incompetence by other newspapers, the besieged Lincoln chaplain might have been considering his position.

It was probably to his relief, therefore, that on the 12th January, the *Glasgow Herald* published an article titled 'Prison Chaplains and the Condemned Cell', which gave a balanced and more sympathetic analysis of the 'difficult and delicate' work required of such men as the Reverend Richter.

It was a measured and scholarly article which reflected on the various criticisms of the Lincoln Chaplain, analysing technical aspects of Confession and the pressing question of the correct way for a cleric to deal with 'obstinate murderers condemned to death'. On the whole, in its consideration of the criticisms of the Reverend Henry Richter by the popular press, with which it was clearly familiar, there was a sense of the writer trying to smooth over uncomfortable difficulties with a quiet reasonableness.

The mask of dispassionate, courteous exploration slipped only once, when the journalist gently mocked 'sensation readers' whom the Reverend Richter might have pleased had he acted differently at the foot of the scaffold, and in so doing, 'wafted the Lincolnshire Clytemnestra to an immediate heaven on the wings of an ecstatic congratulation'.

It was probably the first and last occasion that Aeschylus and Stickney rubbed shoulders in a single sentence, unless, of course, the improbable connection was made by Paul Verlaine in one of his lessons at the William Lovell school a few years later.

In the final analysis, the extreme situation in which, according to the article, the Reverend Richter had found himself did not seem to have been supported by specific training to manage it, leaving the cleric to make a judgement call, caught between his private feelings on the one hand, and his sense of professional obligation, on the other. That was an issue, 'a not unforeseen emergency', which ought in future be addressed by a Prison Chaplain's ecclesiastical superiors, the writer concluded.

This level-headed, pragmatic solution brought to an end the turbulent public difficulties of the Reverend Henry Richter, which had arisen out of his professional vexations with Priscilla Biggadike.

Ironically, the death of the Lincoln Chaplain, aged eighty-four, on the 18th March, 1879, was marked by the tolling of Big Tom, the Lincoln Cathedral bell which had also announced to the city that Priscilla Biggadike, aged thirty-five, was about to die on the scaffold, on the 28th December, 1868.

The Reverend Richter was respectfully buried in the churchyard of St Paul in the Bail, Lincoln; Mrs Biggadike was deposited in the Prisoner's Graveyard, Lincoln Castle, near to Mary Ann Milner and Eliza Joyce.

Appendix One

The Deathbed Confession of Thomas Proctor

In most accounts of the Priscilla Biggadike story, there is a general acceptance that Thomas Proctor was the real culprit, having confessed to the poisoning of Richard Biggadike whilst on his deathbed. Consequently, Mrs Biggadike was absolved and given a posthumous pardon. It also gave the dismal story an added dimension in that if what Proctor had allegedly said was true, then there had been an appalling miscarriage of justice, which made Mrs Biggadike's desperate claim to be innocent, even as she mounted the scaffold, all the more painful.

Finding incontrovertible evidence to substantiate this dramatic story, however, is rather problematic.

According to one recent internet account, the story of the deathbed confession of Thomas Proctor was reported by the *Daily Telegraph*, in 1882, the supposed year of his death. Unfortunately, no such report exists in the newspaper and should the story have existed, it would almost certainly have been picked up by other newspapers, both in and outside Lincolnshire. Similarly, there is no record of Mrs Biggadike having been pardoned, which is hardly surprising, as there does not appear to have been any confession by Thomas Proctor to exonerate her.

A possible clarification of the existence of a supposed confession is to be found, not in a newspaper or government archive, but in a book first published in 1888, written by William Tallack, bearing the rather ponderous title: *Penological and Preventative Principles: with special reference to Europe and America, and to crime, pauperism, and their prevention; prisons and their substitutes; habitual offenders; conditional liberation; sentences; capital punishment; intemperance; prostitution; neglected youth; education; police.*

Tallack was a distinguished and energetic penal reformer who between 1863 and 1866 was the Secretary of the Society for the Abolition of Capital Punishment, and later, the Secretary of the Howard

Association, an organisation from its inception, also dedicated to the abolition of the death penalty.

That Tallack was familiar with the story of Mrs Biggadike is no great surprise, given the letter written just before her execution, by his colleague Thomas Beggs, the Honorary Secretary of the Society for the Abolition of Capital Punishment, who drew public attention to the case in terms of the close relationship between poverty and crime.

Further, two weeks later, Tallack himself wrote a letter to the Press, in which he too expressed a great deal of anguish about the fate of Mrs Biggadike, not so much as a victim of poverty, although that was mentioned, but rather as 'another horrible illustration of the evils of capital punishment'. Published in the *Morning Advertiser* of Wednesday, 6th January, 1869, the letter was explicitly timed to add weight to the work of the Quaker MP, Charles Gilpin, to force a debate in the House of Commons on capital punishment. It was also clear that he saw the circumstances of Mrs Biggadike's execution as an opportunity to highlight just what could go wrong, and did. His evocation of the hanging of Priscilla Biggadike recycled details of what he had read in the newspapers, with some silent adjustments to support his rhetorical intentions. Using a clichéd expression found in many of the press reports published on the 2nd January, she had 'died hard' after her struggle with the executioner, meaning she was 'a miserable, ignorant woman, who had lived in circumstances of utmost poverty and degradation', who was put to death on purely circumstantial evidence. Interestingly, a significant part of Mrs Biggadike's fearful final struggle at the scaffold, according to Tallack, involved 'importunate worryings (by the Chaplain) to confess'.

In his war of words with 'the intelligent Christian state' on the issue of capital punishment, Tallack ended with the predictable reminder to the reader, that the accused woman might well have been innocent. The idea of a miscarriage of justice was clearly part of William Tallack's thinking when considering the story of Priscilla Biggadike, rather more than it had been in that of Thomas Beggs, who seemed to reluctantly accept that Mrs Biggadike was guilty.

There is no reference made to Priscilla Biggadike in the first edition of Tallack's book; but in the second, enlarged edition of 1896, in the context of the dangers of executing an innocent person, he refers to a confession made by a dying man in Stickney:

Some years afterwards, a man in the village where Mrs Biggadyke (sic) had lived, became ill, and on being informed that recovery was hopeless, he manifested great anxiety, and said, 'I cannot die until I have made a full confession of my guilt. It was I who poisoned poor Biggadyke (sic). His wife,

*who was hanged for it, knew nothing of it. I went
into the house, while she was mixing a cake, and put
arsenic into a bowl when she was not looking.'*

Tallack's only comment was that 'some years later it
was proved that she had been unjustly sacrificed'.

The anecdote of the death-bed confession,
supporting his stance against capital punishment, is
presented as fact by the writer. But there is a good deal
of doubt about its authenticity. The dying man had
no name and there is no supporting detail relating
to a possible motive which might have explained the
crime. On a more mundane and practical level, the
concept of a man invisibly moving around a cramped
house whilst Mrs Biggadike was doing the cooking
is risible. It has no more credibility than either of
the two deathbed confessions, reported in 1892,
relating to the execution of Mary Lefley for allegedly
poisoning her husband in Wrangle.

However, the idea of a deathbed confession was
now sewn into the fabric of the Biggadike narrative,
alongside the related idea of it being proved that
Priscilla Biggadike had been wrongly executed.
Whilst there is no mention of Thomas Proctor
in Tallack's anecdote, a shift of perception in the
popular imagination from 'a man in the village' to
the man whom Mrs Biggadike insisted was the real
culprit, would not be surprising, especially when

the information was located in such a respected source.

The story of the improbable deathbed confession, which absolved Mrs Biggadike from the crime of murder, was repeated in 1927, by Eric Roy Calvert, Secretary of the National Committee for the Abolition of the Death Penalty, who explicitly acknowledged Tallack's book as the source of the story. In Calvert's slightly modified and more plausible version, the narrative was shortened and generalised into that of a man who confessed on his deathbed that he had entered the kitchen and put poison in a pudding which Mrs Biggadike was making.

Capital Punishment in the Twentieth-Century was written as a polemic presenting the case against capital punishment and the story of Priscilla Biggadike, 'dragged to the scaffold and executed, protesting her innocence' was a convenient illustration of a miscarriage of justice. In addition to repeating the story of the deathbed confession, Calvert also asserted, but once again citing Tallack as the source, that the innocence of Priscilla Biggadike was 'established after her execution'.

The transmission of the abolitionist myth of Priscilla Biggadike was continued by Violet van der Elst, the eccentric tireless campaigner against capital punishment and one time owner of Harlaxton Manor, near Grantham. In her book, *On the Gallows*, published in 1937, which essentially recycled the words of Eric Roy Calvert, she also was similarly clear that Mrs Biggadike had been 'dragged to the scaffold', but also similarly vague in her assertion that her 'innocence was established after she was executed'.

Reading Mrs van der Elst's version of the Biggadike story, it is indisputable that she drew upon Calvert's book, rather than the earlier account found in Tallack. She uses the same melodramatic description of Priscilla Biggadike's rough handling at the scaffold, employs the word 'pudding' instead of 'cake' in the account of the mystery poisoner and locates the action specifically in the kitchen, rather than in the home. Moreover, she repeats the same date error found in Calvert, that Mrs Biggadike was executed in 1869.

The discovery of hard evidence for a confession by Thomas Proctor would be a valuable contribution to an understanding the Biggadike case, but for the time being, it remains, and probably will always remain, yet another rigmarole story amongst many.

Appendix Two

Key Players in the Priscilla Biggadike Story

ALLENBY, Henry Hynman. Member of Grand Jury at trial of Priscilla Biggadike at the Lincoln Assizes.

ALLISON, Charles Ashlin. Juror at Priscilla Biggadike inquest, Lincoln Castle.

ANDERSON, Sir Charles H J. Foreman of Grand Jury at trial of Priscilla Biggadike at the Lincoln Assizes. Resident of Lea Hall, near Gainsborough.

APTHORP(E), Reverend George Frederick, magistrate and incumbent of Thorpe on the Hill. Interviewed Priscilla Biggadike at her own request, in Lincoln Prison, as a Visiting Magistrate, on 26th

December, 1868.

ASKERN, Thomas. Public executioner. Hanged Priscilla Biggadike at Lincoln Castle, 28th December, 1868. Resident of York.

AVERY, Joseph. Juror at trial of Priscilla Biggadike, at the Lincoln Assizes. Resident of Crowland.

BERRY, Sergeant James. Stickney policeman. Confirmed identity of the dead body, at the Priscilla Biggadike inquest, Lincoln Castle.

BICKNELL, Captain Philip. Chief Constable of Lincolnshire, present at Magistrates' Court in Stickney.

BIGGADIKE, Alice. Daughter of Priscilla Biggadike. Born c.1860. Pauper inmate of Spilsby Union Workhouse in 1871.

BIGGADIKE, Emma. Daughter of Priscilla Biggadike. Born c.1864. Pauper inmate of Spilsby Union Workhouse in 1871. Died 1874, aged ten, buried in Stickney.

BIGGADIKE, Frederick. Son of Priscilla Biggadike. Born c.1856.

BIGGADIKE, James. Agricultural Labourer. Brother of Richard Biggadike. Resident of Stickney.

BIGGADIKE, Priscilla. Baptised 13th January, 1833, daughter of George and Susannah Whiley. Resident of Broadgate, Gedney. Married Richard Biggadike in 1853 at Kirton End. Resident of Church End, Gedney (1861) and then West Fen

Road, Stickney.

BIGGADIKE, Rachel. Daughter of Priscilla Biggadike. Born 1868. Pauper inmate of Lincoln Union Workhouse, November-December 1868. Died pauper inmate of Spilsby Union Workhouse, aged two years and nine months, 1871.

BIGGADIKE, Richard. Born c.1831, Kirton, son of William Biggadike.

BRISTOWE, Samuel Botelier. Counsel for the Prosecution at the trial of Priscilla Biggadike at the Lincoln Assizes.

BROADBENT, Edward Farr. Surgeon. Attended Priscilla Biggadike in prison and witnessed her execution in Lincoln Castle.

BROMHEAD, John. Member of Grand Jury at trial of Priscilla Biggadike at the Lincoln Assizes. Resident of Lincoln.

BROOKS, James. Reporter for the *Lincoln Gazette* and *Lincolnshire Times*. Invited Press witness at the execution of Priscilla Biggadike in Lincoln Castle.

BROWN, George. Correspondent for the *Stamford Mercury*; news and advertising agent. Invited Press witness at execution of Priscilla Biggadike in Lincoln Castle.

BROWNLOW, John. Juror at trial of Priscilla Biggadike, Lincoln Castle. Resident of Martin.

BURTON, T. F. Deputy Sheriff of Lincolnshire. Signatory to witness document at the Priscilla

Biggadike inquest, Lincoln Castle.

BUTLER, Thomas. Juror at Priscilla Biggadike inquest, Lincoln Castle.

BYLES, Lord Justice John Barnard. Sentenced Priscilla Biggadike to death, at the Lincoln Assizes. Resident of Hatfield House, Uxbridge.

CLARKE, Mary Ann. Widow, gave evidence at inquest into death of Richard Biggadike and at the trial of Priscilla Biggadike at the Lincoln Assizes. Resident of Turn Pike Road, Stickney.

CLEGG, Dr Walter. District Coroner, presided over inquest into the death of Richard Biggadike. Gave evidence at trial of Priscilla Biggadike, at the Lincoln Assizes. Resident of Boston.

COLLISON _____. Clerk of Arraigns at the trial of Prisicilla Biggadike at the Lincoln Assizes.

COLTMAN, Reverend George. Magistrate and Rector of St Luke's Parish Church, Stickney. Incumbent of Hagnaby.

CONYERS, Mildred. Gave evidence at the Magistrates' Court in Stickney and at the trial of Priscilla Biggadike, at the Lincoln Assizes.

COOKE, Frederick. Juror at trial of Priscilla Biggadike at the Lincoln Assizes. Resident of Alford.

COOLEY, Thomas. Juror at trial of Priscilla Biggadike, at the Lincoln Assizes. Resident of Moulton.

COOLING, John. Juror at Priscilla Biggadike inquest, Lincoln Castle.

CRACROFT-AMCOTTS, Colonel Weston. MP for Mid-Lincolnshire. Member of Grand Jury at trial of Priscilla Biggadike, at the Lincoln Assizes. Resident of Hackthorn Hall.

DOWSE, Hannah/Elizabeth. Female warder allocated to guard Priscilla Biggadike at Lincoln Castle prison.

DUDDING, Henry. Juror at trial of Priscilla Biggadike, at the Lincoln Assizes. Resident of Riby Grange.

ELLISON, Richard. Banker. Member of Grand Jury at trial of Priscilla Biggadike, at the Lincoln Assizes. Resident of Sudbrooke Holme.

EMERIS, William Robert. Member of Grand Jury at trial of Priscilla Biggadike, at the Lincoln Assizes. Resident of Westgate, Louth.

EMMERSON, Thomas P. Juror at trial of Priscilla Biggadike, at the Lincoln Assizes. Resident of Haxey.

EVRINGTON, Susan. Gave evidence at the Magistrates' Court in Stickney and at the trial of Priscilla Biggadike, at the Lincoln Assizes. Resident of East Fenside, Stickney.

FATCHETT, Thomas. Juror at Priscilla Biggadike inquest, Lincoln Castle.

FARROW, John. Foreman Juror at Priscilla Biggadike inquest, Lincoln Castle.

FENWICK, Edwin. Husband of Elizabeth Fenwick, gave evidence at inquest into death of Richard Biggadike and at trial of Priscilla Biggadike at the

Lincoln Assizes. Resident of Frieston Fen.

FENWICK, Elizabeth. Sister-in-law of Richard Biggadike, gave evidence at inquest into death of Richard Biggadike and at trial of Priscilla Biggadike at the Lincoln Assizes. Resident of Frieston Fen.

FOSTER, James. Governor of Lincoln Castle prison. Witness at execution of Priscilla Biggadike and gave evidence at the inquest on Priscilla Biggadike.

FOX, Thomas. Sub-editor of the *Lincoln Gazette* and *Lincolnshire Times*. Invited Press witness at execution of Priscilla Biggadike in Lincoln Castle.

FYTCHE, John Lewis: Member of Grand Jury at the trial of Priscilla Biggadike, at the Lincoln Assizes. Resident of Thorpe Hall, South Elkington.

GOTT, George. Juror at trial of Priscilla Biggadike, at the Lincoln Assizes. Resident of Gedney.

GELL, John. Juror at Priscilla Biggadike inquest, Lincoln Castle.

HAIGH, George Henry. Member of Grand Jury at trial of Priscilla Biggadike, at the Lincoln Assizes. Resident of Grainsby Hall.

HEMSTOCK, William. Juror at Priscilla Biggadike inquest, Lincoln Castle.

HENEAGE, Edward. Member of Grand Jury at trial of Priscilla Biggadike, at the Lincoln Assizes. Resident of Hainton Hall.

IRONMONGER, GEORGE: boatman, lodger

with Richard and Priscilla Biggadike. Gave evidence at the inquest into the death of Richard Biggadike; at the Magistrates' Court at Stickney; and at the trial of Priscilla Biggadike, at the Lincoln Assizes.

IRONMONGER, Jane. Grandmother of George Ironmonger. Next door neighbour of Priscilla Biggadike. Gave evidence at the resumed inquest on the death of Richard Biggadike, at the Magistrates court in Stickney and at the trial of Priscilla Biggadike, at the Lincoln Assizes.

JARVIS, George Eden. Member of Grand Jury at trial of Priscilla Biggadike, at the Lincoln Assizes. Resident of Doddington Hall.

JESSON, John. Juror at trial of Priscilla Biggadike, at the Lincoln Assizes. Resident of Fleet.

LAWRANCE, John Compton: Counsel for the Defence at the trial of Priscilla Biggadike, at the Lincoln Assizes. Resident of Dunsby Hall, Bourne.

LISTER, Reverend Thomas Henry. Rector of St Oswald's, Luddington. Presided at Magistrates' Court, Stickney.

MAXWELL, Dr Peter. General Practitioner, attended Richard Biggadike and conducted a post mortem on him. Gave evidence at both the inquest and resumed inquest into the death of Richard Biggadike, and at the trial of Priscilla Biggadike, at the Lincoln Assizes. Resident of Stickney.

MASSINGBERD-MUNDY, Charles H. Member of Grand Jury at trial of Priscilla Biggadike, at the Lincoln Assizes. Resident of Ormsby Hall.

MELVILLE, Alexander Samuel Leslie. Member of Grand Jury at trial of Priscilla Biggadike, at the Lincoln Assizes. Resident of Branston Hall.

MOORE, Colonel Charles Thomas John: Member of Grand Jury at trial of Priscilla Biggadike, at the Lincoln Assizes. Resident of Frampton Hall.

MITCHINSON, Dr George. County Coroner. Presided over Priscilla Biggadike inquest, Lincoln Castle.

NAINBY, John Richard. Juror at trial of Priscilla Biggadike, at the Lincoln Assizes. Resident of Barnetby le Beck.

OLDFIELD, Richard. Juror at trial of Priscilla Biggadike, at the Lincoln Assizes. Resident of Sturton and Bransby.

PARKINS, Jarvis. Juror at Priscilla Biggadike inquest, Lincoln Castle.

PEACOCK, Edward. Member of Grand Jury at trial of Priscilla Biggadike at the Lincoln Assizes. Resident of Manor House, Bottesford.

PETTENER, George. Juror at Priscilla Biggadike inquest, Lincoln Castle.

PHILLIPS, John Farr. Governor of Spilsby House of Correction. Gave evidence at the resumed inquest into the death of Richard Biggadike and the trial of Priscilla Biggadike, at the Lincoln Assizes.

PRESTON, John Welby. Member of Grand Jury at trial of Priscilla Biggadike, at the Lincoln Assizes. Resident of Dalby Hall.

PRIESTLEY, Zachariah. Juror at Priscilla Biggadike inquest, Lincoln Castle.

PROCTOR, Thomas. Rat catcher and agricultural labourer, lodger with Richard and Priscilla Biggadike. Arraigned for the suspected murder of Richard Biggadike. Bill thrown out by Grand Jury. Gave evidence at the inquest and resumed inquest into the death of Richard Biggadike, at the Magistrates' Court at Stickney and at the trial of Priscilla Biggadike, at the Lincoln Assizes.

RAWNSLEY, Reverend Robert Drummond Burrell: Rector of St Andrew's, Halton Holegate. Honorary Canon of Lincoln Cathedral. Presided at Magistrates' Court at Stickney.

REED, Ann. Visited Priscilla Biggadike in prison, 26th December, 1868.

RICHTER, Reverend Henry William. Chaplain of Lincoln Castle prison and Rector of St Paul in the Bail, Lincoln. Resident of 23 Minster Yard, Lincoln.

SHORT, John Hassard. Member of Grand Jury at trial of Priscilla Biggadike, at the Lincoln Assizes. Resident of Edlington, near Horncastle.

SMITH, Charles. Juror at Priscilla Biggadike inquest,

Lincoln Castle.

STOREY, George. Juror at trial of Priscilla Biggadike, at Lincoln Assizes. Resident of Stow.

TAYLOR, Professor Alfred Swaine. Fellow of the College of Physicians and Professor of Medical Jurisprudence at Guy's Hospital, London. Gave expert evidence at resumed inquest into the death of Richard Biggadike and at the trial of Priscilla Biggadike, at the Lincoln Assizes.

TAYLOR, George. Juror at Priscilla Biggadike inquest, Lincoln Castle.

TAYLOR, Rachel. Sister of Priscilla Biggadike. Visited Priscilla Biggadike in prison, 26th December, 1868.

TROLLOPE, Arthur. Member of Grand Jury at trial of Priscilla Biggadike, at the Lincoln Assizes. Resident of 16 Eastgate, Lincoln.

TURNER, Henry. Joiner. Gave evidence at the trial of Priscilla Biggadike, at the Lincoln Assizes. Resident of Stickney.

WAITE, Thomas. Retired agricultural labourer. Gave evidence at the Magistrates' Court in Stickney. Resident of Stickney.

WAKEFIELD, John. Juror at trial of Priscilla Biggadike, at the Lincoln Assizes. Resident of Beesby in the Marsh.

WHILEY, George. Agricultural Labourer. Brother of Priscilla Biggadike. Visited her in prison, 26th

December, 1868.

WHILEY, Susan. Sister of Priscilla Biggadike. Visited her in prison, 26th December, 1868.

WRIGHT, Robert. Superintendent of Police, Spilsby. Escorted Priscilla Biggadike to Spilsby House of Correction. Gave evidence at the resumed inquest into the death of Richard Biggadike, at the Magistrates' court at Stickney and at the trial of Priscilla Biggadike, at the Lincoln Assizes.

Bibliography

Archive sources

British Library

British Newspaper Digital Archive (www. britishnewspaperarchive.co.uk)

Lincolnshire Archives, Lincoln

Lincoln Gaol Session Papers
Ref: CoC/4/1/20
Prison Journal of Keeper
Ref: CoC/5/1/3: 1836-1848
Prison Journal of John Nicholson, Governor
Ref: CoC 5/1/4:1848-1856
Prison Journal of James Foster, Governor
Ref: CoC 5/1//5/6: 1860-1868

Prison Journal of Mrs Emily Johnson, Matron
Ref: CoC 5/1/9: 1848-1859
CoC 5/1/10: 1860-1878
Prison Journal of Ralph Howett, Surgeon
Ref: CoC 5/1/14
Prison Journal of James Farr Broadbent, Surgeon
Ref: CoC 5/1/19
Prison Journal of the Reverend Henry W Richter,
　　Chaplain
Ref: CoC 5/1/21: 1839-1845
CoC 5/1/22: 1845-1850
CoC 5/1/27: 1866-1878
　　*Lincoln Castle, Minute of Execution of Priscilla
Biggadike*
　　Ref: 3-LINCOLN PRISON/1

Directories

E R Kelly, *Directory of Lincolnshire with the Port of
　　Hull and Neighbourhood with Map of the County*,
　　various dates
William White, *History, Gazetteer, and the Directory
　　of Lincolnshire and the City and Diocese of Lincoln*,
　　various dates

Census Records

1841-1881

Newspapers

Eliza Joyce

Lincolnshire Chronicle, 30th September, 1842, p.3
Stamford Mercury, 23rd December, 1842, p.3
Lincolnshire Chronicle, 30th December, 1842, p.2
Lincolnshire Chronicle, 3rd March, 1843, p.3
Stamford Mercury, 3rd March, 1843, p.3
Lincolnshire Chronicle, 10th March, 1843, p.2
Stamford Mercury, 10th March, 1843, p.2
Lincolnshire Chronicle, 14th July, 1843, p.2
Lincolnshire Chronicle, 21st July, 1843, p.2
Stamford Mercury, 21st July, 1843, p.3
Stamford Mercury, 26th April, 1844, p.4
Stamford Mercury, 19th July, 1844, p.3
Stamford Mercury, 21st July, 1844, p.2
London Evening Standard, 24th July, 1844, p.3
The Times, 24th July, 1844, pp.6-7
Devizes and Wiltshire Gazette, 25th July, 1844, p.2
Lincolnshire Chronicle, 26th July, 1844, p.2
Stamford Mercury, 26th July, 1844, p.3
Berkshire Chronicle, 27th July, 1844, p.4
Lincolnshire Chronicle, 9th August, 1844, p.3
Stamford Mercury, 9th August, 1844, p.3
Lincolnshire Chronicle, 18th October, 1844, p.1
Stamford Mercury, 18th October, 1844, p.1

Mary Ann Milner

Lincolnshire Chronicle, 9th July, 1847, p.5

Stamford Mercury, 9th July, 1847, p.2

Stamford Mercury, 16th July, 1847, p.3

Morning Advertiser, 22nd July, 1847, p.4

Evening Mail, 23rd July, 1847, p.2

Lincolnshire Chronicle, 23rd July, 1847, p.6

Stamford Mercury, 23rd July, 1847, p.2

Lincolnshire Chronicle, 30th July, 1847, p.5

Stamford Mercury, 30th July, 1847, p.2

John Bull, 31st July, 1847, p.16

Sheffield Independent, 31st July, 1847, p.6

John Bull, 2nd August, 1847, p.15

The Globe and Traveller, 2nd August, 1847, p.4

Liverpool Mercury, 3rd August, 1847, p.4

Hull Packet and East Riding Times, 6th August, 1847, p.7

Lincolnshire Chronicle, 6th August, 1847, p.5

Liverpool Mercury, 6th August, 1847, p.3

Stamford Mercury, 6th August, 1847, p.4

Morning Advertiser, 7th August, 1847, p.3

Northampton Mercury, 7th August, 1847, p.4

The Atlas, 7th August, 1847, p.6

Exeter Flying Post, 12 August, 1847, p.4

Derbyshire Advertiser and Journal, 13th August, 1847, p.3

Lincolnshire Chronicle, 13th August, 1847, p.5

Hertford Mercury and Reformer, 14th August, p.4
Stamford Mercury, 20th August, 1847, p.3
Shipping and Mercantile Gazette, 21st August, 1847, p.4

Priscilla Biggadike

Lincolnshire Chronicle, 23rd October, 1868, p.5
Stamford Mercury, 23rd October, 1868, p.4
Stamford Mercury, 30th October, 1868, p.6
Lincolnshire Chronicle, 31st October, 1868, p.3
Lincolnshire Chronicle, 11th December, 1868, p.8
Stamford Mercury, 11th December, 1868, p.5
Lincolnshire Chronicle, 12th December, 1868, p.8
The Times, 12th December, 1868, p.11
Lincolnshire Chronicle, 18th December, 1868, pp.5, 6-7
Stamford Mercury, 18th December, 1868, p.6
Grantham Journal, 19th December, 1868, p.4
Nottingham Journal, 23rd December, 1868, p.4
The Sun, 23rd December, 1868, p.8
Lincolnshire Chronicle, 25th December, 1868, p.5
Stamford Mercury, 25th December, 1868, p.5
Liverpool Weekly Courier, 26th December, 1868, p.2
The Times, 29th December, 1868, p.10
Lincoln Gazette, 1st January, 1869, pp.2,4
Lincolnshire Chronicle, 1st January, 1869, p.8
Morning Advertiser, 1st January, 1869, p.5
Nottingham Guardian, 1st January, 1869, p.11
Stamford Mercury, 1st January, 1869,p.6

Grantham Journal, 2nd January, 1869, p.4

Manchester Times, 2nd January, 1869, p.4

Lincolnshire Chronicle, 2nd January, 1869, pp.5, 8

Sleaford Gazette, 2nd January, 1869, p.3

South London Chronicle, 2nd January, 1869, p.6

Lloyd's Weekly Newspaper, 3rd January, 1869, p.5

Reynolds's Newspaper, 3rd January, 1869, p.4

Uxbridge and West Drayton Gazette, 4th January, 1869, p.4

Morning Advertiser, 6th January, 1869, p.4

The Sportsman, 7th January, 1869, p.2

Christian Times, 8th January, 1869, p.1

Stamford Mercury, 8th January, 1869, p.6

Richmond and Ripon Chronicle, 9th January, 1869, p.7

Glasgow Herald, 12th January, 1869, p.2

Stamford Mercury, 15th January, 1869, p.6

Boston Guardian, 6th March, 1869, p.2

The Times, 23rd April, 1869, p.6

London Evening Standard, 24th April, 1869, p.2

Lincolnshire Chronicle, 15th October, 1869, p.4

Lincolnshire Echo, 16th March, 2011, p.7

Broadsides

Eliza Joyce

A Full True and Particular Account of the Life, Trial and Confession of Eliza Joyce, Aged 31, who was Executed on the Drop at Lincoln, on Friday, August 2nd, 1844, for Poisoning Emma and Ann Joyce, her daughters.
Printed by R E Leary, 19 Strait, Lincoln

Mary Ann Milner

An Account of the Trial, Conviction and Condemnation of Mary-A Milner, at Lincoln Assizes, July 20th, 1847, for the Murder of Hannah Jickells at Barnetby le Wold.
Printed by R E Leary, 19 Strait, Lincoln

Priscilla Biggadike

Trial and Execution. Priscilla Biggadike for the Wilful Murder of her Husband on the 1st October, 1868, who was tried before the Right Hon. Sir John Barnard Byles, Knight, on Friday, December 11th.
Printed by R E Leary, 19 Strait, Lincoln

Selected Books/Articles

Eliza Joyce

Gagen, N V, *Hanged at Lincoln, 1716-1961*, (Privately printed, Welton, Lincoln, 1998), pp.141-142

Wade, Stephen, *Hanged at Lincoln*, (The History Press: Stroud, 2009), pp.70-72

Watson, Katherine, *Poisoned Lives, English Poisoners and their Victims*, (Hambledon and London: London, 2004), pp.142-143

Wynn, Douglas, *Murder and Crime: Boston*, (The History Press: Stroud, 2010), pp.24-30

Mary Ann Milner

Gray, Adrian, *Crime and Criminals in Victorian Lincolnshire*, (Paul Watkins: Stamford, 1993), pp.2-5

Jakobi, Stephen, Misjudged Murderess: *Female Injustices in Victorian Britain*, (Pen and Sword, 2019), pp. 81-83

Priscilla Biggadike

Calvert, E Roy, *Capital Punishment in the Twentieth Century*, (G P Putnam: London and New York, 1927), pp.125-126

Gagen, *op.cit.*, pp.145-146

Gray, Adrian, *op.cit*, p.12

ibid, *Crime and Criminals of Victorian England*, (The History Press: Stroud, 2011), pp.23, 28 and 44

Hindley, Charles, *Curiosities of Street Literature: comprising "Cocks" or "Catchpennies", a Large and Curious Assortment of Street Drolleries, Squibs , Histories, Comic Tales in Prose and Verse, Broadsides on the Royal Family, Political Litanies, Dialogues, Catechisms, Acts of Parliament, Street Political Papers, a Variety of "Ballads on a Subject", Dying Speeches and Confessions. To which is Attached the All-Important and Necessary Affectionate Copy of Verses*, (Reeves and Turner: London, 1871), p.204

Jakobi, Stephen, *op.cit.*, pp.85-106

Tallack, William, *Penological and Preventative Principles: with special reference to Europe and America, and to crime, pauperism, and their prevention; prisons and their substitutes; habitual offenders; conditional liberation; sentences; capital punishment; intemperance; prostitution; neglected youth; education; police*, (Wertheimer, Lea & Co: London, 2nd edition, enlarged, 1896), pp.246-247

Tulloch, John, 'The Privatising of Pain: Lincoln Newspapers, "Meditated Publicness" and the End of Public Execution', *Journalism Studies*, 7(3),

2006, pp. 437-451, especially pp.447-449 (Onlineathttps://doi.org/10.1080/14616700600680922)

Van der Elst, Viola, *On the Gallows*, (The Doge Press: London: 1937), pp.67-68

Wade, Stephen, *op.cit*, pp.70-72

Wade, Stephen, *Lincolnshire Murders*, (The History Press: Stroud, 2009), pp.34-40

Ward, Arthur C, *Stuff and Silk*, (Gansey Publications: Ramsey, 1948), p.129

Weiner, Martin J, 'Convicted Murderers and the Victorian Press: Condemnation v Sympathy', *Crimes and Misdemeanours: Deviance and the Law in Historical Perspective*, 1(2), November, 2007, pp.110-125, especially pp.115-116

(On line at https://pearl.plymouth.ac.uk/handle/10026.1/8825)

Wilson, Patrick, *Murderess: A Study of the Women Executed in Britain since 1843*, (Michael Joseph: London, 1971), pp.155-156

Selected Internet Articles

Eliza Joyce

www.capitalpunishment.org/joyce.html

http://unknownmisandry.blogspot.com/2011/09/eliza-joyce-english-serial-confessed-poisoner/

http://executedtoday.com/2015/08/02/1834-eliza-joyce-confessed-poisoner/

Mary Ann Milner

www.capitalpunishmentuk.org/milner.html
http:/unknownmisandry.blogspot.com/2011/09/mary-ann-milner-english-serial-killer.html

Priscilla Biggadike

www.capitalpunishmentuk.org/Biggadyke.html
http://murderpedia.org/female.B/b/Biggadyke-priscilla.html
http://historiclincoln   trust.org.uk/Christmas 1868-a-bleak-time-in-lincoln-prison/
http://www.executedtoday.com/2012/12/28/1868-priscilla-biggdike-exonorated-stickney-murderess
http://murderousmonday.blogspot.Com/2012/12/murderous-monday-priscilla-biggadyke.html

General

Bentley, David, *English Criminal Justice in the Nineteenth-Century*, (Hambledon Press: London and Rio Grande, 1998)
Diamond, Michael, *Victorian Sensation, or the*

Spectacular, the Shocking and the Scandalous in Nineteenth-Century Britain, (Anthem Press: London, 2003)

Flanders, Judith, *The Invention of Murder: How the Victorians Revelled in Death and Detection and Created Modern Crime*,(Harper Press: London, 2011)

Fowler, Simon, *Workhouse: the People, the Places, the Life behind Doors*, (National Archives: London, 2007)

Gatrell, V A C, *The Hanging Tree: Execution and the English People*, (Oxford University Press: Oxford, 1994)

Grigg, Barbara, *Green Pharmacy: A History of Herbal Medicine*, (Jill Norman and Hobhouse Ltd: London, 1981)

Loudon, Irvine, *Medical Care and the General Practitioner, 1750-1850*, (Clarendon Press: Oxford, 1986)

Marland, Hilary, *Dangerous Motherhood: Insanity and Childbirth*, (Palgrave MacMillan: London, 2004)

Moyes, Malcolm, *By Force of Circumstances: the Lefley Case Reopened*, (Matador: Kibworth Beauchamp, 2021)

Olney, R J, *Lincolnshire Politics, 1832-1885*, (Oxford University Press: Oxford, 1973)

ibid, *Rural Society and County Government in*

Nineteenth-Century Lincolnshire, (Lincoln: History of Lincolnshire Volume 10, 1979)

Rawding, Charles K, *The Lincolnshire Wolds in the Nineteenth Century*, (Lincoln: Studies in the History of Lincolnshire 1, 2001)

Robinson, Benjamin Coulson, *Bench and Bar, Reminiscences of One of the Last of an Ancient Race*, Hurst and Blackett Ltd: London, 1889)

Seal, Lizzie, *Capital Punishment in Twentieth-Century Britain: Audience, Justice, Memory*, (Routledge: London and New York, 2014)

Showalter, Elaine, *The Female Malady: Women, Madness and English Culture*, (Virago Press: London, 1987)

Steinbach, Susie, *Women in England, 1760-1914: a Social History*, (Wiedenfeld & Nicholson: London, 2004)

Taylor, David, *Crime, Policing and Punishment, 1750-1914*, (MacMillan Press: London, 1998)

Ward, Arthur C, *Stuff and Silk*, (Gansey Publications: Ramsey, 1948)

Whorton, James C, *The Arsenic Century: how Victorian Britain was Poisoned at Home, Work and Play*, (Oxford University Press: Oxford, 2010)

Williams, Montague, *Leaves of a Life: being the Reminiscences of the Life of Montague Williams*, (Houghton Mifflin & Co: Boston and New York, 1890), 2 vols

This book is printed on paper from sustainable sources managed under the Forest Stewardship Council (FSC) scheme.

It has been printed in the UK to reduce transportation miles and their impact upon the environment.

For every new title that Matador publishes, we plant a tree to offset CO_2, partnering with the More Trees scheme.

For more about how Matador offsets its environmental impact, see www.troubador.co.uk/about/